CONSTRUCTIVE CONFLICT MANAGEMENT

Managing to Make a Difference

John Crawley

Pfeiffer
& COMPANY

Amsterdam • Johannesburg • Oxford
San Diego • Sydney • Toronto

PUBLISHED BY ARRANGEMENT WITH NICHOLAS BREALEY PUBLISHING LTD., 14 STEPHENSON WAY, LONDON NW1 2HD, UK. FOR SALE IN NORTH AMERICA ONLY AND NOT FOR EXPORT THEREFROM.

Published in the United States by

Pfeiffer & Company
8517 Production Avenue
San Diego, CA 92121-2280

Page Compositor: Talco Systems Services

Library of Congress Cataloging-in-Publication Data

Crawley, John
    Constructive conflict management: managing to make a difference/John Crawley.
      p.   cm.
    Includes bibliographical references and index.
    ISBN 0-89384-239-7
    1. Conflict management.   I. Title.
  HD42.C73 1993
  658.4—dc20   93-36224
                                                    CIP

Printed in the United States of America.
Printing 1 2 3 4 5 6 7 8 9 10

CONSTRUCTIVE

CONFLICT

MANAGEMENT

Contents

Acknowledgments

*F*irst and foremost, thanks to Katherine, my partner, without whom this would never have been written. Her unstinting encouragement, patience, and optimism kept me going. Her editing skills and extraordinary understanding of language transformed a scruffy text into what I think is a presentable, useful book. Thanks for her love, and tolerance of late night and early morning typing sessions.

Thanks to Andrew Fraley, Karl Mackie, and Shirley Spork in the United States, who read the first draft, for their intelligent and constructive feedback, to Denise Moulton who edited the manuscript with flair and a firm sense of reason, and to Nick Brealey for maintaining faith and keeping me on track.

Introduction

A glance at the bestsellers in the business and management section of any bookstore gives plenty of insight into what is expected of managers. They are "change masters" (Kanter 1985), "actors," "gods," or "captains" (Handy 1992) who are asked to "manage on the edge" (Pascale 1991), "thrive on chaos" (Peters 1988), and simultaneously, or consequently, have a "passion for excellence" (Peters 1989). Add to this the need to adopt patterns of behavior and strategies similar to a whole menagerie of animals from sharks to wolves, and now dolphins. The experts, it seems, expect a great deal from managers, as do their peers, the people who they are responsible for, and their bosses.

How do many people actually become managers? They may have been in an organization for a long time and "know the ropes" better than anyone else. There are those who have extra knowledge, expertise, education, and interpersonal skills that make them suited to leadership. Others rise to management positions because they construct a persuasive application form and curriculum vitae, interview well, or are ambitious and well connected with family or friends in high places. Some are recruited carefully to detailed specifications through effective equal opportunities recruitment procedures.

In their first managerial post they all have one thing in common—no matter how well prepared or trained

1

they are, this is the first time they have had responsibility for other people's work and behavior as well as their own. Placed at the center of a network of subordinates, peers, and superiors, managers have to learn very rapidly how to respond to these people and build relationships that are conditioned and changed by their role as manager.

In some situations the learning curve is extremely steep:

> Theresa, systems analyst, has what some call a personality clash with David, administrator. You are their manager and can no longer ignore it or just join one side or the other. You are responsible for getting them to work together.

> *What do you do?*

> Len, security guard, is known to be making suggestive remarks to Vera, the new receptionist. Before, you may have smiled and joined in with Len, or taken a personal stand and made your disapproval clear, or just hoped he would stop; now you are their manager and have to decide what is best for them both as well as for the organization.

> *How do you handle this?*

> Davina is someone you dislike intensely. The moment she speaks you can feel your blood boil. She always disagrees with you and contradicts you in public. Now she is a member of your team. You are responsible for her work and her relationships with her colleagues.

> *Can you treat her the same? Will you be biased against her if you do reprimand her?*

The pattern of relationships has altered. As part of their job, new managers find out how to handle people bit by bit, through trial and error, hopefully with the assistance of some training, experienced colleagues, and even from business and management books.

Experienced managers are also constantly seeking new ways of dealing with people as the work force becomes more culturally diverse, and as people from other cultures, women, people with disabilities, and homosexual men and women adopt higher profiles in the workplace and in society.

Constructive Conflict Management draws on the knowledge and experience of international peacekeepers, industrial arbitrators, divorce mediators, and organizational consultants who are applying their considerable abilities to one basic question—how can you find constructive ways of resolving conflict so that people are able to express and work through their differences without the risk of, or necessity to, damage one another?

Of course, the manager's job is about organizing, developing systems and monitoring competence as well as ensuring positive interactions and relationships at work. In addition, it is important to remember that there is a social and organizational context to all that we do. Good interpersonal skills will not ensure a conflict-free environment if the economic situation demands regular staff cuts and layoffs.

Constructive Conflict Management targets people skills for managers, and includes very little sociological or organizational theory, because skills do make a difference. Managers, who are dependent on the contact they have with others, will be more effective if they can become proficient at helping people to get along with each other and get along with their work.

Constructive Conflict Management concentrates on common difficult situations in the workplace as these are often the ones when it is most difficult to maintain a positive stance. These situations include

- Personality clashes.
- Threats of physical violence.
- Complaints from customers.
- Harassment charges and bigoted behavior.
- Disputes with your manager.
- Breakdowns in working relationships.
- Disputes in groups and meetings.

A variety of techniques, skills, exercises, and approaches are already being successfully used by

- Arbitrators from the Advisory Conciliation and Arbitration Service (ACAS) dealing with a wide variety of industrial and commercial disputes.
- Project workers in Northern Ireland dealing with sectarian feuds.
- Family conciliators devising alternative services for separating and divorcing couples.
- Mediators bringing victims and offenders together to consider restitution and reparation.
- Community mediators dealing with neighbor disputes and serious community conflicts.

By applying these skills and techniques developed in England, the United States, and Europe in the last two decades, managers will significantly reduce the damage caused by interpersonal conflict in the workplace. They will also facilitate the establishment of healthy, open, and positive working relationships in which people are more able to handle contentious issues and work through their differences.

There are many examples of influential management experts who recognize the value of a more positive, open approach to people in the workplace. The two other books in this series—*Coaching for Performance* by John Whitmore and *Positive Management* by Paddy O'Brien— take different approaches, but underline the value of empowering, not overpowering, staff. Mintzberg's influential work (1980) noted how important frequent face-to-face contact is between managers and their peers and subordinates. Tjosvold, a Canadian professor who has done several studies on cooperation and competition in organizations, concluded that "cooperation, coupled with appropriate use of competition and individualization, can be a major strategy for promoting organizational activity and individual commitment." Richard Walton, examining the effect of advanced technology in the workplace, suggested that businesses would be ill-advised to create technological sweatshops where operators perform limited functions. He asserted that, "one needs practical methods for involving those who will eventually use and/or be affected by a system."

This move to more people-friendly management styles is also seen in the use of Transactional Analysis (TA) in management training, which provides a clear and practical method of recognizing and responding to behavior through the concept of "parent, adult and child ego states."

Pascale (1991) has perhaps the most persuasive argument in favor of pursuing open, direct, and challenging relationships at work. He described the situation at Ford in the United States, where it developed a "collegial" structure with formal and informal space and time allotted for interaction. One engineer was left in no doubt about the benefits of the transformation in the organization: "It's amazing what human nature does without barriers. It has made it easy to communicate, rather than difficult." It is this belief in human potential which underpins this book.

This book will be useful in dealing with conflicts between yourself and others, who

- Report directly to you and to whom you may be assigning tasks.
- Are in your peer group, or in a similar position in the organization.
- Have direct authority over you.
- Are members of the general public, or other recipients of your services and goods.

WHY CONCERN YOURSELF WITH CONFLICT MANAGEMENT AT ALL?

Managers are in a key position to influence conflicts, and thereby make a major contribution to a more positive environment at work. They have

- Authority to make things happen.
- Responsibility for other people's needs.
- Accountability upwards.
- Coordinating, team-facilitating role.

- Responsibility for the quality of work, goods, and service.

The expectations on managers are particularly high at times of conflict. As a manager you are expected to be able to take the pressure and be decisive, but also to help people and not work against their interests. Your quality is measured by how you handle these difficult situations and the people in them.

Improving your ability to handle conflict will have several advantages. You will

- Increase your understanding of other people and yourself.
- Become more open to people's differences and be able to improve their productivity.
- Increase your ability to prevent or reduce the incidence of serious conflict and thereby enhance the quality of the work environment.
- Develop skills which will be useful at times of pressure and will enable you to stay calm and manage effectively.
- Reduce stress levels at work.
- Enhance your own status.
- Save your organization considerable human resources.

CONSTRUCTIVE CONFLICT MANAGEMENT

For the purposes of this book my definition of conflict is

a manifestation of differences working against one another.

Some conflicts can be very explosive, as these differences clash and cause untold damage. All explosive conflicts contain the following components.

Ingredients

These are the differences that are present, such as age, gender, culture, values, beliefs, and assumptions about other people, their interests, status, roles, and responsibilities, and the characteristics and patterns people revert to when under threat.

Combinations and Conditions

The contact that people have, the structures that surround them, and the environment in which they live and work.

The Spark

When differences clash the conflict sparks.

The Burning Fuse

The smoldering conflict includes defensiveness, confusion, jockeying for position, proliferation of issues, and inability to find a resolution.

The Explosion

A dramatic, violent exchange affects the people nearby, as well as those involved when the conflict explodes. This is an adaptation of a descriptive device used by a youth training organization called Leaveners Experimental Arts Project (LEAP).

Conflicts need not always turn out this way. Constructive conflict management will enable you to transform the interaction between employees so that, when the spark occurs, there will be heat generated, but it will not last, destroy the employees, or damage the surroundings. Rather than exploding, the employees will cool, readjust to one another, and settle as shown in Figure 1.

Constructive conflicts are not easy to achieve. In fact, in a world which demands high levels of individual achievement, competitive lifestyles and attitudes, and the pursuit of the interest of oneself above that of others, the development of constructive methods of resolving differences provides all of us, particularly leaders and managers, with a great challenge.

Mary Parker Follett, an influential early twentieth-century visionary, was in no doubt about the value of peaceful methods of resolving conflict.

> From War to Peace is not from the strenuous
> to the easy existence; it is from the futile to the

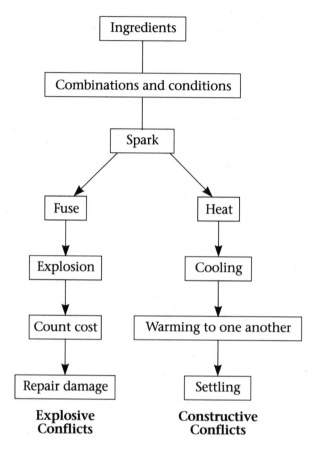

Figure 1. Explosive and Constructive Conflicts

effective, from the stagnant to the active, from the destructive to the creative way of life.... The world will be regenerated by the people who rise above these passive ways and heroically seek, by whatever hardship, by whatever toil, the methods by which people can agree.

The three key words in this are *effective, active,* and *creative.* How often in a conflict have you been made ineffective by your inability to see an opponent as anything but a diabolical enemy? How many times have you fallen into passive agreement with oppressive, unfair decisions made with little consideration of your needs, or let behavior pass which you felt strongly was inappropriate? To be passive is to have an easier life, we assume; only our frustration comes out elsewhere, as we under-achieve when motivation slides, or dump our anger on other people. Have you been put in a situation where you feel there is only one depressing, unsatisfactory way out of a conflict, and that there is no room for creativity? Is this not a particularly energy-sapping experience?

Constructive conflict management offers you an alter-native that will enable you to be active, creative, and effective but, as Follett said, it is not an easy path.

First, you will need to take a close look at yourself and examine how you respond to people, what you know about yourself and conflict, and how well you can han-dle yourself and balance your own perceptions, values, and ideas with those of others. Part One of *Constructive Conflict Management* (Taking a Positive Approach—The Conflict Manager's Challenge) deals with these issues.

Second, if you can meet this challenge, then you will need to develop a repertoire of facilitation, investigation, assertion, and conflict management techniques that will enable you to remain relentlessly positive in your deal-ings with even the most difficult people and manage resolutions to conflicts that are effective, thorough, and achieved through processes seen to be fair. Part Two (Responding Positively to People and Situations—Con-structive Conflict Management Skills and Techniques) and Part Three (Conflict Management Procedures) of *Constructive Conflict Management* give many practical examples and demonstrations of such techniques.

Part Four (Where and How Is Conflict Likely to Hap-pen in Your Organization?) will also help you to look at your organization, predict where conflict is likely to occur, and work constructively with it.

YOU NEVER STOP LEARNING

Some people are very good at managing terrible, danger-ous conflicts. There can be no more fierce antagonism than that between Arabs and Israelis in the Middle East, or Christians and Moslems in Lebanon. Even to get people talking, rather than shooting or bombing one another, is a major achievement. The humility of the men and women who mediate is amazing as they shuttle between war zones, dodging insults and bullets from all sides. They facilitate exchange, and even progress, on a variety of issues and demands. They are asked back—a true sign of respect from the disputants. It is not the power that attracts them, nor the sense of achievement, though they have understandable pride in their work.

The power of learning and search for understanding is what motivates them and gives them their strength. They are hungry to find out more about what works, how people behave, and how others react to them. They even admit that they get it wrong sometimes.

So even if you have consummate dispute resolution skills and a deserved reputation for being calm and able under pressure, read on, and you can learn something from what many others have to teach.

WORKPLACE EXAMPLES

A fictitious organization, Troubled Associates Ltd., is used to demonstrate conflict resolution skills and methods. The setting is the head office, where there are many conflicts. As you will see, although these threaten to make life difficult for the organization, the managers and staff cope well, and you will learn a lot from them. Conflicts within the head office, between peers, and between employees at different levels of status and authority are the focus. These are managed by a variety of people. Troubled Associates Ltd. is an organization approaching conflict constructively, and many of the techniques and skills would be equally appropriate for dealing with conflicts off-site, in other regional offices, or with contractors, suppliers, or customers and clients.

Figure 2 is an organizational chart to introduce you to the set-up. As the book progresses, you will get to know more about the fictional team, and you may well recognize many familiar types of situations and people.

Figure 2. Organizational Chart of Troubled Associates Ltd.

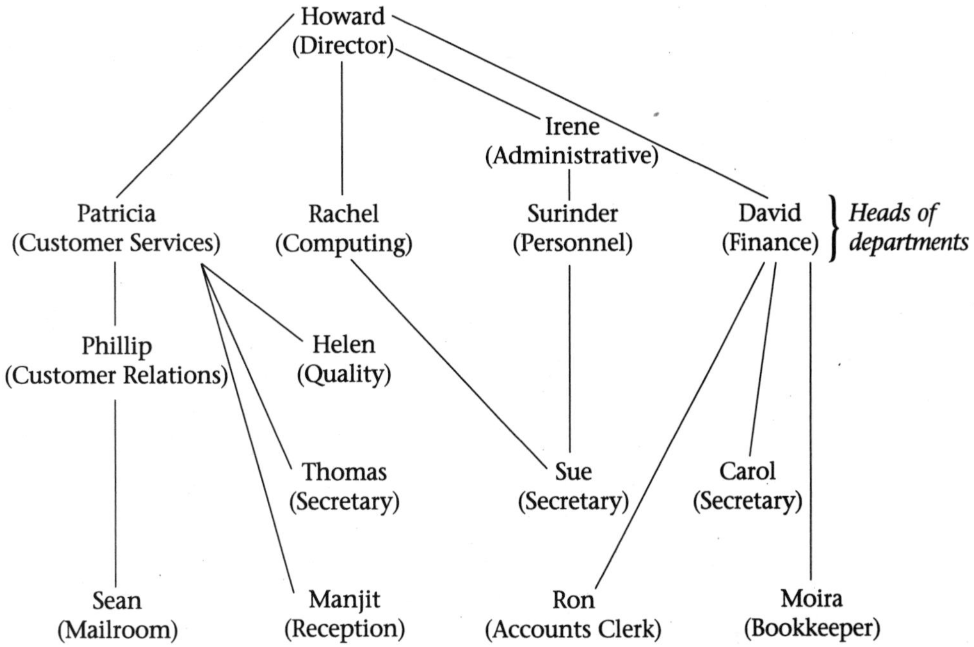

Howard
(Director)

Irene
(Administrative)

Patricia
(Customer Services)

Rachel
(Computing)

Surinder
(Personnel)

David
(Finance)

} *Heads of departments*

Phillip
(Customer Relations)

Helen
(Quality)

Thomas
(Secretary)

Sue
(Secretary)

Carol
(Secretary)

Sean
(Mailroom)

Manjit
(Reception)

Ron
(Accounts Clerk)

Moira
(Bookkeeper)

Part One

Taking a Positive Approach—The Conflict Manager's Challenge

INTRODUCTION

For many years managers were expected to treat their staff as subordinates, keeping them in their place, acting out the role of controller, expert, disciplinarian, and occasionally patron. More recently their role has changed, and they are expected to facilitate more openly, make connection with and between people, and encourage as well as control. Tom Jennings, who was head of employee development at IBM, refers to one aspect of this in a 1991 article in *The Independent:* "Most management development over the last twenty years has been about telling people they can't just tell people what to do; they must work to develop others."

Few people doubt the wisdom of this switch, but it is important to remember that such a transformation poses a substantial challenge to managers. Rosabeth Moss Kanter (1985) refers to a set of old organizational assumptions, using words such as *closed, segmentalized*, and *controlling* to describe organizational structures and systems. If, as a manager, you have grown up in this kind of environment, then the "new assumptions," which Kanter and many other management gurus believe are necessary to manage change and regenerate organizations, require you to make a major shift of attitude to openness, innovation, flexible goals, and the need to connect people rather than keep them separate. New managers are expected to join this movement toward more trusting, open, collaborative work relationships, and yet they are almost all products of an education system that places little emphasis on self-development and even less on the development of others. They will have had little encouragement or opportunity to seriously challenge their own attitudes or develop their relationship skills.

In addition to the basic task of developing a positive, more open style of manager-staff relationships, you are now faced with the challenge of taking a constructive attitude even when people are unreasonable, unreliable, and combatant, as they often are during conflicts. It is at times like this when principles of trust and cooperation fly out of the window, particularly if you are directly involved in the conflict.

To help you achieve and maintain a clear, constructive attitude during even the most difficult conflict, four basic guidelines may help.

A Recipe for Constructive Conflict Management

1. Be clear about what you see, how you judge, and how you react to people and situations.
2. Understand and take charge of your own feelings and behavior.
3. Step back and take a balanced view.
4. Respond positively.

These four guidelines contain the basic elements of the constructive conflict management approach.

- Clear perception and good judgment
- Self-awareness and control

- Ability to analyze and balance different views and positions
- Openness to others

By maintaining this balance between oneself and others, while keeping good contact with what is going on, a manager can remain calm, and develop positive, effective responses (many of which will be covered in Parts Two and Three) to difficult people and situations. This process is summarized in Figure 3.

Figure 3. The Constructive Conflict Management Process

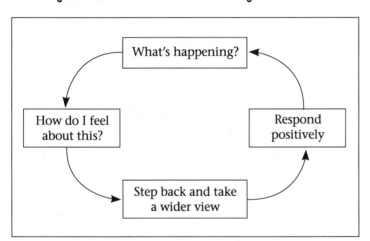

In practice, this is how it works. At the first contact with a conflict—for example, if you walk in on a conflict (as in the example in Chapter 4, which looks at a potentially violent argument)—you need to respond quickly. You tune in to the situation and get an initial idea of what is happening, register and take control of your own feelings, make a provisional assessment taking into account as many elements as you can, and then respond.

From the start you are consciously processing, keeping yourself sharp, and remaining open to the people and the situation. This produces a more measured approach, even though you may feel your own emotional level rising.

Once you respond, the other parties will react, so you begin again, fine-tuning your original perception, feelings, assessment, and responses. In many instances, as the situation develops, you need to shift to another way of seeing, modify your feelings, and alter your original assessment and response.

This is a flexible, ongoing process, balancing emotion and reason. You get a clear, quick idea of the facts, but restrain the tendency to prejudge or make assumptions by frequently seeking more information. There is a great emphasis on discovery and facilitation. Questioning techniques are one of the key elements of conflict management. With this kind of approach you turn a conflict into an opportunity to learn and encourage learning, instead of being a vehicle for combat that causes animosity and division.

Approaching conflicts this way can initially seem threatening and disorienting to managers who are used to being the guardians of order, administering judgment. While being responsible for resolutions that are seen to be fair and appropriate, the conflict manager's role is often not that of judge or expert, but as the catalyst who can bring the parties together and change their patterns of thought, communication and behavior. It is particularly challenging to adopt this approach when you are one of the parties to the conflict.

There are several advantages that will make it well worth the investment of your time and energy.

- You will build up your own strengths and grow more aware of your limitations by getting to know more about yourself.

- You will build your understanding of others and enhance your ability to form more collaborative work relationships by finding out other points of view and gathering information.

- You will learn how to use your emotions and intellect constructively, while gaining respect for others.

- You will be able to remain true to yourself while encouraging others.

- You and your management of difficult situations will be seen to be fair and reasonable, which will be beneficial even when outcomes to conflicts are not exactly as disputants wished.

- You will facilitate resolutions which work, and which at worst narrow the gap between winners and losers and at best give everyone the chance of winning.

By the end of Chapter 3 you will have a much better idea of the kind of skills and attitudes you need to successfully use this approach. Part two, a practical section, follows examining particular skills and techniques.

What's Happening? 1

"*Seeing* is believing," or so a widely quoted seventeenth-century proverb tells us. How can what we see be anything but the truth? Why is it that multiple eyewitness accounts of crimes are notoriously unreliable? People give their version of what they saw with conviction, and one person is often as certain that the culprit's hair was fair as another is convinced it was black. We simply do not experience reality in the same way, particularly when it bursts in front of us so unexpectedly and passes by so fast.

During conflicts it is common for people to see themselves and their situation very differently from their opponent. They cling desperately to their version of the events and see, hear, and believe only what they want to.

This chapter will help you get as clear a focus as possible on what is happening during conflicts, and it will help you to rise above your own prejudices and assumptions. It is divided into three sections.

1. Factors influencing perception
2. Improving faculties of perception and observation
3. Good judgment

FACTORS INFLUENCING PERCEPTION

You are affected emotionally by what goes on around you, reacting to or identifying with people and situations in ways specific to the "filter" of your personal history. Three factors are important here.

1. How you filter what you see through your previous experience
2. First impressions—what you do and do not see
3. How you organize what you see

Perception Exercise

The aim of this exercise is to simulate your contact with a real situation and examine your perceptions. The simulation will be most realistic if you read the instructions on the next page before looking too closely at the picture opposite. You may make notes if it helps.

Instructions

1. Look at the picture for one minute.
2. After one minute think about the following:
   (a) Is there anything you like or dislike in the picture? How do you feel about what is going on? What do you think the people involved are feeling?
   (b) What exactly is happening? Note down the details you think are important.
   (c) What has happened immediately prior to this? What is happening now and what do you imagine will happen next?
3. Spend up to fifteen minutes recording your impressions.
4. Give the picture to a colleague with the same instructions.

5. Discuss your responses. What are the similarities and differences? Exchange what you think are the reasons for your own responses and try to establish what influences our perception.

There are three influences worthy of discussion.

- Personal filters
- First impressions
- How you organize what you see

Personal Filters

When asked questions like, "How do you feel?" and, "What do you like or dislike?" people will

- Comment on and interpret the picture differently.
- Use tone and language to convey their strength of feeling.
- Side with one person or the other.
- React strongly to a particular part of the scene.

Individuals are bringing a part of themselves into the scene, applying what they have learned about people and situations. Without this capacity to learn from previous experience, new situations would become almost impossible to manage. So individuals store incidents, people, places, and the emotions connected with them.

You can remember experiences that changed the way you felt about something and affected how you behaved afterwards. There are also many others that you process and use unconsciously. A baby on first encountering a bright red and yellow flame approaches it with glee and curiosity. Then it touches the flame and is burned. From then on it will not actually think about it, but will react differently—with caution—from a distance. You construct a set of emotional responses based on your significant experiences. They are extremely reassuring, as they allow you to make situations familiar and know where you stand emotionally.

People, places, situations, faces, shapes, and shadows activate your filters, coloring what you see and feel. This is often different from what other people see and feel.

Your filters are often most profoundly triggered into action by your first impressions.

Your first impressions have a profound impact on your reaction to anything. They condition and shape what you see. Why do they affect your perception so much? First impressions

- Carry immense emotional weight. You need to make extremely fast decisions about how threatening or safe a person or situation is. Your instincts, previous experience, knowledge, and emotions are activated immediately to assess the risk value of that person, or fit them to your personal impression of the world.

- Are a way of making the unfamiliar familiar. Right or wrong, you see people in the light of what you already know. You fit them quickly into one set of types or another. This is reassuring, as it is easier for you to decide how to relate to people if you consider them to be a certain familiar type.

First impressions are powerful, but not always reliable. Much of the work in this book is about balancing such instinctive responses with reason, and being aware of the often changing nature of reality as we perceive it.

Connections

Seeing is also about organizing images. We are constantly making connections between the different parts of what we see in an attempt to make sense of the world.
Picture these four consecutive images:

1. One man stands in a Wild West street with a gun.

2. Another man stands in the same street with a gun.

3. One man draws his gun and shoots.

4. The other man falls to the ground clutching his stomach.

This is the visual style of television and films. Four quick images suggesting an event: Two men are having a gunfight and one shoots the other. Most people would not question that this is the scenario displayed. Yet how do you know that one man shot at the other? How do you know that the shot was only just before the fall? Maybe they were not connected so closely in time. Maybe these two men were in the street at different times. Perhaps the second man had indigestion after eating the snake that the other man shot.

Television has hooked into people's ability to connect separate incidents into a living scenario. But are people also becoming too dependent on the visual image? Is it true that, "through television people are weaned from language" (Adorno 1991), or, "whoever has been weaned from language has never learned to listen" (Slembek). People need to rediscover their ability to make careful, accurate connections, and not always follow the apparently obvious track or signals.

Conventions

There are strong visual conventions that cause individuals to associate certain signals with a particular event or that provoke predictable kinds of behavior. These are different across cultures and if you are working with a culturally diverse work force, it is useful to get to know some of these conventions (Mole 1992). They have a significant impact on our reading of people and situations.

In England, a police car or motorcycle is painted with a broad red and blue stripe. All drivers know this. When they see a car with a broad red and blue stripe on the horizon, or behind them, they look at the speedometer and, if they are speeding (as they often are), immediately slow down and continue to drive slowly and carefully until the police car is out of sight. Many times this is a false alarm, as pizza delivery vans, messenger bikes, and transport companies often have a corporate appearance similar to police cars—no doubt calculated to cause other cars to slow down and let them pass. The red and blue stripe has become a visual convention that affects people's behavior.

These visual conventions apply to people as well. An advertisement in the 1980s showed a businessman dressed in a dark gray suit and bowler hat walking confidently down a busy city street. Behind him a young woman was running toward him. She had green spiked hair, tight ripped pants, and large boots. She grabbed the man by the shoulders and threw him to the ground. The audience assumed that he was about to be robbed. The camera panned up to show a large heavy piece of furniture just about to come crashing down onto the pavement. The woman had pushed the man out of the way and probably saved his life as he had not noticed the danger. She was his savior, not an assailant.

IMPROVING FACULTIES OF PERCEPTION AND OBSERVATION

You make sense of the world around you through a mixture of observation and interpretation. The training workbook of the San Francisco Fire Department's Peer Mediation Program (Roberts 1991), which was used to manage deep-rooted conflicts within the department, makes the distinction between observation and interpretation clear, "Interpretation is subjective, partial and not necessarily factual and observation is objective, impartial and approaching certainty."

An ability to understand and interpret behavior is an asset to a conflict manager, but interpretations should be balanced by solid, sharp observations. Your powers of observation can be enhanced by

Interpretation is subjective

- Perception checking.
- Positional awareness.
- Structuring what you see.
- Witnessing.
- Focusing.

Observation can be enhanced

The San Francisco Fire Department taught all its officers this technique when it became apparent that the stressful nature of their job (high excitement and danger, mixed with long periods of calm and inactivity) was causing considerable misunderstanding and conflict in the department. The major problem was that people were constantly jumping to conclusions. A particularly

Perception Checking

common example of this was a tendency to treat interpretations of behavior as fact. For example:

"Why are you so annoyed?"
(Who said you were?)

"What's the matter with you?"
(Who said anything was the matter?)

"Don't lie! Tell the truth."
(Who said you were lying?)

Check your perceptions

Perception checking is a verbal procedure that has two main functions.

- It helps us to establish what is happening.
- It tells others that we are interested in them.

There are three stages.

1. Describe the behavior you have noticed.
2. Suggest what you think the behavior means. (It is important to keep this tentative, using phrases like "I wonder," "perhaps," "maybe," or "it seems.")
3. Request feedback about what the behavior means.

Examples of Perception Checking Questions

"When you banged your file down on the desk and got up and left, I thought you were pretty angry. Is that true? How were you feeling?"

"You said you were pleased with the report, but your tone of voice and the way you fidgeted with the pages made me feel that there was something else you wanted to say, but had difficulty saying. How do you really feel about it?"

"When you sat alone in the cafeteria, as we usually sit together, I thought that I might have done something to offend you. Are you okay? What's going on?"

Perception Checking Exercise

Develop perception checking statements for the following situations.

1. You made what you thought was a very good suggestion at your last meeting with your boss. She seemed quite interested and said she would check on the matter right away. Two weeks have passed now and nothing has changed.

2. Last month you lent $20 to a colleague. He said he would pay you back within a week. You still have not received the money three weeks later, and the colleague has not mentioned it.

3. A month ago your secretary was coming in late, and explained that she was having trouble with child care. You agreed for her to start work thirty minutes later than normal, since this would make it possible for her to be on time. A month later she is now beginning to arrive five or ten minutes late again two or three times a week.

Suggestions

1. I've noticed that you have not talked to me about my suggestion from the meeting two weeks ago. I thought you agreed to "get back to me right away." Does the delay mean that you have simply not had the time, or is it maybe that you are not really interested any more?

2. Hi, Richard. Do you remember that you owe me $20 from three weeks ago? Since you have not paid me back I thought you might have forgotten. Is that true?

3. Your time-keeping was improving Dianne, but I have seen you arrive late a couple of times recently which makes me think that maybe you have underestimated the time you needed to get your baby ready. Can you tell me what's happening?

   or

   I am beginning to think that giving you a later start isn't going to help. What do you think?

Positional Awareness

Obtain optimum view

When you are responsible for handling a conflict between others it is useful, indeed necessary, to decide where you should be in order to get the optimum view of the situation. If you come upon a violent conflict, for example, get to a position where you can see as much of what is going on as quickly as possible, without getting involved, and then decide how to act. For any conflict involving others you should endeavor to be in a position where

- You can see and hear all parties clearly.
- They can see and hear you.

Sensitivity to Others

Be sensitive to others' space

Sensitivity to relative height, distance, and closeness communicates a message of trust to the other party and says you are willing to deal with them. Adjusting and balancing physical positions can be the first step to resolution. For example, sit down if you are standing and towering over your counterpart. This physical awareness will enhance your own comfort levels and sharpen observation skills.

Change Places

In some disputes, especially those about working environments, you actually need to change positions with the disputants to get the picture from their perspective. If a secretary is complaining of the heat at a window, or a foreman is finding the noise insulation in the workshop fails to dampen excessive machine noise levels, you will find it helpful to go and see for yourself what their conditions are actually like.

Look at all angles

In their efforts to help solve long-term neighborhood disputes over such issues as car parking, antisocial behavior, and property maintenance, community conciliators often examine the environment of both disputing neighbors. They begin by visiting each party separately in their home. This experience of life from the individual party's perspective is very informative and often helps the conciliators to understand the conditions which contribute to the dispute. Problems can be defined more clearly if you have time and resources to see them from all available angles.

When investigators arrive at the scene of a crime they seal off the area, then approach the gathering of evidence systematically. First, they do a broad sweep, collecting and recording what is easily noticeable. Then they organize a squad to do an intensive, inch-by-inch survey, dividing the area into grids and painstakingly working through each area in detail. They do this to be sure that they have done a thorough job of observation. Systematically structuring your approach to any conflict may also help you. Asking yourself five basic questions will guide your observation.

Structure What You See

- **Who** is involved?
- **What** is happening?
- **Where** is it? **Where** are people in relation to one another?
- **Why** is this happening? **Why** are they doing this?
- **How** did it come to this? **How** are they behaving?

Ask questions

After asking yourself these questions, several analytical approaches will help illuminate conflicts or impending conflicts.

Ranking

Ranking is an analytical approach that gives an initial impression of priorities and urgent needs. This is particularly necessary when safety is an issue. When ranking, decide

- What is the most important feature?
- Who is most powerful?
- Who is most at risk?
- What is the next most important feature?

Prioritize

How Do You Look?

Organize how you look at the scene and consciously structure the actual process of observation. Think about the scene systematically.

- Left to right
- Top to bottom

Structure your observations

- Key features and then take a broad view
- Section-by-section in a detailed examination
- Center out or edges to center
- Obvious to unobvious elements

Individuals respond differently to visual signals. Try some of the above systems with the picture from the perception exercise at the beginning of the chapter. Do you notice different things? Which methods suit you best? Try them on a simple live scene. Later the book discusses the structured approaches to discovery through questioning, listening, and facilitation. Why not try to structure your process of observation as well?

Checklists

Remember nonverbal behavior

Checklists are very useful. They act as reminders at times of stress. They can guide our management of the situation, and also what we are able to detect from observation. When interviewing people at the first stage of a complaint or dispute, it can often be useful to make a record of their nonverbal behavior to supplement what they tell us about their feelings and thoughts. A checklist will help you organize your observations but do not be too mechanical or pedantic with checklists as you may annoy the disputants or affect their perception of you. The following checklist helps you to notice different kinds of nonverbal behavior.

Witnessing

Witnesses are people who were in a position to see what was going on and who may corroborate different versions of the truth. They may have seen something you missed; be able to validate a statement, view, or fact; or present an alternative view which will throw new light on the situation. In this sense they are useful when trying to understand what has happened.

Use your witnesses effectively

The following are some key points to remember when using witnesses.

- They are providers of information, not necessarily tellers of truth. Listen to them, but also evaluate their reliability.

CHECKLIST

Nonverbal Behavior

■ Posture—how would you describe this person's posture? Relaxed, tense?

■ Hand gestures—does this person use his or her hands when talking, or in other ways, such as playing with an object?

■ Body movements—does this person sit still or move around, such as fidgeting in the chair?

■ Facial expressions—how much facial expression is there and what kind?

■ Eye contact—does this person look at other people when conversing with them? When not talking, where are the eyes focused?

■ Vocal quality—includes tone of voice, pitch, volume, rate, fluency.

■ Touch—do you notice this person touching others or letting them touch him or her?

■ Appearance—includes clothes, hair, makeup, facial hair, jewelry.

■ Space—does this person create his or her own space and how close does he or she let others get? How much space does he or she use?

- You need to develop a variety of questioning and listening skills to use witnesses effectively.

- Using witnesses is time consuming. Evaluate how necessary and useful they are.

- When you have disputants together and are acting as a third party, be aware of the effect of witnesses on the parties, and maintain balance in numbers, authority, and status.

- Expert witnesses are particularly useful for difficult, technical disputes, but consider carefully how they will function. For example, will they be allowed for all parties?

- The status of witnesses may affect what they are prepared to say.

Focusing

In the late 1960s Eugene Gendlin (1981) developed the focusing process that was used in therapy with people who had previously been unable to make progress in certain psychological and emotional areas. By becoming aware of their own physiological responses to certain people and situations, they gradually learned to understand and control spontaneous reactions which had previously seemed uncontrollable.

Be aware of yourself

Gendlin's focusing process encourages people to look inside themselves first, register what is going on, be as much in control of their feelings and physiological reactions as possible, and then focus out on what is happening.

The principle of self-awareness, added to concentrated, lucid observation, is fundamental to positive conflict management. You will be surprised at how well you grow to understand what is happening in conflicts by remaining positive and focused on your own internal responses, as well as the behavior taking place before you—like a photographer with your lens polished—maintaining optimum positioning and being in control of your relationship with your subject. You will get the best possible pictures of what is happening if you can also exercise good judgment about the footage you record.

GOOD JUDGMENT

Exclusive Views

John Haynes, an eminent family conciliator and trainer, has noticed how separating and divorcing couples build up exclusive views of one another. They come to him and say only things that will make their partner or ex-partner look bad. Because they are locked into their separate positions, they see the situation quite differently from their partner (Haynes 1989). In fact, their definitions of the problem clash continually. They believe that the problem lies with the other partner, not with themselves.

Figure 4. Exclusive Views

Person A	Person B
You are the problem. You never listen. I'm the only one who ever cared for the kids when we were married.	You are the problem. You never give me a chance. And look what a mess you made of it.

Figure 4 shows how these misunderstandings of problems lead to exclusive views.

When helping these couples manage their conflict, Haynes defines his task as moving the parties from their exclusive views of the problem to mutual definitions. He engages them in a process which moves them toward a shared definition of the problem. He does not ask them to change their basic beliefs, but to cooperate on the basis of shared aims and interests.

Seek shared definitions of problems

Any manager entering the field of conflict needs to understand how his or her own belief system is likely to affect interactions and to avoid forming limited, one-sided views of people and situations.

Examining Your Own Beliefs

Your own beliefs have an effect

Belief systems are sensitive, personal, and absolutely necessary. They provide you with a basic framework from which to relate to the people and situations you encounter. An effective conflict manager possesses a strong set of positive values about other people, but also needs to examine and be in control of his or her beliefs, assumptions, stereotypes, and prejudices.

Stereotypes

Stereotyping is a process of simplifying judgments about a group of people so that all members of that group are seen as having certain, usually negative, traits.

Stereotypes Exercise

This exercise is useful for raising group awareness of stereotypes. It can be done with four to thirty people.

Instructions

1. Give a sheet of paper and a pen to each person and ask them to write the numbers one to ten down the left-hand side.
2. From the list below, read out the first word only. Do not read the whole list in one go.
3. Ask the group to write the first word that comes into their mind, and not to censor their replies, but to be as spontaneous as possible.
4. Repeat the process with the second word, and continue through to number ten.

List of Words for Stereotypes Exercise

- Women
- Police
- Teenagers
- Typists
- Homosexuals
- Blacks
- Shopkeepers
- Managers
- Factory workers
- Politicians

Discussion

Exchange papers and call out the responses in order, recording a selection on a flip chart. Discuss the following issues:

1. Did you find yourself censoring? Why?
2. Were you surprised by anything that came to mind?
3. Were the responses positive or negative?
4. Is there any objective truth in them?

This exercise is useful for reminding you how pervasive stereotyping is, even in your beliefs. It is almost impossible not to come to some general conclusions about other people based on our experience of them. This experience comes through personal contact, television, radio, and newspapers, and the influence and information gained from friends, family, and coworkers. Stereotypes invariably contain a mixture of truth and fiction. Women are mothers biologically, and defined as nurturers by many societies. Bus drivers are mainly male and a number are black. This does not mean that women should only be mothers, or black men should be bus drivers. Stereotypes are essentially both limited and limiting. They ignore the individual for the convenience of the general, imposing characteristics on everyone regardless of their actual truth. They are judgmental in a limiting way, based on what appear to be predominant or generally acceptable facts, rather than specific characteristics and circumstances.

Prejudice

Prejudices, like stereotypes, are strongly connected with feelings and attitudes. They are feelings or attitudes about a group or individual based on partial knowledge, which begin to form during childhood, and are profoundly affected by the communities and societies within which we live. They are built into our systems and happen with us hardly being aware of them. How do they influence our behavior?

Prejudice Exercises

These exercises (Beer 1990) are for you alone. You will not be expected to share the responses with anyone. You can destroy the papers after you have finished, so be honest with yourself.

Bias

1. Think of five trivial things that might bias you toward someone and write them down.
2. Think of five trivial things that might bias you against someone and write them down.

3. Do the items fall into any distinct categories such as age, background, attitude, appearance, mannerisms, voice, posture, ethnicity, gender, sexual orientation, status, role, or preferences (choice of music, books, etc.)? If so, which?

Action

Hold bias back

As you come into contact with people, use the conflict management process to get to understand and balance out your biases. No one can be entirely neutral or devoid of prejudice, but it is possible to hold bias back, to become aware of the effect it has upon you, to focus on others through questioning and listening, and to respond in a balanced way.

Behavior

1. What do you do when you dislike someone? For example, do you avoid eye contact, turn away or tense your body, act overly polite, smile or laugh a lot, talk more or less than you would otherwise, listen carefully, or inattentively? Jot down some behaviors you exhibit.

2. Do you have a prejudice which you feel is stronger than any others? What do you think has caused it? What experiences lie behind this prejudice? Does your behavior reflect your feelings? If so, how?

3. How do you think you might behave under the following circumstances?

   - You attend a school parents' evening and are talking to your son's teacher, and he states that he is homosexual.

   - You meet a new colleague for the first time and she is in a wheelchair.

   - You enter a room at a party and everyone in there is black. Whether you are black or white, how would you react?

Know your prejudices and control them

The purpose of these two exercises is to provide a simple, non-threatening framework for you to get a sense of your prejudices. This will enable you to predict situations in which you need to exercise particular emotional and intellectual control. The best antidote to prejudice is knowledge.

Action

The third exercise gives you the opportunity to explore how differently people judge others, and to build up your understanding of the nature and influence of prejudice. If you work on issues of prejudice with groups, be prepared for strong feelings and differences of opinion that will be difficult to break down. Careful, sensitive facilitation and the establishment of clear ground rules will ensure that scapegoating and victimization are minimized, and that discussions do not lead to polarization of positions and fragmentation of the group.

Comparing and Discussing Prejudices Exercise

Instructions

1. You will need a group of four to ten people to do this exercise.
2. Copy the descriptions of people contained in the box that follows.
3. Each person reads the descriptions and ranks these people from the given information, from the least objectionable (1) to the most objectionable (5). Each person must have a rank.

Discussion

After you have finished ranking these yourself, compare your results with the others in the group. Describe your reasons for your ranking with one another. Why did you find some more objectionable than others? Is there any consensus in the group? What are the distinct variations and similarities and why do they occur?

Sally is friends with Joanne and Syreta. During lunch with Syreta, Sally talks about her night out with Joanne and how flirtatious Joanne was which resulted in them getting lots of attention—unwanted by Sally—from men. During lunch with Joanne a week later, Sally relates a story about Syreta which makes Syreta look bad. The next day Sally has lunch with both of them and says what good friends they both are to her.

Pete works with you. He is very humorous and is popular with customers and contractors, but does not get along too well with other coworkers, particularly women. Occasionally he goes off on long lunch breaks, and you have heard that he spends a lot of time in the bar drinking after work.

Tony is quiet and pleasant most of the time, but you have seen him with his wife and family and he seems very rude to them, even abusive at times. He smacks his children in public. He believes a woman's place is in the home.

Nilgun is an unmarried woman who is very ambitious. She has attended a number of executive training courses which she paid for herself. She makes it very clear that she considers herself a valuable member of your organization, speaks up in meetings for other women, and always corrects any sexist jokes or comments in quite an aggressive way.

Barry is sixty-eight years old and is a devoted Christian. He attends church at least once a week. He reveals in a private conversation with you that he is homosexual, and has had a relationship with another homosexual man for twelve years.

Action

Sometimes prejudices in groups, work teams, departments, or whole organizations can cause major dysfunction. In Part Two there is a workshop model which will help you address some of the issues connected with group dysfunction. If you acknowledge there is a problem, however, and that it is one your organization is committed to overcoming, then there are trainers and consultants in this field who offer a variety of methods to tackle the problems of prejudice, discrimination, and inequality.

Contrary to many people's beliefs, engaging in a long-term process of prejudice reduction or limitation in an organization is a liberating, though difficult, experience. We have little to fear in the process of true understanding, but there is much to be afraid of in the blindness that many prejudices cause.

Discrimination

Discrimination could be described as acting on a prejudice, and involves showing bias, singling out or treating a person or group of people differently because of an emotionally held belief about them. It is not always negative, but is always selective. Discrimination in the workplace is often a cause of conflict. If you were managing the person who you ranked as most objectionable in the previous exercise, could you be sure that you would not pass him or her over for promotion, for example, in favor of one of the others? Would you give the person ranked least objectionable all the best jobs? Probably not, but the danger is obvious; if you rely too much on emotionally formed opinions of people, based on convention, assumptions, and partial knowledge, the quality of judgment and decisions would be questionable. There are many examples in the book of effective methods of ensuring that you build interactions based on understanding and knowledge characterized by openness, trust, and mutual respect.

Getting Beyond Stereotypes and Prejudices

When you encounter people who set off prejudices you experience an emotional surge which affects your behavior. The source of these emotions is in an earlier experience, which may have been a brief encounter with some persuasive information in a conversation, book, television show, or film. You cannot change that experience, but you can alter your attitude to it.

Consider the individual

Getting beyond stereotypes and prejudices (which will be examined closer in later chapters) is a continuous process. Emotional and psychological changes are necesary to replace long-standing, ingrained stereotypes and prejudices with more accurate, fair, and complete views of people. There are practical steps which can be taken, however, to move yourself and other people away from stereotypical views of people and situations. Consider these examples.

- Use questions to understand more about people and their behavior.

    — "Could you explain a bit more about your beliefs?"

    — "Is it true that...?"

- Read and talk to people about their background, beliefs, and behavior.
- Listen carefully and actively, paying attention to details.
- Discover new words that give you the capacity to avoid stereotypical descriptions.
- Facilitate communication between others that avoids stereotypical language and perceptions.

When you do feel the emotional weight of past prejudice rising, once again, the use of the four steps in the constructive conflict management process (see Figure 3) will ensure that you react more positively. Accurate perception will keep you sharply focused on the present and, by turning into and controlling your emotions, you will be able to moderate the effect of the prejudices you have built up.

Get to know the person   Questioning specifically about the person is particularly useful. Concentrate on getting to know more about the person who sets off your prejudice alarms.

"What is it like being homosexual in a school like this?"

"Do you think that affects your relationship with students and teachers?"

These questions prevent you from making false assumptions, such as

"Gay! I bet the men in the school run away from you!"

"I'm not letting you near my son anymore."

There are many examples later in the book of skills and techniques that will enable you to overcome your prejudices through a combination of investigation, facilitation, and active listening. These skills will also be useful for encouraging others to interact positively and overcome their negative views of one another.

How Do I Feel About This? You and Conflict

2

*O*f the 150 or so people working in conflict management in the United States interviewed in 1991, at least 80 percent admitted that "a strong, full sense of self" is one of the fundamental requirements of their trade. This chapter aims to increase your awareness of yourself with particular regard to conflict.

A variety of exercises will assist you in understanding your characteristic beliefs about the images and messages of conflict and responses to conflict. It concludes with a chart of constructive conflict management characteristics (Figure 6) against which you can rate yourself.

CONFLICT MANAGEMENT INSTRUMENTS

There are several established instruments for evaluating your conflict management behavior (Thomas and Kilman 1974), such as models (Blake and Mouton 1971), styles (Hall 1969), and the Management of Differences inventory (MODI) (Kindler 1988), which provides a list of "strategic styles."

You will be presented with several checklists and charts that provide you the opportunity to create your own conflict collage—a collection of thoughts, beliefs, and behaviors that you associate with yourself and conflict. There are eight sections to the collage.

1. Do you believe in win-win resolutions?
2. Are you like fire or ice?
3. Do you like to be in control and in charge?
4. Are you a persecutor, rescuer, or victim?
5. What are your people hooks?
6. What are your situational hooks?
7. What messages do you have about conflict?
8. What are you good at and what would you like to change?

Do You Believe in Win-Win Resolutions?

Two checklists of beliefs follow. The first list contains beliefs that keep people from acting for mutual gain and paralyze cooperation. The second list comprises those that facilitate resolutions in which all parties have a chance of getting something that they want, otherwise known as win-win resolutions. Do you hold any of these beliefs?

This book contains ideas and suggestions for you to increase your levels of understanding of people and their behavior and to enlarge your repertoire of constructive responses that help you work toward win-win resolutions. Being more skillful with people, and thereby improving the quality of contact you have with them, will counteract many of the more negative views you hold about people's capacity to manage their differences.

Are You Like Fire or Ice?

An industrial arbitrator in New York had a vivid way of describing the attitude she took to her clients. She was working against a background of mistrust and obstruction in a major dispute that had been going on for some time. Her first task was to get the parties to trust her.

CHECKLIST

Beliefs That Lead to Impasses

- It is impossible to solve anything. Life and its difficulties are too complex.

- I feel helpless, so let's argue.

- Stand firm, don't give up.

- Things don't work out.

- I can't expect too much.

- Someone has to suffer.

- You ask stupid questions.

- There are a lot of things that are none of my/your business.

- This is just the way it is.

- I just can't get anywhere with certain people.

- There will always be winners and losers.

- I can't trust anyone.

Well, you can be like ice, remote, hard, and distant, and eventually you may chill them into agreement. Or you can give them fire, burning them down with passion and conviction, mixed with a touch of human warmth so that they like you and respond to you. Me? I like to give them a combination.

If I need more ice then they get cool water that wakes them up but doesn't freeze them out. If it's more heat they need then I turn up the fire and they can dip their hands in, but don't get burnt.

If fire is human passion, conviction, humor, and warmth, and ice is a distant, hard, tough quality, which do you use most at times of conflict? Or do you use both of them during conflicts?

CHECKLIST
Beliefs That Lead to Win-Win Resolutions
■ It is possible to solve problems. We can handle the complexities of life.
■ I don't need to argue to be powerful.
■ I am willing to let go.
■ Many things do work.
■ I expect a lot of myself and others.
■ Much human suffering can be eliminated.
■ There is no such thing as a stupid question.
■ There is very little that is none of my/your business.
■ There are other ways.
■ I can get somewhere with anyone.
■ It is possible for everyone to win.
■ It is possible to trust myself and others.

Do You Like to Be in Control and in Charge?

People understand differently what it means to be in control or in charge. A recent study of gender-based perceptual biases in mediation (Burrell et al.) uncovered distinct differences in the parties' perception of the untrained mediators.

> Female mediators were viewed as less controlling... even though they behaved in a more controlling fashion. Men were perceived as more controlling, even though their behavior was less controlling... even though they [the women] pursue their role with as much fervor as their male counterparts, they are perceived to be less in charge of the interaction.

Interactions with others in conflict situations place people under extreme stress, which makes it difficult to focus on objective reality. In the above study, people reverted to their stereotypical assumptions. Women and men, according to this study, are assessed very differently with regard to their capacity to be in control or in charge.

Many people do not expect women to be in charge and often either react to them as though they are not or, once it is clear the woman is the person in authority, consider her to be incompetent. A senior woman manager who attends an event with a subordinate male staff member often has to contend with behavior which denies her position, as person after person greets her male colleague first, assuming him to be the senior party.

Bearing this in mind, ask yourself three questions. During conflict situations

1. What do you think being in charge and being in control mean?
2. Do you think you are in control or in charge?
3. What do others think of you?

Being "in control" in a conflict situation is not as advantageous as we often believe. Amy and Thomas Harris (1986), in their sequel to *I'm OK, You're OK,* suggest that controlling other people is like "trying to keep five basketballs in a swimming pool all underwater at the same time. It is tiring, precarious if you are in the deep end, and it can't be done." Being in control of yourself, however, is extremely useful. This will become more likely as you get to understand yourself and improve your responding skills.

Are You a Persecutor, Rescuer, or Victim?

The Karpman Drama Triangle (Harris 1985), shown in Figure 5, is a useful way to understand some of the seductive positions we take up in our interactions with others which often lead to conflict.

The triangle contains three types of roles which do not get individuals what they want. The three roles are persecutor, victim, and rescuer.

The persecutor invites a person to strike back and does not encourage cooperation. For example:

"You spend too much time at lunch."
"You're always moaning."

People who initially take the position of persecutor take the view "I'm okay, you're not okay." For example:

Figure 5. The Karpman Drama Triangle

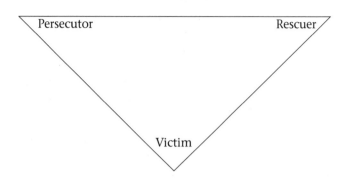

"Why do you always have to be such a pain in the neck?"

In fact, they do not really believe they are okay and, when challenged, often switch to the victim position. For example:

"Why am I such a pain in the neck? Because you always nag me, that's why you idiot!"
"I don't nag you! How can you say that? I try really hard to be good to you."

These two people are switching from persecutor to victim, attack to defense. Rather than taking on any of these roles, assertively asking for what you want and describing the behavior which concerns you are more effective ways of avoiding conflict and getting what you want if you experience behavior that you do not like (see Parts Two and Three).

Another switch is from persecutor to rescuer. Rescuers depend on rescuing other people for their identify and self-esteem, offering unrequested help and not believing others are able to cope with things on their own. People who feel guilty about persecuting switch to rescuer and give assistance that is not clearly contracted and is more than is needed. For example:

"You're absolutely useless...I'm sorry I said that about you. Have a chocolate. What, you don't like chocolates! You ungrateful..."

This person has switched from persecutor to rescuer to victim to persecutor.

Is any of this familiar to you? Do you find yourself involved in relationships where you are doing all the giving and feeling indignant about getting nothing back? Do you take on extra work and feel upset when no one notices? Are you a friendly manager who behaves in ways that you consider to be supportive and encouraging, only to find that people take advantage of you, taking liberties with time-keeping or discipline in general? If so, it is time to get out of the triangle and get what you want in another way.

What Are Your People Hooks?

An experienced conciliator with the Advisory Conciliation and Arbitration Service (ACAS) concluded a lengthy session with the representatives of major trade unions and a group of employers. The issues were complex, tactics sophisticated on both sides, and she really had to keep her wits about her. Throughout she was resourceful and honest, and controlled the warring factions in a way that enabled them to put their points across and negotiate effectively. They were very nearly at the point of agreement when one of the employers stood up and gave a lengthy political speech. All attempts the conciliator made to quiet him failed and her co-conciliator took over, allowing some angry exchanges. When she calmed down, she moved back to the negotiations.

When they came out the first conciliator looked tired and said, "God, he always does that; I just knew he would. I could kill him!"

This level of anger was surprising, especially coming from a woman whose behavior in the meeting epitomized reason. "There is always one! When they start, I know how grateful I am that I work with a partner, I get so angry!"

You are a very unusual person if there is not also one person who hooks you. When hooked, you experience emotions that are out of proportion to what he or she does, and you lose your composure, forgetting or scrambling patterns of behavior and skills that normally work well for you.

What hooks you? Look at the two following checklists and see if any items particularly affect you. If nothing on either list registers, is there another type of person or behavior that really gets to you? Use these checklists to compile a picture of exactly what it is about people that make them difficult for you to deal with.

Very few people are actually difficult by nature, but people do learn kinds of behavior which they believe will satisfy them, give them control over others, and get them what they want. Of course, you too will be difficult for other people, especially at times of conflict. As you begin to learn positive conflict management skills, some people will become easier to manage and you will have a better chance of resolving your differences with others and helping them to resolve theirs. Also, like the conciliator, consider working with a partner if you are going into a situation or dealing with people who you feel may pose you particular problems.

What Are Your Situational Hooks?

Particular situations and subject areas also hold specific perils. Discrimination is one such area. For instance, during a mediation, although the dispute was outwardly about who would repair a boundary fence, there were obvious signs as the discussion progressed that racism was lurking under the surface. One family regularly made assumptions about the other's behavior and values, and occasionally used language laced with racist overtones. Not only was the affronted family infuriated by the racist language, but the conciliator had a difficult time remaining calm and impartial as well.

Conflicts contain many elements, some of which may strike a raw nerve. Monitor your behavior as you encounter conflicts in the workplace and take note of the disturbing ones. What are the ones that trouble you the most?

CHECKLIST
Types of People

- Speechmaker—always wants to make lengthy speeches, never listens.

- Steamroller—pushes everyone around.

- Undercover agent—manipulates and attacks behind the scenes.

- Honest Joan—is always the first to be up front about feelings.

- "Me! Me! Me!"—turns every story around so they are constantly talking about themselves.

- Quiet type—says very little even when asked.

- Motormouth—always talking.

- Macho type—acts the way he thinks a man should.

- Liberated woman—asserts women's rights.

- Climber—ambitious and wants to get ahead at all costs.

- Lazy—never does quite enough work.

- Complainer—is never satisfied and always tells you.

- Everything's lovely—always smiles and says everything's okay, even when feeling bad.

- Perpetual pessimist—always looks on the negative side.

- Eternal optimist—looks too much on the bright side.

- Latecomer—bad time-keeper.

- Indecisive—can never decide what decision to make, or make it.

- Staller—keeps putting things off.

- Risk-taker and crazy-maker—push their behavior to the limits of boundaries.

- Aggressor—pushes, shoves, bullies, shouts, and takes up all the space.

CHECKLIST
Types of Behavior and Characteristics

Think of specific instances when any of the following behaviors or characteristics might have affected you strongly. What was it that got to you?

- Tone of voice?
- Gestures?
- Eye contact?
- Not listening?
- Touching?
- Posture and body position (upright, cramped, turned away, facing you directly)?
- Unwillingness to see other points of view?
- Unreliability?
- Incompetence?
- Expertise?
- False view of self?
- Flattery?
- Criticism?
- Untrustworthiness?
- Pettiness?
- Pedantry?
- Arguing on points of principle?
- Having no principles?
- Not doing what is promised or delegated?
- Competitiveness?
- Lack of ambition?
- Not being assertive?
- Physical appearance?
- Dress?
- Foreignness?
- Attitudes?
- Sexuality (homosexual, heterosexual)?
- Age?
- Disability?

CHECKLIST
Types of Conflict

- Disagreements over resources.

- Personality clashes.

- Disputes with your superiors.

- Differences of personal standards—what is acceptable moral or offensive behavior?

- Questions of belief, such as religion.

- Political conflicts—who has power, what is fair, what do you have to do to get power?.

- Role clashes—who does what, is accountable to whom, and responsible for what?.

- Customer or client complaints.

- Resistance to change.

- Disputes over allocation and performance of tasks.

- Allegations of harassment in the workplace.

- Cross-cultural confusion—differences over attitudes, norms, beliefs, and behavior that have cultural associations.

- Disagreements about methods of work.

- Complaints leading to disciplinary proceedings.

- Disputes over pay and work conditions.

- Meetings or groups where people cannot agree or one person wants something different from others.

Parts Two and Three give many practical suggestions for a variety of conflict situations.

What Messages Do You Have About Conflict?

Each person has strongly ingrained messages about success, love, and self-value which have accrued since childhood. These dictate how people behave, although sometimes people may not consciously acknowledge what those messages are. At times of stress, such as conflicts at work, these messages provide replicable responses and predictable outcomes.

A workshop at a conference explored the relationship between popular songs and "script messages," which are the constructs of messages through which we play out our lives. There was a very high correlation in the group between the messages implicit in the songs people liked and the script messages in their lives. Many people had not previously been aware of the parts of their script represented by the songs. A popular song of the 1980s, "I will survive," reminded one person that she did have a tremendous capacity for self-sustenance, although she often felt out of control and weak. The songs not only echoed people's lives, but also threw insightful light onto them.

What messages do you have about conflict? How do you act them out? These messages could be

- Something you remember your parents telling you.
- A motto from a club or a group to which you belonged.
- Words remembered from a friend.
- Title or lines of a song.
- Extracts from a book.
- Phrases from your religion.
- Something you heard in a film, on radio, or on television.
- Pieces of learning from a training course or management book.
- Slogans or other fragments you remember.

Some examples of these conflict messages include

- Fight for your rights.
- Turn the other cheek.
- Don't let them get away with that.
- You should be seen and not heard.
- Come out fighting.
- Don't let them walk all over you.

- War, what is it good for? Absolutely nothing....
- Fight the good fight.
- There is no such thing as a just war.

The checklists earlier in this chapter about beliefs connected with conflict contain other phrases that may remind you of your own messages about conflict.

Finally, what are you good at and what would you like to change? Often this is phrased as, what are your strengths and weaknesses?

What Are You Good At and What Would You Like to Change?

Think of a minimum of three things that please you about your capacity to deal with difficult people and situations. Write them down and keep them. Add to the list as you notice more.

What would you like to change? Think of specific examples when you think you could have handled people and situations more effectively.

CONSTRUCTIVE CONFLICT MANAGEMENT CHARACTERISTICS CHART

The characteristics listed in Figure 6 are in no particular order of priority; they are equally important. They form the basis of the kinds of desirable human interaction that should be encouraged.

Rate yourself from one to ten in each area. Then think if there is any rating you would like to improve. Make this your target and add it to the chart. Keep the chart so that you can monitor your development. Only a saint could match up to this specification at all times. There are bound to be situations that make you want to scream, lose control, and be selfish and uncooperative.

You always can improve

If you continue to develop these characteristics and concentrate on using constructive conflict management skills and techniques, you will be able to come through even the most difficult conflict with your integrity intact and a much more positive attitude to other people.

Figure 6. Constructive Conflict Management Characteristics

Characteristics	Self-Rating	Target (10 is maximum)
■ Ability to understand and deal with difficult emotions		
■ Empathy and ability to earn trust		
■ Openness and sensitivity to others		
■ Emotional balance (understanding of own feelings and how they affect you)		
■ Ability to balance your feelings and views with those of others		
■ Self-awareness and integrity		
■ Ability to take non-judgmental stance		
■ Capacity to learn from experience		
■ Willingness to be assertive		
■ Ability to think creatively and deal with complex factual material		
■ Thoroughness and professionalism		

MAKING THE MOST OF CONFLICT

Learning informs feelings and behavior. Conflicts challenge us to learn about ourselves and others, but we will not learn if we cannot control the gut reactions some people and situations set off in us. Effective conflict managers choose how to behave, staying aware of their feelings, and expressing them appropriately where necessary.

Step Back and Take a Wider View 3

*O*nce you strive for clarity of perception and begin to understand and take charge of your emotional and behavioral responses, you then have to learn to step back and take into account factors other than those associated with your own perspective. If there were only one perspective then there would be no conflict.

The conflict manager's job is to encourage a process of communication and understanding through which a resolution, a narrowing of differences, can be sought. Constructive conflict management commits you to take other people into consideration, even if you are involved directly in a conflict with them. There are also other elements to take into account.

SELF, OTHERS, AND THE CONSEQUENCES

Imagine you are in charge of a rowboat on a river. There are five other people and yourself with an oar each. In midstream, after an hour of steady progress, an argument breaks out. Two people refuse to row further. One wants to have a rest since he is tired, the other thinks the boat is difficult to row but wants to push on. As they argue, another person says timidly that he is getting concerned because he cannot swim and the boat is out of control. There are two others who continue to row but since they are on the same side, the boat starts to go round and round in circles, and you are so busy working out what to do that you have not been rowing effectively to straighten out the boat. You now have a boat going nowhere, full of unhappy people.

Careful planning went into the trip, and everyone was happy when they set off, but now things have changed. As the person in charge, everyone is looking to you for a solution. They have forgotten the cooperative mood that set the context for the trip, are fast losing their patience with one another, and feelings are running high.

The argument has brought many issues to the surface, and you are not achieving what you set out to accomplish. Furthermore, differences have materialized that were not evident when you planned the trip. There is a need for action, but also an opportunity for everyone in the boat to learn.

The conflict in the rowboat contains four separate elements.

- Yourself—what can you do? What do you want?

- Others—what are they doing? What do they want? What are they likely to do to you?

- Situation—what does it tell you? What limitations does it put on action? What does everyone need to know?

- Consequences—what will happen in the future? How will the outcome affect people?

All conflicts in which you have a role as manager have these same four elements. These elements determine the outcomes and the resolutions, which are neither ideal nor perfect. The basic aim of positive conflict management is to seek resolutions which achieve the best possible balance between yourself, others, the situation, and the consequences. This is irrespective of how fierce or insignificant, long-running or instant, complex or straightforward the conflict is, and of who is involved.

Keep these four perspectives in your mind—self, others, situation, and consequences. They will guide your action and, using them, you will become adept at analyzing conflicts quickly as they happen. Establish a key group of questions to ask yourself under each of the four headings. Who, where, what, when, and how questions are the most useful. Use the checklist at the end of this chapter to help you build up a repertoire of useful questions to ask yourself about any conflict. Select from it, or add ones that you find more helpful. This emphasis on inquiry is continued in Part Two which covers many techniques for questioning disputants.

Ask questions

Considering the four elements of self, others, situation, and consequences immediately helps you to

■ Take a step back emotionally.

■ Focus on what is going on around you.

■ Be more in charge of yourself.

■ Understand other people's points of view.

■ Be realistic and reasonable in your approach.

■ Move the conflict away from the past where nothing can be changed.

■ Think of the future where change can happen.

In the rowboat example the payoffs would be immediate. You could

- Establish sufficient calm to continue the trip in safety.

- Open a dialogue about how best to manage the rest of the journey.

- Row more effectively, navigating the river's difficult currents.

- Learn a great deal about the strengths and weaknesses of the team.

- Identify issues that need to be tackled when the trip is over.

This form of conflict analysis places the manager in the role of investigator and facilitator. Tasks associated with this role are in stark contrast to the tasks people assign themselves when they are involved in conflicts, as demonstrated by Figure 7 below.

Figrue 7. Contrasting Tasks of Conflict Managers and Participants

Conflict Manager	Conflict Participant
Seeks facts	Makes assumptions
Thinks about the situation from several angles	Narrow-minded
	Argues from own point of view
Gets people to explain	Does not listen
Looks for what is best overall	Singularly pursues own ends

Approaching difficult situations and people using conflict analysis means you will be constantly increasing your understanding of the psychology of disputants, and anticipating sharp moves or combatant gestures. Your responses will be much more measured as you are less likely to get hooked by such behavior.

THREE WORKPLACE CONFLICTS

This section covers three examples from Troubled Associates Ltd. where the benefits of this four-sided conflict analysis can be seen. You will have the opportunity to decide what you would do if you were the manager.

1. Read the examples and think about them from the four different perspectives of self (you are the conflict manager), others, situation, and consequences.

2. In each example there are two questions under each category of self, others, and situation in order to keep things simple.

3. The situations are described from each person's point of view, and then analyzed in terms of the likely consequences of acting too much from one of these perspectives.

Example One

Carol, a twenty-six-year-old, born in England to black Jamaican parents, is secretary to David, the white, English head of finance who is thirty-one years old. She has a complaint about Ron, the accounts clerk, who is sixty years old and is also white. Carol tells David that Ron has been aggressive toward her, which she could tolerate, but that now he has started to make remarks which she believes have a distinct racial bias. She knows these are not the most extreme kind of racist comments, but still finds them objectionable. She has told Ron she does not like it, but he has continued to make remarks like, "why are you giving me all those black looks?" and, "keep your curly hair on." Carol is upset and angry.

Some of the Factors to Consider

Self

David

- Comfort—how comfortable does David feel with this?
- Competence—does he consider himself competent to deal with it?

Others

Carol

- Interests—how important is this to her?
- Personality—what kind of person is she—reliable, truthful, resilient?

Ron

- Status—how powerful is he in the organization?
- Role—what part does he play in the department?

Situation

- Policy—are there policy guidelines in this area?
- Procedures—is there a procedure that instructs you to act in a certain way?

David's View

David feels comfortable with the emotional level, and sufficiently knowledgeable and competent to deal with this issue. He sees it as a challenge. Carol works hard and he does not want her to loose motivation. She is tough enough to look after herself, so David assumes this is a professional complaint, and not personal. Ron has been hostile and resistant to David in the past because David has only been in the company a short while, yet has a higher position than Ron. David looks forward to this opportunity to put him in his place. The company has no policies with regard to harassment, so David has an opportunity to influence policy if he can deal with this successfully.

Carol's View

Carol was initially surprised by Ron's behavior but tolerated it quietly at first, calmly telling him that she did not appreciate it. Eventually she found the remarks annoying and warned Ron that she would have to do something about it if he did not stop. Carol sees herself as a reasonable person. When Ron did not stop she decided to complain to David, even though she knew it could create a lot of fuss. Carol decided to complain, because she thought the company should take a stand on issues like this to show they valued their black and female staff. She is not sure what David's reaction will be, but this is an important professional matter, which she feels quite upset about.

Ron's View

Ron sees himself as a character. He likes to work, but gets bored if everything is too serious. Having been with the company for thirty years he expects some respect, and finds it difficult at times dealing with the various people in the company. There was a time when he felt he had something in common with everyone, but not now. Carol "took him too seriously," and the more she objected the more he wanted to tease her. He did not think this was a complaint David would take seriously. He is confident that David would not want to "stir things up" as this would be bad for his department.

Situational Factors

There are no written procedures with regard to harassment, but it is in David's job description to ensure the best possible working relationships between staff. It is not clear what happens if David cannot manage this situation successfully, or where else Carol can go.

Consequences

1. There is an immediate benefit for Carol in David's approach, since her complaint is taken seriously, but at the point of contact with David she will need a caring, sensitive approach. David risks being too detached and professional and not giving sufficient acknowledgment of the discomfort Carol feels. Harassment is always experienced as hurt, regardless of how everyone else, including the other party involved, sees it.

   The long-term consequence for Carol and other staff who have difficult experiences with colleagues may well be that they will not bring such issues before David if David is too detached. As a result, tensions may accumulate and some people will begin to lose motivation.

2. Ron is not aware of Carol's feelings, nor does he feel he has transgressed any company rules. This is going to make him immediately resistant to a direct challenge. If David is confrontational and blaming, Ron may well become defensive and seek allies, thus polarizing opinions and generating

wider ill feeling. Ron may not be able to learn after so many years in the company, but this is an opportunity for education as well as a question of discipline.

3. As there are no guidelines, David is right in thinking he may set a precedent. Immediately he will be judged by the parties on what he does. In the long term, this incident may well provide the stimulus to develop policies in this area, but David will be hindered if he puts pressure on himself and the parties to get it all perfect this time.

What would you do? How would you manage this situation?

Suggestion

Give acknowledgment

1. David needs to balance reason and emotion with regard to Carol and Ron. Acknowledging Carol's situation requires a mixture of professional respect and empathy to give her the confidence that she is being taken seriously and to establish the trust which will be needed to get a workable resolution. Ron is likely to be difficult, but will be less so if David is open and straight with him, and seeks cooperation and acknowledgment of the problem. David can channel any disapproval he may feel into clear statements about standards and should not be overindulgent (see Chapter 6, Dealing With Prejudiced Behavior).

Take it step-by-step

2. In order to counteract his own desire to "do well," David should take a step-by-step approach and not pressure himself or the parties.

Listen and question

3. David has enough information while hearing Carol's complaint to take a balanced approach. If he listens more actively (see Chapter 5) and uses open questioning (see Chapter 7), he will give Carol more of a feeling of acknowledgment, while also getting the information he needs.

Example Two

Surinder is the head of personnel. He is a thirty-five-year-old Indian man, who has been with the company for three years. He ordered 2,000 staff appraisal sheets, which he redesigned with the help of a printer who has had links with the company for twenty years. When the sheets are delivered there are two major mistakes. He has checked his instructions and knows that they were correct and clear, but the printer denies this. Surinder is meeting with Doug, a white, forty-eight-year-old printer's representative, who has been the link between the two companies for fifteen years. Doug insists that this mistake was not a printer's error, and will reprint only if Surinder is prepared to authorize payment for the extra work.

Some of the Factors to Consider

Self

Surinder

- Principles—is there a point of principle which is important?
- Preparation—how well do you know the background? Are there any other options?

Others

Doug

- History—what was done in similar circumstances before and how does this affect the present? What is accepted practice?
- Relationships—are there powerful issues? Are there important allies or enemies?

Situation

- Deadlines—are there important time restrictions?
- Cost—what are the budget implications?

Surinder's View

The printer responsible for the error should bear the cost of rectifying it. Surinder has checked previous transactions and there have been errors before, all of which his company has paid for. This time he is determined to establish a new principle. The deadline is urgent, because a new procedure involving the forms is scheduled to start in a week's time. Surinder is prepared to postpone this procedure if the dispute cannot be settled in time. His main aim is to establish a clear, businesslike arrangement, especially since links between the printer and his company have been somewhat informal in the past. There is money left in the budget, but he will not make it available for this reprint.

Doug's View

Doug agrees that the written specifications were clear, but suggests that Surinder's accompanying telephone instructions were not. In the past there have been misunderstandings and Surinder's predecessor always took responsibility for them and paid any extra cost incurred. In fact, there have never been any problems with payment as Surinder's company is wealthy and successful. Doug knows the director well and he thinks that this might sway Surinder his way. The deadline is no problem to him, but he wants an assurance of payment before he reprints.

Situational Factors

The deadline is there because a whole new appraisal system is starting. Training and induction procedures are scheduled to begin immediately after the deadline. It would be a major problem if this date had to be changed. In addition, competitive quotes are never obtained for printing jobs. These printers have been used for as long as anyone can remember. No one has checked whether or not the current printers offer good value for money.

Consequences

1. Surinder is right in wanting to establish a principle as this will be very constructive for future dealings. However, the extra work and trouble caused by rescheduling the new procedures would cause immediate and future extra cost.

2. Doug does not want to lose the business from this company as they are regular customers and timely payers. If he does reprint, he will have immediate costs due to the reprint, but future benefits from continued good will.

3. Surinder is concerned about his status and authority and will need to reassure himself that, whatever the consequences of this dispute, he has the authority from and confidence of his senior management.

What would you do? How would you manage this situation?

Suggestion

1. The most important immediate need is out of Surinder's control—the reprints must be done on time. This supersedes other needs. Even if some payment is made for the extra printing, reprinting is still the most economical approach.

Prioritize needs

2. A principle should be established and some guidelines drawn up for future contracts. This can be done by adopting a progressive approach, such as starting from a very firm position of principle, but being prepared to temper this in return for future agreements.

Be prepared to compromise

3. Surinder will also encourage Doug to accept some responsibility and make a financial move in Surinder's direction. If he will not, then he should be made aware of the future consequences, that other printers will be contacted for future work. This is a mutual process of balancing long-term and short-term interests.

4. Any prestige or rights Doug has outside the competence of his firm is an issue for later. Surinder does have to weigh the director's influence in two ways: First, if the director really is an influential figure in this, then what would be the cost of earning his displeasure? Second, does Surinder want to continue in a company which places the informal associations of its top management above formal working relationships between responsible staff and contractors?

Example Three

Manjit is twenty-five years old, Indian, and has been a receptionist for the company for the last six months. She is pleasant, but sometimes connects people to the wrong extension. Her manner with visitors is courteous; however, she has in the past kept them sitting in the reception room for too long or sent them to the wrong part of the building. Helen, the quality control manager, who is thirty-five years old and black, is temporarily taking the place of Patricia, the head of customer services. She has a very angry customer on the phone who is complaining of extreme rudeness and inefficiency by the receptionist. The customer describes how she was made to wait a long time and was given two wrong extensions. When she criticized Manjit she got a rude response and asked to speak with the manager. The customer says her company will terminate its contract if she does not get a written apology.

Some of the Factors to Consider

Self

Helen

- Role—is she the right person to be dealing with this?
- Time—what are the other immediate commitments on her time?

Others

Customer

- Feelings—are they congruent with the situation?
- Reasons—is it clear what has happened and why this conflict has arisen?

Manjit

- Awareness—is she aware there is a problem?
- Competence—what is her record of competence?

Situation

- Context—what can be achieved by phone? Does this restrict the approach?
- Rules—are there any rules or guidelines for situations like this?

Helen's View

She is writing a report for the director that she must complete urgently and is running out of time. She wants to help, but is aware that this is quite a serious complaint. Helen does not normally deal with customer complaints, nor does she have the authority to decide on what action to take. She wants to apologize politely and refer the customer to Phillip, the customer relations officer, right away.

Customer's View

She is very angry and wants to be heard. She believes that companies should be run efficiently and that receptionists are key people required to handle their calls and visitors politely. This incident has upset her principles and inconvenienced her. She is aware that her company is a good customer, which gives her the right for attention, and is determined to have her say.

The written apology would be beneficial for both sides, she believes, as it would assure them of better relationships in the future.

Manjit's View

Manjit is not aware how strongly this customer feels, but knows a complaint has been lodged. So far, no one has given her any reason to doubt her competence and she waits with interest for feedback on this issue. She would not like to think she has upset someone.

Situational Factors

1. Phone conversations are different from face-to-face ones as they impose visual and electronic distance between the parties. This should not minimize their importance, however. Phone behavior has an immense impact on people, especially those phoning for services from outside an organization. In this instance, the customer had already spoken to three different people on the phone.

2. There is an employee handbook that provides guidelines and training for all managers in dealing with customer complaints. This was considered

necessary when other managers were covering for the customer relations officer.

3. Helen must make a quick decision since one minute's phone silence is much more likely to frustrate the caller than one minute's face-to-face silence.

Consequences

1. Although Helen is in a difficult position due to her own work commitments, passing this customer back to reception will probably make matters worse.

2. If these kinds of complaints cause disruption frequently for Helen, then she should take the first opportunity to discuss this problem with Patricia and other concerned parties.

3. The risk of loss of business must be taken into account, plus the effect of such an incident on the organization's image.

4. Manjit needs to have a clear sense of her level of competence, and also the consequences for both customers and the organization of misconnections and delays. This is an opportunity to be specific and provide a better framework with which to monitor her competence. But she is reprimanded or blamed without any previous hint of censure, this will not have a positive effect on her self-image and desire to improve.

What would you do? How would you manage the situation?

Suggestion

Listen

1. Under the circumstances, particularly as the employee handbook clearly outlines managers' shared responsibility to take customer calls, Helen takes time to listen to the complaint and to assure the customer that she is being taken seriously.

Feedback

2. Helen has no direct responsibility for Manjit, but should inform both Manjit and her supervisor of the outcome, and give them both feedback on

Manjit's behavior so that her needs can be taken into account.

3. Helen should evaluate what the impact of handling complaints is on her time schedule. If there is a problem, she should register that with the team leader as soon as possible. Customer complaints place serious demands on the listener's concentration, particularly if they are feeling harassed or short of time as Helen is (see Chapter 8 for more on dealing with an angry customer).

You may disagree with some of the analyses of these situations and the suggested aims and outcomes. Conflict management is, of course, concerned with outcomes, and people will feel most satisfied when they are pleased with the outcome. However, much research also shows that disputants are equally concerned with process, such as how they were treated and whether the conflict manager and the other people involved were sensitive to their positions, needs, and interests.

Summary

Remember: self, others, situation, consequences

Analyzing conflicts from the perspective of self, others, situation, and consequences will enhance your capacity to be sensitive to others and ensure that you are in touch with reality. This will gain you respect and facilitate well-grounded, workable agreements.

By now you should understand more about the constructive conflict management approach. Parts Two and Three will give you a great deal of practical information about how to put the approach into practice and achieve healthy, positive workplace relationships, which will survive and prosper from conflict.

QUESTIONS TO ASK ABOUT CONFLICTS

Following are questions you may ask yourself to help decide which conflict management steps to take. Obviously you will only have a short time to think if a conflict arises or is brought to your attention and needs immediate action, so develop a core group of useful questions for such circumstances.

After you have gathered more information, take time to consider the situation again. Questions such as those on the checklist below will help you sort out the complexities of conflicts which always have four sides, not just one.

CHECKLIST
Questions to Ask About Conflicts

Self (the person responsible for managing the conflict)

■ General—what can I do? What do I want? What are my responsibilities?

■ Interests, values, needs, principles, beliefs—how do these affect my position? Can I manage this conflict fairly? Am I comfortable with the people and issues involved?

■ Boundaries—are there any issues, kinds of behavior, or situations that I would prefer not to deal with? If so, what can I do?

■ Personality—how much of my own personality (humor, sensitivity, warmth, strength) can I use?

■ Style of management—will this fit in with my overall style of management? Is that important?

■ Strengths and weaknesses—what resources of strength can I draw on? Are there any weaknesses I should avoid, or that will cause me to act more cautiously?

■ Knowledge and competence—is there any specialist knowledge I require? Am I competent to manage this conflict?

■ Power, authority, status—do I have the power and authority to act effectively? Will the conflict affect this or my status?

■ Role—is it appropriate for me to be dealing with this?

■ Relationships—what are my relations with the parties? What effect will this have?

■ Resources—do I have any other demands on my time?

■ Personal experience—what has worked for me in the past?

CHECKLIST

Questions to Ask About Conflicts (continued)

Self (the person responsible for managing the conflict)

■ History and context—what else do I know? Are there any other important personal factors which need to be taken into account?

■ Add any others you find useful.

Others (the other parties involved in the conflict)

■ General—what do I know about them? What do they want?

■ Previous knowledge—have they been in similar situations before? How do they normally behave?

■ Interests, needs, values, beliefs, principles—how important are they to the parties? Will this affect how they behave?

■ Personality—are they reliable, sensitive, intolerant, difficult? Does this affect the approach I take?

■ Boundaries—are there limits to what the parties are prepared to accept? How do I manage these boundaries?

■ Strengths or weaknesses—are there particular strengths the parties have and how are they likely to use them? How will their weaknesses affect them?

■ Behavior—is there any excessive behavior? Are the levels of feelings congruent with events, or exaggerated? How can I deal with this? What does the body language tell me?

■ Awareness—how aware are the parties of the effect of their behavior and attitude?

■ Knowledge—do they have more knowledge in this area, and will this have an impact on the situation?

■ Competence—have the parties acted competently? If not, what course of action will be taken? Is the issue at stake really about levels of competence between parties?

■ Power, authority, and status—what is the power balance within the conflict? Is there inequality? If so, how should it be approached?

CHECKLIST
Questions to Ask About Conflicts (continued)

Others (the other parties involved in the conflict)

■ Role—how do the respective roles of parties have an influence on the conflict? Is there a lack of clarity about role, or role clashes?

■ Relationships—what relationships do the parties have? Do they need a close working relationship?

■ Resources—how is the conflict affecting their work? How much time can be spent working on the conflict? What is the cost of the continuing conflict?

■ History and context—what else do I know? Are there any other important factors which need to be taken into account?

■ Add any others you find useful.

Others (those not directly involved in the dispute)

■ General—how does the conflict affect them? How much of this do I take into account?

■ If after your initial assessment you realize that this conflict involves others, or is having an effect on others in the workplace, consider how bringing them into the process might be useful.

■ If their views are important, give them the same consideration as the other parties, and use the factors above as a guide.

Situation

■ General—what does it tell me? What does everyone need to know?

■ Rules—am I guided by organizational or legal rules about behavior, competence, and performance? Are the parties aware of these rules?

■ Procedures—are there existing procedures and structures to work from? How do you make them known?

■ Resources—are there cost and resource limitations? For example, if the dispute is over money, how much is available?

CHECKLIST
Questions to Ask About Conflicts (continued)

Situation

- Deadlines and time factors—do these impose limitations on possible courses of action? Can they be changed?

- People and management resources—how much time and energy can be spent on these people and this situation? How will this affect future work (for example, efficiency and motivation)?

- Company culture—is there a particular style of interacting, negotiating, or behaving which is influencing the situation?

- History and context—what else do I know? Are there any other important situational factors which need to be considered?

- Add any others you find useful.

Part Two

Responding Positively to People and Situations— Constructive Conflict Management Skills and Techniques

INTRODUCTION

Constructive conflict management requires a positive attitude to people problems and a strong sense of self, combined with a broad repertoire of responding skills. This part of the book demonstrates a wide variety of such skills.

Organizational behavior specialist Dean Tjosvold has conducted several studies of conflict in the workplace. In his 1985 study, he acknowledges the importance of procedures and cooperative goals (see Part Four, Chapter 24) for producing "productive conflict," but emphasizes that "managers and workers should...interact effectively" to ensure achievement of their goals. He cites several examples of this effective interaction, including discussing problems fully, feeling accepted as a person, influencing collaboratively, trying to understand each other's perspective, and integrating each other's ideas. In his study these elements were "highly related to each other and to positive outcomes."

"Effective interactions," characterized by the above elements, are achieved through a mixture of managerial skills. These are the tools that help repair broken relationships, tighten up leaky teams, and renovate cracking or crumbling trust and confidence. Your capacity to influence interactions positively will be greater if you have more basic tools at your disposal. In this part of the book you will find examples of new tools to add to your managerial kit.

Part Three contains structured processes, particularly mediation, which utilize these basic skills, and should be used in conjunction with Part Two.

Two Points to Remember

1. There is work for you to do, but also for the other parties.

2. You need progressive procedures of conflict management which include grievance procedures and disciplinary hearings.

Work for the Conflict Manager and for the Other Parties

The consultants and trainers who prepared an innovative program of peer mediation for the San Francisco Fire Department in 1991 made a very useful distinction between the work of the mediators and the work of the disputants. Conflict management requires all parties in a dispute to contribute to its effective resolution. Neither you, nor one of the other parties, should be doing all the work.

Example

Two heads of department come to you, their boss, because they are not able to agree on the allocation of staff for the new year. You called a meeting because they have both told you separately that they are finding it very difficult to talk to one another directly about this. Your aim is to facilitate communication. So, what is your work, and what is theirs? Figure 8 clarifies this.

Figure 8. Whose Work?

Aim	Conflict Manager's Work	Other Parties' Work
To facilitate communication	■ Restate information	■ Identify issues
	■ Encourage perception checks	■ Talk about views of the other
	■ Assist with summary	■ Work to understand how the other is affected

Sometimes parties will not or cannot do their part of the conflict management work. They may not be able to get themselves out of the pattern of escalation, oppression, and rejection. There may be other factors such as psychological incapacity or alcohol or drug abuse, or it may be that the situation simply cannot be settled by cooperative processes. On these occasions you need other options.

Progressive Procedures of Conflict Management

Within your organization you should have discipline, grievance, counseling, and appraisal procedures (see *Notes for Managers* series from the *Industrial Society Press on Effective Discipline, Appraisal and Appraisal Interviews* and *Industrial Relations,* or *Supervisors' Survival Kit).* There will probably be unions or staff associations to which people turn when conflicts arise. Whatever role you have in these procedures and groups, constructive conflict management skills will enhance your capacity to deal with conflict effectively before it escalates.

For example, active listening, facilitation, investigation, and assertion skills can transform appraisals from difficult, touchy meetings into frank, thorough, realistic exchanges in which differences are discussed, achievable targets set, and appraiser and appraisee have a clear idea of their responsibilities and tasks. This way, potential conflict is converted into constructive, ongoing discussion.

When people are not willing or able to participate in a constructive conflict management process you do need other procedures. For example, if your meeting with the departmental heads above does not work and they still cannot agree, then you could act as arbitrator (see Part Three), removing their responsibility for making the decision. If, as a result of your decision, one of them insults you and walks out, slamming the door, then you will probably want to use a disciplinary procedure as a method of censure. Whatever procedures you have in your organization, the skills in this section will assist you in gathering information, understanding the background, and making fair decisions.

Finding Your Way Around Part Two

The chapters in Part Two have the following themes.

1. Workplace situations representing different types of conflicts, including

   - Potentially violent disagreements.
   - Complaints about a colleague.
   - Prejudiced behavior.
   - Personality clashes.
   - Angry customers.
   - Conflicts with your boss.
   - Conflicts in groups.

2. A brief description of the steps to take

3. Detailed examples of helpful skills and techniques

4. Exercises to aid understanding, where necessary

5. Summary of useful skills

In Part Three there are four examples of structured processes—mediation, arbitration, and two step-by-step problem-solving methods—where many of these skills can be applied.

A Potentially Violent Disagreement

4

Situation

Patricia, the forty-year-old head of customer services, opens the door of the mailroom and sees Sean, the mailroom worker, and Phillip, the customer relations officer, involved in a rowdy argument. Sean is seventeen years old and left school a year ago. This is his first job, which he has had now for six months. Phillip is twenty-seven years old and has been in his position for two years. He worked for another organization before that. They are quarreling loudly and Sean is threatening to hit Phillip if he does not "lay off." They notice Patricia come in, but do not stop arguing.

PROCEDURES AND PRECAUTIONS

Disputes like this can escalate, drawing in innocent bystanders or anyone who seeks to get involved. The first rule in situations like this is to ask for help if you do not want to confront the situation yourself. Also, familiarize

---

Dealing with Violent Disagreements

Stop the fight.

↓

Calm and separate the parties.

↓

Initiate the resolution process.

↓

Gain agreement on what to do next.

---

yourself with the two Ps before acting in any situation where there is a threat of physical violence.

Be familiar with procedures

- Procedures—guidelines, codes of behavior, disciplinary procedures

Take precautions

- Precautions—making the situation as safe as possible for yourself and the parties involved

Procedures

Procedures are the protocol for dealing with different situations; they cover your responsibilities with respect to your organization and the people in it. They include

- Job descriptions.
- Guidelines for conduct and behavior.
- Complaints and grievance procedures.
- Disciplinary procedures.

Use or compile written guidelines

Patricia will find it easier to fulfill her role as manager with this clash between Sean and Phillip if she has familiarized herself with any written guidelines that might appear in an employee handbook, organizational induction package, contract of employment, or code of health and safety. Equal opportunities policies and practice guidelines should include clear guidelines on dealing with racist and sexist behavior.

Time spent developing and communicating such materials to staff in the workplace is time well spent. If you have the time and resources you can develop such materials through a collaborative process of negotiation with representatives from your work force.

Unwritten norms also exist within the culture of the workplace. Conflicts often occur due to misunderstandings over personal and cultural codes of behavior and it will be much to Patricia's advantage if she has some knowledge about such codes. For example, there may be a long-term understanding that working hours are quite flexible, so that as long as people work their full weekly hours it does not matter if they start late or finish early. It is useful to check out these kinds of understandings if you encounter behavior that surprises you.

Remember unwritten rules and norms

Get to know your organization, the people in it, and the available procedures for dealing with difficulties. Working within the boundaries of your organization, rather than treating each individual situation as a unique occurrence, will mean that you should also have the backing of senior staff in any action you take.

Precautions to be considered include the following points raised below.

Precautions

Alarm Systems

These are particularly important when dealing with large numbers of the general public, handling valuable materials, or working in a environment where there is a lot of contact with potentially volatile people and security is of paramount importance. They can be verbal or electronic signals, and should have clear, effective, and reliable response mechanisms. No one would phone 911 for emergency services if there were no response at the other end of the line.

Alarm systems

Support

Who else is around? You may not have to handle a situation alone. If Patricia does decide to act, who could come to her aid? How soon? She should thoroughly check this out beforehand if she has time.

Support

Prior Knowledge and Experience

Reflect on what you know about the parties and situation that will help you predict the outcome. Are these people

Knowledge and experience

normally aggressive? Have they been involved in such behavior before?

Knowing Your Limits

Know your limits

You should be familiar with how you respond in various situations and your people and situation hooks. If Patricia knows that she gets very angry with men who behave like this, and that this only makes things worse, then she should be particularly careful. If she has a choice, it might be safer and more productive not to get involved.

Special Training

Special training

If you are likely to have to sort out violent conflicts frequently then you should ensure that you have special training. Even then, there are some violent incidents, particularly those where a victim is suffering severe physical abuse, where the only solution if you are alone is to call the police. It is not the purpose of this book to encourage you to take unnecessary physical risks.

KEEPING YOUR HEAD WHEN OTHERS AROUND YOU ARE LOSING THEIRS

When situations happen as suddenly and unexpectedly as this, you have little time to analyze what is going on in depth, see the whole picture, or be absolutely clear about what to do. Get into the routine of using the first three steps of the constructive conflict management process.

- Good observation—be clear about what you see.
- Be aware of how you feel and how this may affect your behavior.
- Think quickly about what is best for yourself, others, and the situation, and what the consequences will be.

This should calm you down, and instill your actions with assurance and composure.

Keep your head

Breath control, positive body language, and visualization will also help calm you down. As a result, you should appear less threatening and more conciliatory to the parties.

Most people's breathing changes in association with strong emotion, either in ourselves or others. Regulating breathing helps slow our movements, as though our heart has more space to beat and our brains more room to think. Consciously breathe deep into your stomach initially, then relax your shoulders, keep your head up, and keep breathing at a comfortable pace.

Breath Control

Control breathing

Patricia needs to appear confident and positive rather than defensive or aggressive. Below are some examples of typical behavior to avoid and to adopt.

Positive Body Language

Defensive

Avoid defensive behavior. Do not avoid eye contact, clench fists, cross arms, or shift position from foot to foot and side to side.

Avoid defensive behavior

Aggressive

Avoid aggressive behavior. Do not stare at others, point, move or gesture suddenly toward them, or circle around them.

Avoid aggressive behavior

Confident

Act confident. Look others in the eye, stand straight and at ease with a balanced posture, change position slowly and deliberately if you think your position is not giving both parties the same sense of you.

Act confident

Positive

Take up an open stance. Move toward others steadily, using a gesture of welcome or greeting such as a handshake.

Be positive

Gestures are a powerful accompaniment to words, but do not assume everyone will understand them in the same way. In general, defensive or aggressive behaviors are to be avoided and confident, positive behaviors are to be adopted.

Visualization

Visualize positive outcomes

Visualization refers to the way we make visual images out of thoughts and feelings, and it can be used to energize us or to change our emotional condition, particularly at times of stress.

In this instance, visualizing a positive outcome will reproduce the sensations associated with success and suppress the fear of failure. Patricia might choose to

- Remember another time when she, or someone she knows, did well under similar circumstances.

- Construct an image in her mind which is calming and enriching, such as a warm sun, a fond hug, or the smile of approval of a friend or peer.

- Create a succession of visualizations of a successful outcome, modifying it as conditions change, but constantly focusing on the positive.

Visualization is also useful for generating options when verbal discussion is not helping, and for instances where there are different levels of understanding caused by extreme variations of linguistic competence.

STOP SIGNALS—INTERRUPTING AND DEFLECTING THE ARGUMENT

Internal calm should be matched by appropriate verbal responses. In such situations this is extremely difficult. Sooner or later the disputants will have to stop and face the consequences of their behavior. How do you stop them?

Use careful stop signals

Stop signals should

- Be clear and unambiguous.

- Not add heat to the situation.

- Deflect the disputants from their argument.

- Be delivered in a powerful, even tone of voice.

Questions are particularly useful in this respect, although they may seem initially a little unwieldy. Try practicing various phrases and tones of voice on colleagues or friends, getting them to put themselves in the role of an angry disputant.

Patricia would first have to interrupt Phillip and Sean.   *First interrupt*

"So what's going on here?"

This leading question in a slightly aggressive, disapproving tone could lead to Phillip's reply of

"I'm going to teach him a lesson."

Sean could answer with

"We're arguing—what does it look like?"

Or Patricia's first interrupt could be less critical.

"Why are you behaving like this?"

This approach encourages them to disengage and think, even though they may not like one another's answers. Phillip may say

"He's hopeless."

Sean could interpose with

"He never leaves me alone—always moaning!"

Patricia would need to rapidly follow up with questions that encourage elaboration.

"Hold on a minute, what do you mean? I'd like to get to the bottom of this."
"What are you going to get out of this, Sean and Phillip?"

As this question is forward-looking and deflecting, it encourages them to think about where they are going and to back off from what they are doing and what brought them to this stage.

If they appear to be pausing or disengaging, then   *Then deflect*
continue the deflection process by bringing in other perspectives.

"Seeing you two like this really upsets me. It would really affect everyone else in the office if they saw you too."

(Voices disapproval, tempered with a sense of caring.)

"If you two are this angry it really would be much better to let me help you sort this out without violence."

or

"This is really doing neither of you any good; I don't want to see you get yourselves into trouble."

(Communicates the effect of their behavior.)

"If you continue to fight I will definitely have to deal with this as a disciplinary matter."

or

"Do you realize fighting is an offense punished by instant dismissal?"

(Gives information about the worst consequences for them.)

WHAT NEXT?

Redirect energy

Positive interactions are designed to achieve more peaceful, fair agreements, reached in an atmosphere of cooperation and to reduce the possibilities of an explosion while redirecting the energy of the conflict into a more productive exchange. Whether or not you achieve this you will have to decide what to do next and communicate this to the parties. In a situation like this, the first step is to stop the fighting. If they do not, then this becomes a matter for disciplinary action. Assume that they do stop. Patricia will then move to initiate the resolution process.

Five Stages to This Resolution Process

1. Put the conflict on hold.
2. Be open about what you are doing.
3. Work for the first agreement.
4. Ensure you make agreements that will work.
5. Finalize the agreement.

Patricia has calmed and separated Phillip and Sean.

A police officer in Coventry, England, had a simple technique for such moments when the disputants are still emotionally engaged in their conflict, though distracted for a moment and separated by his intervention. If there are seats in the room, he sits each person down in turn with plenty of space between them until all are seated, then sits down himself. He says; "Okay. You sit down, then you sit down, then you sit down. Now I'll sit down. Now we'll stay sitting down and try to figure this out." He uses the pause in hostilities to control the physical setting so that the conflict cannot continue as it was, as a fistfight.

This is a useful model to follow; achieving a measure of physical control is a prerequisite for effective conflict management. Once you have achieved this, do not move right into the investigation stage, as the parties will most likely still be excessively agitated. At this moment they are vulnerable to a resurgence of destructive anger and are not yet ready to express themselves constructively. Continue the holding process by telling them what you will be doing next.

A key way of developing the parties' trust in you and demonstrating your desire to be even-handed is to communicate lucidly how you are aiming to handle the situation. Positive conflict management is dependent on this openness and respect for the people involved. In this instance it also serves other positive functions.

Put the Conflict on Hold

Put conflict on hold

Be Open About What You Are Doing

Communication intention

- Demonstrates authority and control over the process.
- Diverts thoughts from the immediate conflict.
- Informs parties what is expected of them.

Work for the First Agreement

The first step toward agreement on issues is agreement on process. In protracted international or multiagency negotiations a great deal of time is spent designing a process that will ensure equal participation, balancing of power, and realistic agreements.

Agree on process

Patricia has several options, such as seeing Phillip and Sean one at a time now, seeing them together, seeing them later, or sending them to the director. At this stage of the dispute she needs to assert her authority, but decides to give them a choice of options so that they can take some responsibility for the first agreement. Giving a choice to the parties, and offering them a chance to demonstrate responsibility can be an effective way of getting them on a positive track. In this instance, as feelings are still running high and Phillip and Sean have up to now exercised very little sense of responsibility, Patricia should frame those options in a way which restricts the parties' room for disagreement.

Frame options carefully

Not Useful

"Okay you two, what would you like to do now?"
This question is too open.

Useful

" I want to sort this out now you're both calmer. There are four ways we can proceed...(give choices). Think about them. You can choose one. Shall I repeat the options? I'll ask you, Sean, what you think first, and then Phillip. If you cannot agree, I will make the decision."

Offer options that reflect your aims

Patricia's aim is to give limited choice to the disputants, and also to move things along, and her framing reflects this. Think carefully about how you frame options, as they should reflect your aims.

Agreements are of little use if they do not work. Good feeling generated by unworkable agreements which are vague, badly thought out, unrealistic, or not fully understood, soon dissipates. Workable agreements are a fundamental part of effective conflict management.

A workable agreement

- Is carefully framed.
- Takes what you consider to be the important factors into account.
- Is clearly communicated and acknowledged by all parties.
- Is understood.
- Can be checked and followed up.

Basic questions such as *who* will do *what, how*, and by *when* must be asked, and the agreement tested in the light of resources, commitment, and other elements of the surrounding reality. Agreements that break down reflect badly on the disputants and on the conflict manager too.

The first agreement in any dispute is particularly important. It is often concerning a matter of process or how the conflict is going to be addressed. For most interpersonal conflicts, such as those this book concerns itself with, you are advised to spend time at the beginning of the conflict discussing and gaining agreement on the resolution process. Willing participants are much more likely to achieve effective, lasting agreements than passive victims caught in an alien process.

Patricia's carefully framed proposals gave Sean and Phillip what they needed to make a basic decision. Depending on their choice she now has to be more specific, remaining in control of the process. For example, if the decision is to see them separately first, then together

"You first Sean. Phillip, just wait outside in the hall for fifteen minutes then I'll call you in and Sean will wait outside. Then we will all get back together."

Ensure You Make Agreements That Will Work

Make workable agreements

Test out agreements

Willing participants are best

If she is to see them either together or separately later on, she states when and where. Alternatively, if she is sending them to the director, when, and what happens until then must be decided.

Conflict is often caused, and frequently prolonged, by broken agreements. How often have you agreed to something that is so vague that everyone will have a different understanding of what has been agreed?

> "Okay, let's all agree that we will do a lot better in the future."
> "I think we're all agreed that this is simply not satisfactory."
> "Let's agree never to be so inefficient again."

Do not be seduced into easy agreements about practical issues.

Finalize the Agreement

Patricia will restate the agreement and make sure that both disputants acknowledge her.

> "So, Sean, you've agreed to see me now, with Phillip [checks with him], and you, Phillip...."

Measurable decisions

Then she can move on to the exploration and investigation stage.

If Patricia cannot gain agreement, then she will decide. An effective decision is one that can be measured. The same factors apply as for workable agreements.

> "As you cannot agree, I will see you both together now."

SUMMARY

Useful Circumstances

- Procedures—disciplinary, recruitment, and grievance
- Precautions—alarm systems, support, prior knowledge and experience, knowing your limits, and special training

- Keeping your head when others around you are losing theirs—breath control, positive body language, visualization
- Stop signals—interrupting and deflecting

  1. Put the conflict on hold.
  2. Be open about what you are doing.
  3. Work for the first agreement.
  4. Get agreements that work.
  5. Communicate it to the parties and gain agreement.

Limitations

- Special training is required for high-risk situations and actual violence.
- If defusing or calming techniques do not work then you will need another option, such as disciplinary procedures.

A Complaint by One of Your Staff Against Another

5

Ron is the accounts clerk referred to in Chapter 3. He has been with the organization for thirty years. Recently there have been complaints about him making remarks that have upset people. Ron has always had a reputation for straight talking, but he is beginning to have a negative effect on people. Carol, the secretary to David, head of finance, wishes to make a verbal complaint about Ron's persistent racist remarks. In this chapter we are dealing with the first stage of the complaint: interviewing the complainant.

ACTIVE LISTENING

If you observe friends and colleagues, you will see many examples of bad listening.

- Interrupting people
- Not checking understanding

Interviewing the Complainant

Show concern and acknowledge the speaker's feelings.

↓

Collect information.

↓

Clarify the situation and check what is wanted.

↓

Remain in control as the listener.

- Answering with irrelevant, unconnected information
- Misinterpretation and misunderstanding

How many times have you asked for directions on the street, paid scant attention to the speaker, and found yourself only able to remember half the directions? Watch any television show presenting people with different political views, and see how often they avoid questions, interrupt, and just say what they want to say regardless of what has been said before. How often have you given clear verbal instructions only to find out later that they were misheard or misunderstood, when the work is returned done inadequately? Why is it so difficult for people to pay real attention to one another? Stress, external distractions, and the quantity and complexity of information affect the capacity to listen.

The development of electronic media has also influenced the way we interact and manage our "social reality."

> The social reality of people becomes more and more part of the visual and audiovisual media which favors the sense of distance personified in pictographs, cameras, plastic money, TV, and the computer. This social reality virtually keeps us from communicating with one another; it keeps us from searching for the goals people pursue in dealing with one another. Hearing, which is so important for oral communication, has lost its meaning in the visual world. (Slembek 1988)

There is also a commonly held misconception that it is easier to be in control when we are speaking, rather than listening. To the contrary, active listening enables the listener to gather information, affirm and acknowledge the speaker, and also remain in control. There are a variety of active listening techniques which overlap somewhat. They are sprinkled liberally throughout the rest of the book, since they are fundamental for positive conflict management.

Listen

Listening checks (Burley-Allen 1982) are questions asked by the listener to verify what has been said or what the situation is. These are useful in all conflict situations.

Listening Checks

Clarifying Check

This will help David obtain and clarify facts, check that what he is thinking is right, and understand what is being said by Carol. For example, he may ask

"Will you clarify what you mean by...?"
"I would like to know a little more about...."
"What exactly did you mean when you said...?"

Check understanding

Accuracy Check

If David is getting a lot of information and wants to be sure he has an accurate picture of what is going on, or if he wants to encourage further discussion, he could do an accuracy check. This is done by restating the basic ideas and issues as he has heard them, emphasizing important facts. This lets the speaker know he is taking time to listen, and also gives her the opportunity to correct him and continue adding information if she thinks it is necessary. For example:

"As I understand it the problem is.... Am I hearing you correctly?"
"What I think you said was...?"
"It would help me to be clear that I understand if I summarize what I have heard...."

Check accuracy

Feeling Check

Carol feels strongly about her complaint, and David uses a variety of feeling checks to

- Show he is listening and understanding.
- Reduce anxiety or other negative feelings.
- Let the other person know he understands how she feels.
- Let the other person know it is okay to have the feelings she has.

Check feelings

"You feel angry that Ron is so insensitive."

(Reflects Carol's feelings. There is more about reflecting in Chapter 16.)

"I hear you saying that you believe Ron is deliberately trying to provoke you."

(Paraphrases what Carol is saying in his own words.)

"It's annoying for you to have this happen."

(Matches the speaker's depth of feeling—light or serious.)

"Am I right in thinking that you also feel hurt and insulted by the fact that Ron does this so publicly?"

(Perception check.)

Summarizing Check

Carol is given a sense of the value of her emotions by David's ability to reflect, paraphrase, and be clear about them. He also needs to move her forward to get a good assessment of what the key facts and issues are, and what can be done. By sharing hypotheses and checking summaries with Carol, he invites her to join him in a process of analysis and assessment. This is "empowering" at a fundamental level, and also allows David, once again, to verify what he has learned about the situation. For example:

Summarize

"Let's see, so far we have looked at these factors...."
"These seem to be the main issues that concern you...."
"To summarize the main points as I heard them...."

Throughout the meeting David also uses many forms of acknowledgment, which show Carol he is interested, though neutral, and encourages her to keep talking. For example:

Acknowledgment

> "I see...."
> "Mmm hmm."
> "I get the idea."
> "I understand."
> "I can see this is a very serious subject to you."
> "Thanks for speaking to me."

*Acknowledge and
build trust*

He also maintained steady, though not insistent, eye contact and a relaxed upright posture, nodding his head at times.

WHAT NEXT?

By now Carol will feel that David understands, and is taking her seriously. He should then outline what the options are. Disciplinary or grievance procedures are one option, but David is going to try some constructive conflict management first.

Outline options

Because the dispute has not become too deep-seated yet, he senses that there is a chance for Ron and Carol to settle their differences without having to involve disciplinary measures. The first step is to meet Ron. Carol may well feel strongly that Ron should be "punished," and this is still an option, but David feels a more constructive approach initially will lead to a more lasting resolution. He wants to get Ron and Carol together, so that they can work through their differences.

First, David must gain Carol's approval. As he has built up trust by listening sensitively to her, she agrees that she would meet face-to-face with Ron providing she were clear how the meeting would be run. David intends to run the meeting as a mediation (see Chapter 13). This would provide the structure for Carol to feel confident that her rights and values are not going to be violated. Now David has to deal with Ron in a way that would prepare him for some mutual problem solving.

Gain approval

SUMMARY

Useful Circumstances

- Listening checks
  - — clarification check
  - — accuracy check
  - — feeling check
  - — summarizing check
- Acknowledgment

Limitations

- The complainant should enter into a constructive conflict management willingly. If the dispute contains a deep-seated, long-running difference, the use of grievance or disciplinary methods may be the only answer.

- Constructive methods, such as mediation, have been used effectively in some extremely harsh conflicts, but you should not coerce either party into such a process.

Dealing With Prejudiced Behavior 6

Prejudiced behavior is characterized by an unreasonable adherence to negative beliefs and assumptions
about people. It manifests itself most obviously in racist,
sexist, and other targeted violence, harassment, and
abuse. But what about the run of the mill prejudiced
individual or coworker?

Managers have a responsibility to ensure that interpersonal relationships at work are as positive as possible.
Many managers believe that prejudiced employees often
put a wrench in their psychological and emotional
works. When managers hear a comment or witness other
behavior that they know to be offensive to some of their
staff, they react in one of two extreme ways.

- They freeze, say nothing, or ignore the comment,
  thus avoiding the issue, and consequently colluding with the behavior.

- They get hooked, reacting strongly by saying, "How dare you! I find that really offensive!" or, "We don't use those words here!"

This kind of criticism is understandable, but it is unlikely to change the behavior of the prejudiced individual.

Prejudiced behavior is based on emotionally formed beliefs and invites an emotional response. Interrupting the emotional, irrational cycle that sustains prejudice is the most effective method of dealing with prejudiced behavior.

The competent handling of disputes involving this kind of behavior will reflect positively on an organization and so would suggest that all organizations develop a protocol for handling this type of complaint. Broadly speaking there are three ways of doing this.

1. Train the whole team. There are specialist organizations that will help you deal with issues such as racism, sexism, and ageism in the workplace in a nonthreatening, constructive way. They encourage sharing of mutual fears and concerns, gaining of knowledge about one another's cultures and background, and the development of personal and organizational strategies for building a workplace tolerant to differences.

2. Institute team-building exercises and strategies. People in your team will be more able to understand and respect sensitive issues and to avoid offensive behavior if they are encouraged to get to know one another and to share mutual goals and values. There is a group-building workshop model in Chapter 11 that will give you some ideas on how to do this.

3. Take a lead in developing positive responding skills. The remainder of this chapter demonstrates several such techniques.

If prejudiced behavior continues after you have adopted a constructive approach, then you may need to bring grievance or disciplinary procedures into play. The Equal Opportunities Commission (EOC) and Commission for Racial Equality are helpful in this respect.

Dealing with Prejudice

Respond effectively to difficult behavior.

↓

Explore the reasons behind the behavior.

↓

Prepare for problem solving by getting the individual to think about his or her behavior.

Situation

This is the other half of the Ron–Carol situation. David is meeting with Ron.

SENDING POSITIVE MESSAGES

David knows that Ron will be ready for him. Most people who regularly use biased remarks are accustomed to getting either hostile responses or subtle and supportive winks and nudges. They like to take sides, have strong views, and manipulate others into positions of favor or disfavor.

David is not going to give Ron what he wants, either approval or disapproval. He has set up a meeting with Ron, describing it as "a chance to discuss the situation between himself and Carol." He avoided saying "the complaint about you" or the "problem," as these are value laden. David also insists that he wants Ron to talk freely about his point of view, and tell David what facts he thinks are necessary.

Avoid approval or disapproval

Without showing approval or colluding with Ron's behavior by indirectly giving support by joining in or not taking a stand, David is sending positive messages to Ron that he is prepared to listen.

Do not collude

LISTENING AND MOVING CLOSER

Ron says

> "She's just the same as all the rest—lazy, and gets upset about the slightest thing!"

David moves slightly closer to Ron, and with a calm, warm tone says

> "What makes you think that? Tell me more."

Listen to learn

Do not confuse listening with approval.

Listening carefully gives us the chance to learn and the speaker the chance to experience an unfamiliar response. Ron is accustomed to the avoidance or confrontation which his remarks cause. Avoidance gives him permission to continue. Confrontation fuels his anger and resistance. David's willingness to listen contradicts Ron's previous experience. This is not the interaction he was expecting. It will be difficult for him to feel so bad about himself under the circumstances.

Empathize

Throughout this interaction David is using one of the key constructive management characteristics—empathy. Empathy is a capacity to relate to, acknowledge, and engage with a person in a positive way, without judging. It is different from sympathy through which we form emotional alliances and take sides. Both are natural, acceptable qualities in many situations, but for constructive conflict management it is empathy which achieves fair, balanced results, not sympathy which can be misleading and divisive.

Explore behavior

Exploring Ron's behavior through listening and questioning is the first step to breaking down his resistance to change. Neutral questions and empathetic responses will help David do this.

NEUTRAL QUESTIONS EXPLORING BEHAVIOR

Ron is there to answer a charge of verbal harassment. David clearly needs information, so he does not want to make Ron defensive, nor does he want Ron to believe he has an ally. Neutral questions are ones that do not suggest or lead to value judgments or interpretations. Here are examples of questions that are not neutral.

"Why do you have such a problem with Carol?"	(Judging)	*Critical*
"What have you done to improve your habit of annoying people?"	(Asking for information to confirm your assumptions)	
"Why have you been behaving like this?"	(Probing for motivation can often lead to defensive responses.)	
"So what's this little tiff with Carol all about?"	(Devalues Carol's complaint)	*Colluding*
"What do you think about Carol's complaint?"	(Diverting him from his own behavior and seeking judgment on Carol)	
"What on earth have you done to Carol this time, Ron?"	(Humor disguising the forming of an alliance against Carol—the suggestion is that Carol is overreacting.)	
"Could you tell me more about your view of Carol? I'm interested to know."	(Open question inviting Ron to describe his own experience)	*Neutral questions*
"Ron, can you help me understand how you get on with Carol?"	(Open question, with an affirmative message—David is seeking to understand.)	
"When was the last time you spoke to Carol? What happened? How often do you speak to one another?"	(Specific open questions)	

These neutral questions gather information in a nonthreatening way and encourage Ron to think about his own behavior.

Designing questions that are not threatening, blaming, or approving is a difficult task. Just listen to people around you or on television and radio for countless examples of inflammatory, loaded questions. Neutral questions are a simple, but important part of conflict management.

EXPRESSING EMPATHY

Counselors have a wide variety of empathetic responses, using the full range of verbal and nonverbal language. They are responses which acknowledge the other person, while not betraying a sense of approval or blame. For example:

Empathize

"I see."
"Thank you for telling me that."
"I can understand how you feel."
"Mmm mmm."
"Okay, so that's much clearer now."
"Was that painful for you?"
"It sounds as though that hurt a lot/you were very pleased/angry."

A nod of the head with open, relaxed eye contact and body position also express empathy.

There are many examples of these kinds of responses throughout the book. Try out as many as you like, and add your own to establish your verbal and nonverbal empathy vocabulary.

CHALLENGING QUESTIONS

Challenging questions confront the usefulness or relevance of certain attitudes to a mutually successful outcome (Lawyer et al. 1985). They get the parties thinking about what they are saying and prepare for problem solving or working toward agreements. For example:

"Ron, could you tell me how you think your attitude to Carol affects your working relationship?"

"Ron, you have said a lot about your fears about immigration. How is that pertinent to what we're talking about?"

Challenge to prepare for problem solving

"I'm wondering if you're aware that you've not talked about Carol at all, but black people in general."

Challenging questions should be asked in a clear, warm tone of voice with positive body language.

CONCLUSION

David uses a considerable amount of self-control here. It is easy to get hooked by prejudiced individuals. Avoidance and confrontation serve our needs, but are not necessarily effective for changing behavior and attitudes. This process of acknowledgment and exploration will open the way for problem solving, where you can explore mutually acceptable outcomes. There are examples of how to move into the problem-solving stage later in the book, such as step-by-step problem-solving approaches (see Chapter 23). Setting up a mediation in which both parties can explain their differences and work their problems out will be another option (see Chapters 13 to 22).

Exercise self-control

SUMMARY

Useful Circumstances

- Sending positive messages.
- Decreasing defensiveness.
- Listening and moving closer.
- Asking neutral questions.
- Expressing empathy.
- Asking challenging questions.

Limitations

- This approach depends on the response from the biased individual. The person may not be able or willing to respond to this positive approach.

- This approach is not a replacement for disciplinary measures, particularly if the behavior has been persistent, is against policy, and is the source of a complaint. It is the first stage in a progressive process.

- People affected by prejudiced behavior, in this instance Carol, should be kept informed of your actions.

A Personality Clash 7

*T*here are certainly people who clash at a level that is difficult for them and others to understand. When in close contact they are not themselves and their behavior is often indifferent, uncooperative, or downright aggressive to one another. Labeling these as personality clashes is restrictive; consider them instead as behavior clashes. Managers cannot hope to change someone's personality, but they can achieve a measure of success by focusing on behavior and getting the parties to do the same.

Focus on behavior, not person

Situation

Rachel and Irene work at opposite ends of the main office on the main room. Howard, who is fifty-five years old, has been with the company twenty years, and director for the last seven. Rachel is head of computing and joined the company two months ago. Irene, who is Howard's administrative assistant, is forty-six years old with ten years' company service.

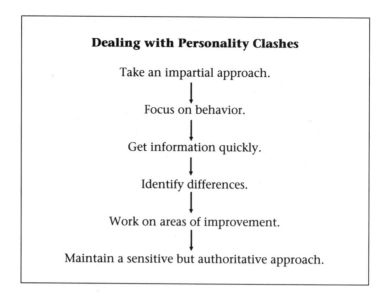

Dealing with Personality Clashes

Take an impartial approach.

↓

Focus on behavior.

↓

Get information quickly.

↓

Identify differences.

↓

Work on areas of improvement.

↓

Maintain a sensitive but authoritative approach.

Irene did not like Rachel the first time she met her. Rachel has tried to build a working relationship with Irene, but there have been some angry exchanges, which Howard overheard from his office. These happen particularly when Rachel wants to see him. Rachel believes Irene is influencing Howard's opinion of her. Rachel is responsible for computerizing the accounts and administration so she needs frequent easy access to Howard for consultation and feedback.

Howard has an important meeting in fifteen minutes and hears Rachel and Irene arguing outside. He decides to get them together and find out what the problem is between them. Neither of them has spoken to him about this issue before.

TAKING AN IMPARTIAL APPROACH

Howard only has a short time, but he is determined to have a positive influence on this conflict; he believes that he will achieve this by being even-handed and not taking sides from the beginning. He can demonstrate this in various ways.

- Check that his perception of their behavior is correct.

"Am I right in thinking that you have had several disagreements recently?"

Check perception

- Remain respectful, but also encouraging.

"I would like to meet with you both in my office now. I have some time, and I think it would be useful to discuss ways of helping you work together."

Maintain respect

Howard uses an assertive statement followed by a statement about what he hopes to achieve. He did not refer to a "problem" nor did he hint at blame.

- Describe clearly how he is going to process the meeting.

"It would help me understand what is going on if you both tell me what you are unhappy about. I will ask you first Irene, then Rachel. Then we will try to think what we would like to change."

Communicate intention

- Use ground rules to control behavior.

"Before we start, I would like to be clear that you do not interrupt one another. I will do my best to give you equal time and space. Please feel free to be honest about one another, but frame your references to one another respectfully. Do you both understand?"

Use ground rules

- Create a supportive physical environment.

Find a comfortable, preferably neutral space. Place their chairs where the parties can see one another and you can see them. Adjust your body language to include both parties. For instance, sit facing each of them and steadily turn your head from one to the other as they speak. From this position you can also observe them effectively. More about this is discussed in the chapters on mediation in Part Three.

Create a safe environment

OPEN, CLOSED, AND FOCUSED QUESTIONS

Open questions are broad and invite a narrative answer. If you have a great deal of time, as in a full mediation, open questions will be useful starting points. Focused questions require more specific answers, and closed questions most specific of all. Use a combination to get information quickly and clearly from people, particularly when they are inclined to over elaborate or talk about many issues. For example:

"What are you unhappy about?"	(Open question)
"Tell me more about your working relationship."	(Open but more focused)
"What causes you and Irene/Rachel to argue?"	(Focused)
"Can you think of two or three things about Irene/Rachel that make it difficult to work with her?"	(Focused)

By varying your questions, you get specific information and avoid too much diversion or repetition.

KEEPING THEM ON A POSITIVE TRACK— SPECIFYING AND CHALLENGING QUESTIONS

Use specifying questions If Irene and Rachel begin to quarrel, then Howard can direct them onto a more positive track by reminding them of the ground rules and using specifying questions. These encourage the speaker to be as clear, accurate, and detailed as possible.

Rachel

"Irene is just an obstructive and difficult old hag!"

Howard

"I can hear that you're angry, but it is not helpful to insult one another. What specifically do you mean by obstructive?"

By acknowledging Rachel's feelings followed by a behavioral reminder and a specifying question, Howard has deliberately excluded the second half of her comment as the least useful for the process of resolution (see Chapter 6 for more on selective summary).

Irene

"She doesn't know what she's talking about. She's only been in the company two months!"

Howard

"It would help me to understand if you don't just make general accusations. Would you be willing to tell me what it is about Rachel's relatively short time in the company that is difficult for you?"

Challenging questions (see Chapter 6) are also useful as a way avoid being sidetracked by issues less helpful to a positive resolution. Examples of these might be

Rachel

"I'm fed up with her acting so high and mighty. She can't even spell properly."

Howard

"Your last statement has confused me. What do you think is the connection between her attitude and her spelling?"

Irene

"She thinks she's so clever and that I'm stupid. She's one of these feminists."

Howard

"I'm not sure I see the connection, Irene. How is the fact that you describe her as a feminist relevant?"

Ask for examples

Use challenging questions to avoid being sidetracked

VERIFICATION BY CLOSED QUESTIONS

As there is little time, Howard will try to establish at least one or two basic facts and issues. The level of feeling may prevent him from gaining an agreement, but the questioning process will have enabled each to at least give some reason for their behavior which will be helpful to him and to them. Closed questions can be used to verify some of the basic information or to identify differences. For example:

Rachel

"From the first week I was here, Irene hardly ever said hello to me when I came in."

Howard

"So Rachel, being welcomed as you arrive in the office is important to you."

This acts as an accuracy check and is a closed question.

"Irene, as far as you are aware, do you often say hello to Rachel in the morning?"

If Irene agrees that she does not, this verifies Rachel's statement; if she disagrees, Howard has identified some area of difference.

GENERATING OPTIONS

Questions are also useful for encouraging the parties to come up with their own suggestions for resolving the situation.

Use open questions to get suggestions

"What would you like to change about the current situation?"
"What would you find helpful in this situation?"
"What do you think is the best way forward from here?"

All these questions are open-ended and give the parties freedom to generate solutions. Howard may need to use specifying and closed questions to obtain more detailed information.

"What is the single most important thing you would like to change in this situation?"
"What if we agreed that you both try to remember to say hello to one another in the morning and have lunch together with me tomorrow to talk about how

Use closed questions to check facts

you joining the team has affected the way we work together?"

This hypothetical question includes something for each party: Rachel was concerned about verbal welcomes and Irene about her responsibility for computerizing Howard's accounts.

Hypothetical questions containing suggestions that the third party, in this instance, Howard, has introduced are useful for breaking deadlocks, or moving the process on to a rapid conclusion. Howard should be very careful not to coerce the parties into a resolution that they see as unfair or which is unworkable. For example:

Use hypothetical questions to prepare for movement

"Well. what if we just agree to be more friendly in the future?"

This is not specific enough and for this reason is unworkable.

"So would you like to just make sure that you say hello to each other in the morning?"

There is clearly some need for a balanced resolution to this dispute as both Irene and Rachel have valid points. Irene would get very little from this suggestion, because this solution addresses Rachel's issues. Therefore, this is unlikely to be a mutually agreeable solution.

Something for each party

EVALUATING THE CHANCES OF A RESOLUTION

Now comes the part that happens in each conflict when you have to decide whether or not a collaborative process of decision making is going to be possible. If, in the participants' view, it is, then there are various ways of generating options, testing them out, and forming agreements with the full participation of the disputants. Mediation and seven-step problem solving are two good methods of achieving this (see Part Three). If collaboration is not possible, then an arbitration may be effective; it uses many of the investigative and facilitative methods of mediation, but the arbitrator makes the decision, not

Decide process

the disputants, on the basis of a fair exploration of the evidence. The difference between these two approaches is discussed more fully in Part Three.

Throughout this situation, Howard should be clear whether he is encouraging Rachel and Irene to find their own solutions, or collecting information so that he can make a decision. In the brief fifteen minutes since he interrupted the argument, Howard has quickly gathered information and helped Rachel and Irene listen to and respond to one another. When asked if they have any suggestions to improve the situation they both agree that they should talk to one another more, in the same constructive fashion, and that they will report back to him tomorrow with some ideas. As he leaves he can detect a much more friendly, interested tone in their voices. Once given the chance to actually deal with one another without the cloud of their prejudices and mis-apprehensions, they are eager to find out more about one another.

SUMMARY

Useful Circumstances

- Neutral third party approach
- Clear process information
- Use of ground rules
- Neutral territory and balanced body language
- Open, closed, and focused questions
- Keeping the parties on a positive track using specifying and challenging questions
- Verification by closed questions
- Specifying future questions
- Hypothetical questions

Limitations

- It may not be possible to deal with all the issues uncovered by these methods in one brief meeting, moreover feelings may be very deep-seated and need more unpacking. In this case, Howard should arrange for a future meeting, and decide whether he is to act as a mediator or arbitrator. Either way, he will be able to arrive at a fully considered decision, which should have something for both the parties.

An Angry Customer Calls for the Manager

8

*I*n London during the 1950s, there were many large department stores with sales associates in black clothes, with their hands behind their backs like maids and butlers, willing to attend politely to the customer's every need. The customer was always right and repeatedly reminded of that fact.

Now, in the 1990s, the outward appearance of face-to-face retailing has changed a great deal. There are far fewer staff, but one underlying element has remained constant, retail shops need customers. This is true for all organizations: banks need investors, voluntary organizations need contributors, and social work agencies need clients.

The relationship an organization has with its customers and clients is affected by many factors: customer need, obligation, and desire; choice, supply, and quality of goods and services; and organization efficiency. (See the following checklist.) Whatever the external characteristics of the relationship between you and your customers, Charles Handy (1992) suggests three basic facts to consider.

Customers are forever

1. Customers are forever—treat them as though they will always be there. "Any faults would show up in the end, so there should be no faults.... Good products (and services) make good clients and good clients keep you in business, whatever you are doing."

CHECKLIST

Factors Affecting Client–Organization Relationship

- Need—do they need you as much as you need them?

- Choice—is there anywhere else they can also get what they want?

- Supply and demand—do you have enough of what they want? Do they want more than you can ever give?

- Quality—is what you are offering of long-lasting good value, or special quality, or especially well suited to wants and needs?

- Obligation or necessity—do they have to come to you by law, or through basic human need such as health, or because you offer a basic service or product such as water?

- Desire—do people believe they really need something, or think that they will be better people for having the product or service you are offering?

- Efficiency—are you good at what you do? Are you reliable, productive, organized?

Customers are everywhere

2. Customers are everywhere—customers are not just the people at Macy's or Kmart, or those buying homes from real estate agents, but parents of children in school, or people calling in for advice on social security benefits.

Customers come first

3. Customers come first—find a way of talking and listening to your customers or clients; allow them to influence your thinking. "The customer decision is the first, not the last." If you want a par-

ticular kind of client, then you organize your business around your clients. If you have no choice of client then this too will affect how you organize, present, and evaluate your services or products.

Customer-oriented thinking should go beyond systems, structures, service charters, and promises. The daily interactions between organizations and their users, customers, and clients, play a vital part in shaping external perceptions. The quality of these interactions should be consistently high. Your credibility, efficiency, capability, and, ultimately, success or failure is challenged by each of these interactions.

How often have you deserted a trusted retailer because of an insensitive, unhelpful sales associate? How often have you lost a client because the receptionist was distracted or cold or put callers on hold for too long? How many times have you gained business because an inquiry was dealt with in a positive friendly way, and even though you could not provide what the customer needed that time, they returned to your organization when they wanted what you have to offer?

Customer-oriented thinking encourages customer satisfaction and devotion. But not all customers are satisfied by the service they receive. One of the most difficult situations of all is dealing with an angry customer. Constructive conflict management skills can turn this potentially risky situation into one of mutual benefit for the customer and organization.

Situation

Mr. and Mrs. Patel have used the services of Troubled Associates Ltd. several times. Three months ago they registered a complaint which was followed up to their satisfaction. However, a month ago, another problem arose and has not yet been addressed. They arrive at the company unannounced and Manjit, the receptionist, a twenty-five-year-old Indian woman who has been with the company three months, tries to establish what they want. She also has to take incoming phone calls, however, and Mr. and Mrs. Patel become angry and frustrated, feeling that they are not getting sufficient attention. They demand to see the most senior person available. Phillip, the customer relations officer, is called to the reception area.

NOTE ON CROSS-CULTURAL AWARENESS AND COMMUNICATION

Understand differences

In many parts of the country the work force is changing, reflecting the United States' enlarging diversity of culture and ethnicity. This presents a particular challenge for managers. Whether you are from a "minority group" or managing people who are, you will be presented with differences of behavior, norms, speech patterns, attitudes, home background, religion, and other beliefs which are associated with a particular culture. You will be a more effective manager if you attempt to understand these differences, avoid prejudgments, and take constructive steps to create open, trusting, working relation-

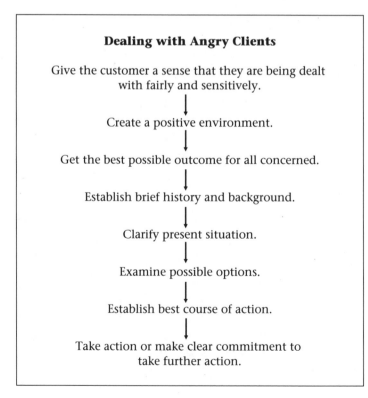

Dealing with Angry Clients

Give the customer a sense that they are being dealt with fairly and sensitively.

↓

Create a positive environment.

↓

Get the best possible outcome for all concerned.

↓

Establish brief history and background.

↓

Clarify present situation.

↓

Examine possible options.

↓

Establish best course of action.

↓

Take action or make clear commitment to take further action.

ships across cultures. Using the first three stages of the constructive conflict management process will be very useful in this respect. Many of the skills illustrated in Part Two will allow you to overcome any problems you have dealing with people who are different from yourself. These skills help you to establish self-control and to concentrate on objective reality. They are also extremely valuable when dealing with the general public as customers or clients.

TAKING CONTROL OF YOURSELF

All angry customers have one expectation—that they are in for a fight. Paying customers who believe they have not had value for money, have faulty goods, or have received bad service, have every right to be angry. Think of an instance when you have been in the position of an angry customer; you felt like an innocent victim. How often have you met with a tone of indifference, condescension, or hostility?

The tone of an interaction with an angry customer is important. Assume that Phillip will be consciously using the constructive conflict management process and the suggestions and processes in Part One, including

- Clear observation.
- Awareness of one's personal feelings, prejudices, and assumptions.
- Breath control and positive body language.
- Taking a wide view—looking at the problem from the point of view of self, others, the situation, and the consequences.

In addition to this, when dealing with customer or client complaints, it is essential to separate the complaint from the person. Remember that

- You are focusing on their complaint and the issues connected with it, not their behavior or personality.

Focus on complaint

- Their complaint is usually not directed at you as a person, even if it is aimed at your workplace, where you have strong connections, or even if it is directly connected with your own work role.

These two factors should affect your approach in the following ways:

Don't take it personally

1. Acknowledge the parties' feelings, but focus primarily on the issues. Your task is to build a relationship with them purely on the basis of reaching the best outcome. How you actually feel about the person is not relevant to the resolution of the conflict. For example, if Mr. and Mrs. Patel seem unreasonable and vague to Phillip, he should not seek initially to make them more reasonable, but more precise. By getting all the information from them, he will communicate to them that he values their complaint, whether or not he considers it reasonable. Do not let angry customers upset you. Conflicts are often prolonged when emotion is met by emotion. Reason will prevail if you concentrate on the facts.

Don't get upset

2. Remember that the customer is angry at what has happened, possibly at you and your colleagues as a function of your organization, but not at you as a person. By doing so you will be less defensive. When people feel under attack for their work, it is easy to feel threatened. Defensiveness is not constructive when dealing with angry customers, although you have every right to be angry if a customer uses personal remarks. In such an instance, use some of the techniques presented in Chapter 6 on dealing with prejudice or use assertive behavior. These methods will enable you to get the interaction on a more positive track. Overall, make sure that from the very beginning you are in control of yourself, and also able to be open to the customer.

PREPARATION

If you have a moment, take time to prepare. It is better to have a brief delay to help you prepare before meeting the customer rather than have frequent interruptions during the interview as you check procedures and files. At some stage in the proceedings you are likely to need

- Knowledge of guidelines and procedures.

- Information on file about previous contact with the customer.

- Details of current work plans, resources, and schedules that may affect the remedy for the complaint, such as how quickly repairs can be done, goods replaced, or services reinstated or modified.

Be prepared

Phillip can prepare by

- Asking Manjit to check the customers' full names, addresses, and date of last contact, and to let him know immediately so that their file can be accessed.

- Collecting the file or instructing an assistant to bring it to reception as soon as it is found.

- Taking relevant information with him regarding work schedules.

- Instructing an assistant to contact reception in a few minutes to check whether he needs anything else.

- Checking on the way to reception whether a room is available.

INSTANT JUSTICE—OR AT LEAST A SENSE OF JUSTICE

"Justice deferred is justice denied" is a phrase commonly used by lawyers, and in many senses it is true. It is frustrating for a customer to go away without a full remedy, particularly if, as in the case of Mr. and Mrs. Patel, they have already experienced a considerable delay. But there are some complaints that cannot be fixed instantly, and in these cases it is essential to communicate a sense of fairness and justice to the customer. This

Communicate justice

can be done through your attitude, tone, behavior, and the processes you adopt.

MAKING GOOD INITIAL CONTACT WITH THE PARTIES

Phillip approaches the Patels and tries to establish positive contact with them. His tone is open and respectful, describing his position and giving his name. He immediately acknowledges them and that they have a complaint, avoiding language, gestures, and tone that are likely to antagonize the Patels.

Establish positive contact

"Hello. I'm Phillip Walters, customer relations officer. Thank you for being patient; I came as soon as I could. I understand you are Mr. and Mrs. Patel and that you have a complaint?"

Attend to comfort

Now is also the time to check to see whether the customers have any immediate needs. For example, is their car parked safely, do they have constraints on their time, do they have any immediate physical needs? A chair is particularly important when dealing with customers who are elderly or have disabilities. This communicates an interest in the present welfare of the customers and obtains information about their expectations, as well as focuses them on the present.

CONTROLLING THE ARENA

After introducing himself, Phillip will now do what he can to control the physical environment in which this meeting takes place. To the Patels, this is their arena where they have come for a fight. Philip wants to create a space where

Control environment

- He and the Patels can meet in a situation of mutual respect.
- The idea of the company and the Patels as adversaries can be dissipated.
- They are separated from the scene of the most recent incident that has upset them.

This may not always be possible. Some customers actually prefer a public space so that they can be seen to be getting attention, and they know this is also humiliating for the manager.

Wherever you are, however little time and space you have, you should exercise control over as many of the following factors as possible.

Physical Position

Everyone should have equal space. They should not be too close to be threatening or too far away to be remote. A sitting position is the most conducive to calm.

Give customer space

Touch

A handshake or similar greeting can be useful at the beginning, but touching angry customers is not recommended. For example, try to avoid physically steering them in a particular direction, unless they are being very obstructive or causing problems for others. Verbal warnings should always be used before physical action.

Judicious use of touch

Body Language

Stand directly facing the customer, with your weight balanced equally on each foot, in an upright, relaxed posture. Keep your arms and hands reasonably still. Welcoming and acknowledging gestures can be useful. For example, extend both hands palm up as you introduce yourself and nod as you listen.

Be aware of body language

Distance

If the customer's complaint is about an incident that has just happened, removing them quietly from the scene of the incident will enable them to have a more detached view. This will also prevent escalation or recurrence of the conflict.

Remove from scene of incident

Privacy

Preferably use a separate room, or at least a place that is not too public. If this is not possible, then you should at least move the customer tactfully to one side so that you

Provide privacy

are not distracted or influenced by the reactions of others. Check that everyone is comfortable with the location.

Comfort

Attend to comfort

Even if there is no private space and no seats, you should do everything you can to be attentive to the comfort of the customer. Tea, coffee, or a cold drink can be a useful calming device. If the customer insists on standing in a public space, you could use the lure of a more comfortable, private space to get him or her away from the public platform.

Interruptions

Reduce interruptions

You will be able to maintain the flow of information and response more easily if you reduce interruptions to a minimum. If you are in a spare room disconnect the phone or instruct the receptionist not to put calls through if you feel you may need access to the phone. On the other hand, if this will be a long meeting, breaks can be very constructive, and you may find it interesting to experiment with the timing of the arrival of refreshments or fresh information. Carefully planned breaks can be useful because they

- Interrupt negative behavior from the customer.
- Give you and the customer breathing space.
- Allow security to check on you if you have a volatile customer.

GETTING THE CUSTOMER TO TELL THEIR STORY—DOOR OPENERS

Angry customers need no encouragement to let off steam. Phillip's task here is to be sensitive to the Patels' feelings. His main responsibility, however, is to establish what their complaint is and what the key issues are. As they have already spoken to Manjit and complained before, he should be sensitive to their frustration. There are various door openers he could choose. Door openers are phrases, often accompanied by gestures, that encourage people to talk in difficult situations. They are invitations to get started, and they involve four stages (Lawyer et al. 1985).

Use door openers

- Reflecting on what you see (behavior)
- Inviting people to talk, either stating or implying you are able and willing to take time to listen
- Waiting to allow the other person to initiate communication
- Active listening

For example:

"I can understand that you're frustrated, but I have plenty of time, and assure you, I will give you my best possible attention. Would you like to give me the details of your complaint?"

"I am sorry it took a little while to find a room. I can see that this is a serious matter for you, and wanted to be sure we could discuss it in full, without being interrupted. Perhaps you could tell me...?"

MANAGING THE TIME FRAME— SELECTIVE SUMMARY

One of the most distracting behaviors when people get into a conflict is a tendency to blur the past and the present, or to subjectively reconstruct the sequence of events by replacing present events with past ones and reconstructing memories based on present experience. Angry, anxious people often recite a catalog of incidents, seamlessly assembled, persuasive in their collective intensity. The impression is that they are all recent and connected but, on closer questioning, they have actually occurred over a very long period of time. Also other incidents, which contradict this seamless version of the conflict, are initially excluded.

Each person has developed his or her own sense of the relationship between the past and the present and the nature of the conflict. They are locked in a subjective time zone, and it is up to the conflict manager to establish a shared perspective of time, cause, and consequence. This is managing the time frame—establishing and agreeing on a sequence of events from the past to the present, so that the parties can concentrate on the future.

For example, Mr. and Mrs. Patel's complaint has recent history and also an immediate past. Phillip needs to know what is important, but also wants to concentrate on the present needs and future wishes of the Patels.

Mr. Patel

"That silly girl at reception paid no attention at all, just like the people before. I can't understand how a company like yours can be efficient one minute and hopeless the next. Yesterday I thought that I wouldn't wait any longer."

Mrs. Patel

"Go in and talk to them, I said. Don't just talk to them on the phone like last time. When you wrote before it was okay, but this time they've been giving us the runaround. Go in and complain, I said."

They are both constructing stories without regard to the sequence in which the events occurred or where the events occurred, and in general being very vague. Phillip uses three selective summary methods to help get the details and time frame clear. Selective summary is the process of assembling and reflecting back key information, issues, and ideas which you believe will help move the parties forward. Phillip uses

Use selective summary

- Selective specifying questions.
- Paraphrasing.
- Chronological summarizing.

Selective Specifying Questions

Right at the opening Mr. Patel mentions Manjit and her inability to give them sufficient attention. Phillip chooses not to focus on this, as he does not believe that it is important with respect to the overall conflict. If he is wrong, Mr. Patel will almost certainly tell him now or return to the issue later. Instead, Phillip concentrates on clarifying the history.

"Mr. Patel, am I right in thinking you are generally upset by the response to your complaints? Could you say when you complained before, and what happened?"

Perception check

"What happened before which gave you the impression you were not being listened to?"

Specifying questions

"Mrs. Patel, when you referred to Mr. Patel writing, what did you mean? Was there a letter connected with the same complaint?"

Piece by piece, Phillip is encouraging them to fill in the gaps in his understanding, selecting what he needs to know to be able to give them a fair hearing.

Paraphrasing is the process of restating the main idea that the speaker is trying to convey and repeating it back to them in their own words. It lets the speaker know whether or not you understood them. Paraphrases should represent a small portion of what is being said and should be framed in a way that enables the speaker to correct them if he or she wishes.

Paraphrasing

So Philip might say

"So it seems that you have spoken to three or four different people about this and that so far nothing has been done?"

Paraphrase

"If I understand you right, you have also had another complaint some while ago, which was dealt with satisfactorily?"

A chronological summary is a brief statement that places key events in an accurate time sequence. Phillip might try to reconstruct the Patels' story.

Chronological Summarizing

"Well, thanks for helping me understand this. I would just like to check with you, Mr. and Mrs. Patel that I have got the overall picture. First, a year ago, you had a complaint which was handled perfectly well. Then a month ago you had another problem and have

Chronological summary to verify

complained three times. Despite assurances of action, nothing has been done so far, which is why you are here. What you want now is rapid action."

Mr. and Mrs. Patel agree that this is an accurate summary. So, now the time frame and facts are clear. Phillip can consider what next.

EXAMINING THE EVIDENCE

A few minutes into the meeting, Phillip's assistant arrives with the Patels' file. Before examining this, Phillip makes sure that

- The customers get a chance to tell their story as this will settle them down and communicate that he is taking them seriously.
- He listens actively, acknowledging, checking, and questioning when necessary.
- He introduces the company's evidence sensitively, especially if it contradicts the customers (see Chapter 22 on arbitration for more about evidence).

The files confirm that the facts are as Mr. and Mrs. Patel describe, so Phillip has no clash of evidence to deal with. Sometimes customers' stories are not as accurate, and then the conflict manager has to act as an "agent of reality."

Being the Agent of Reality

This is an important role for the conflict manager. The manager's aim is to get the best possible outcome for all concerned, and this should always include due consideration of the situation and the consequences. The tasks of an agent of reality are to

- Assess and balance people's needs against what is possible.
- Communicate difficult decisions clearly and fully.
- Make workable agreements.

To function in this way conflict managers need

- Knowledge of procedures and guidelines.
- Accurate information.
- Knowledge of resources.
- A clear idea of the limits of authority and powers of discretion.

Where there is a clash of views or facts, time should be spent identifying and exploring differences and working out a commonly held view of events (see the chapters on mediation in Part Three). In this instance, there is no clash between the customers' information and the company records. Phillip has proved he is organized by bringing in work schedules and accessing the file. He has the authority to commission work, give refunds, or set repairs in action.

MAKING A WORKABLE AGREEMENT—GAINING AUTHORITY AND CHECKING RESOURCES

Phillip quickly phones to confirm resources and makes an appointment for the Patels to have new work done to remedy the problem. Not all angry customers' complaints work out quite so comfortably, as is true for many conflicts, where the resolution does not epitomize calm, reason, or logic. The above skills will greatly reduce the level of anger and produce the opportunity for frank exchange and negotiation.

A workable agreement is also dependent on the customer's willingness to accept the limitations of what an organization can and cannot do. If a positive, sensitive tone is adopted throughout, even when you are denying the customer's wishes, the customer is more likely to accept what you decide.

If your organization is not able to provide someone with decision-making and resource-allocating authority to deal with angry customers, you must ensure that

- Customers know this.
- You have a rapid mechanism for gaining authority and checking resources when you have explored the complaint.
- The person receiving the complaint uses the same skills as above so that you do not have to be called in to calm down an even angrier customer.

SUMMARY

Useful Circumstances

- Take control of yourself with clear observation, prejudice awareness, focusing, and breath control.
- Separate complaint from person so you are not being aggressive or defensive.
- Prepare procedures, file information, and resources information.
- Make good initial contact by checking immediate needs.
- Control the arena with physical position, touch, body language, privacy, comfort, interruptions, and distance.
- Use door openers.
- Manage the time frame.
- Use selective summary—specifying questions, paraphrasing, and chronological summarizing.
- Check evidence.
- Be an agent of reality.
- Make workable agreements—check authority and resources.

Limitations

- Particularly resistant customers may need to be handled more like violent disputants (see Chapter 4) in the early stages.

- If your organization is being accused of serious negligence, the person who is receiving the complaint may have to check with senior staff before deciding on whether or not he or she is the right person to be dealing with this issue. In this instance, the best you can do is collect information in the same way and agree on the next best step.

- The whole time scale for this process is variable, but you have to consider the other demands on your time as conflict manager and be as clear as possible with the customers if you have any constraints on your time. Communicate this early on, then use these skills to streamline the questioning and gathering of information.

A Conflict With   *9*
the Boss

ASSUMPTIONS ABOUT BOSSES

The word *boss* often evokes a stereotypical image that is usually male, powerful, more wealthy than ordinary workers, and likes ordering people around. Recently there was a British television program in which a senior police officer and a junior constable worked together. The senior officer was a woman and the constable was a man. Still other police officers constantly approached the man and addressed him as "sir," assuming that he was the senior officer. How many times have you been surprised when meeting someone who did not meet your image of a boss?

There are many different kinds of bosses, and it would be simplistic to propose that they all look alike and behave in a similar way. It is equally simplistic to suggest that people respond in the same way to those in authority, especially at work. However, people have certain assumptions about bosses, and these influence relationships with those who manage them, particularly when conflicts arise. These assumptions also have a significant effect on the way people behave when in the role of boss.

Some Commonly Held Assumptions About Bosses

If you believe any of these assumptions just a little, then imagine how your behavior toward your boss will be affected.

"They are powerful people."

(Powerful people don't have to listen. They can afford to make mistakes, but will criticize yours. You must be very sure before confronting them, and even then you will probably feel very threatened.)

"They need to be in control."

(People who need to be in control will not let you take responsibility and will check all the time that you are doing the right thing.)

"They expect deference."

(If someone expects deference they will be annoyed if you confront them, even if you are assertive, not aggressive. They will not believe you respect them unless you show due deference.)

"They should be treated differently from peers or less senior staff."

(If there are different rules for how you behave with bosses, you cannot be yourself. You cannot learn the rules. You cannot relax with them or trust them.)

"They are more clever than anyone else."

(Clever people are seldom wrong, and even if they are, will persuade you that they are not, or that you are wrong. You either have to be more clever, or bow to their superior knowledge to earn their respect.)

"They have to work harder than anyone else."

(People who believe they work harder than anyone else have little time for their staff and expect similar commitment and even sacrifice from others. Although they are always busy there is always more to do, and they are reluctant to take a break, or even step back and take advice, or consider what others are doing. This means that work piles up even more. The company depends on them working hard.)

So how do you get what you want from people who have authority over you? How do you overcome your apprehension? Can you really achieve anything with an unreasonable boss? You can if you stick to three basic aims.

- Be realistic.
- Be yourself.
- Get to know and understand your boss so that you are interacting with the real person, and not through your fears and stereotypes.

Situation

Rachel, the head of computing involved in the conflict with Irene, the director's administrative assistant, has been with the organization now for almost a year. She gets along well with Irene now, but is exasperated by her immediate boss, Howard, the director. He very seldom gives her positive feedback, usually picking out the one or two mistakes in her work. She is setting up a new computer system and knows there will be mistakes, but would like some positive feedback as well.

Three or four times Howard has been quite dismissive of Rachel, once cutting her off in mid presentation in a meeting with other departmental heads, but otherwise in private. He says things like, "Not now Rachel; we can

---

**Establishing Authority When in a
Conflict With Your Boss**

Get the boss to take notice of you.

↓

Get some idea of the boss's expectations.

↓

Understand his or her behavior.

↓

Behave assertively, making feelings clear
and communicating what you want.

↓

Influence the boss in a positive fashion
while retaining integrity.

---

talk about that later," but does not then make himself available even when requested by memo or phone. Howard has also postponed three supervision sessions. Rachel has a yearly appraisal coming up and has a very strong sense that Howard does not value her work.

Even though Rachel feels she has good reason to be aggrieved, she is also aware that her seniority and authority in the organization are limited by her relatively short time of service and the newness of her position. There was no head of computing before her, and she alone is responsible for establishing the status of her department. Her potential power in this conflict is limited by these factors, especially as she is in conflict with the most senior officer in the company.

On the other hand, this is an opportunity to establish authority, so how does Rachel do this without alienating her director?

THREE WAYS TO GET THE BEST FROM YOUR BOSS

There are three ways to get what you want from your boss.

1. *Listen actively*. Make positive use of the contact you have with your boss, finding out what your boss

wants and what expectations she or he has of you, and seek to explore and understand his or her behavior.

2. *Behave assertively*. Find ways of clearly expressing what you feel, and saying what you want.

3. *"Influencing-up."* Develop a set of genuine, positive responses that acknowledge and affirm, while emphasizing your own strengths and maintaining your integrity.

This three-way approach is not confrontational, nor is it weak and accommodating. It gives you a good chance of getting the best you can from your boss from the beginning of your working relationship.

The meeting does not start well. Howard comes in, does not sit down, and says that he has five minutes.

Howard

"I've only got five minutes. What do you want, Rachel?"

Rachel

"I'd like to talk about how I'm getting on with the system."

Howard

"I'm sure you're doing fine. No need to talk about that."

Rachel

"My appraisal is due in three weeks, Howard, and we have not met for more than ten minutes in the past two months."

Howard

"There'll be plenty of time for that. Don't fuss. I'm very busy you know, and I hired you to do all this computer stuff. This company would fold if I didn't put in so many hours. Do you know how many hours a week I work?"

This feels familiar to Rachel, and she is getting frustrated, but controls her feelings and decides to use this brief

Listen to explore behavior

contact to explore Howard's behavior and the basis of his resistance. What causes him to avoid her? Remember, when dealing with difficult or resistant bosses, make the most of the contact you have with them. Active listening is extremely useful in this respect.

ACTIVE LISTENING

There are a variety of techniques, already covered, which would be constructive when dealing with a resistant boss. Rachel may ask the following types of questions.

Meaning check

"When you say we don't need to talk, Howard, are you saying that you don't want to talk right now, or that we don't need to talk at all?"

Reflecting content and feeling

"If I understand you right, you are saying that computers don't interest you much, and that you hoped I would be able to set up the system entirely alone?"

Specifying questions

"Thanks for reassuring me that we'll have time to talk soon. Could you tell me when that would be?"

"So what time do we have to stop talking?"

Focused questions

"When you say you've only got five minutes do you actually mean five minutes, or just very little time?"

"What do you mean when you say 'Computer stuff,' Howard?"

Paraphrasing

"So I believe, Howard, that you're saying that you will have some time to talk soon, even though overall you don't envisage spending too much of your time discussing the computer set-up."

Four Types of Behavior

1. Aggressive
2. Passive
3. Manipulative
4. Assertive

ASSERTIVENESS

Each behavior has various disadvantages and advantages.

Agressive Behavior

Aggressive behavior is based on a lack of respect for others.

Advantages
- You may get less aggressive people to do what you want.
- You may be admired by some people.
- You may experience yourself as powerful.

Disadvantages
- People will resent you.
- You will often cause people to retaliate, either directly with aggression or indirectly with manipulation.
- In the long term you are unlikely to get and keep what you want.

Passive Behavior

Passive behavior is based on a lack of respect for yourself.

Advantages
- You may feel virtuous because of being unselfish or self-sacrificing.
- You can avoid confrontation and not notice the effect other people have on you, or you on them, which seems comfortable.
- You can have a "quiet life."

Disadvantages
- People do not really respect martyrs and may end up resenting you.
- Other people will take advantage of you.
- You will find it difficult to respect yourself or get what you really want.

Manipulative Behavior

Manipulative behavior is based on a lack of respect for yourself and others.

Advantages
- People may be persuaded to do what you want.
- You can avoid dealing directly with situations you find difficult.
- You will not have to risk asking directly for what you want and being refused.
- You may feel more clever than others.

Disadvantages
- People may well not understand what you want if you do not make it clear.
- People dislike being manipulated and will resent it.
- You will lose other people's respect.
- Long term, it is unlikely that you will get what you want.

Assertive Behavior

Assertive behavior is based on respect for yourself and others.

Advantages
- People understand clearly what you want.
- They do not feel pressured or browbeaten.
- You are more likely to get what you want in both the short and long term.
- Other people respect you.

- You will keep your self-respect.

- Your relationships will survive disagreement.

Disadvantages
- You risk your requests being refused.

- You risk confrontation with other people.

Assertiveness is therefore appropriate for positive conflict management, because it is based on a sense of one's own strength, and the value of others.

Assertiveness is also about

- Knowing your strengths and limitations.

- Choosing how to manage your feelings and those of others.

- Avoiding being hooked by others' nonassertive behavior.

Be assertive

Rachel feels strong because she

- Believes she has done a good job.
- Is used to discussing difficult issues.
- Is a good listener.
- Is aware that she may not get what she wants right then but that does not mean she has failed. There may be another time, another way.

Know Your Strengths and Limitations

You will find it easier to be assertive regardless of the situation or people if you are

- Realistic and honest about your own position and open to what others have to say.

- Aware of the other factors influencing the situation.

- Willing to get what you want, but also aware that you may not.

Choose to Manage Your Feelings and Those of Others

Paddy O'Brien (1994) talks about "gentle focused strength," which is realistic and effective, and is gained through being assertive. If you are in a situation where you are likely to be overwhelmed by fear or anger, do not let either your feelings or those of others take you over. There are many ways of doing this, such as focusing, breath control, analyzing the situation from a wide perspective, visualization, positive body language, and physical positioning (see Part One).

Rachel is a little angry, but consciously decides to move her anger to one side and focus on how she thinks Howard is experiencing her and the situation. When he came in, she thought he looked a little uncomfortable. To avoid making assumptions about his behavior she uses a perception check.

Perception check

"Howard, you look a little uncomfortable. Are you okay standing?"

He says he is fine. Rachel would rather that he sat, but is prepared to accept Howard's assurance and focus on her own comfort.

Acknowledge others

By listening actively, Rachel maintains her own balanced emotional level, and by affirming Howard enables him to feel more comfortable.

Avoid Being Hooked by Others' Nonassertive Behavior

When individuals are provocative, dismissive, disruptive, manipulative, or nonassertive in other ways, they are sending out signals that can hook us into a cycle where we behave in a similar way. Ultimately, no one gets what they want in these cycles.

Do not become provoked

If Rachel chooses to be provoked by Howard's apparent lack of time for her, and his reference to computer stuff, then she will most likely get even less attention from him. It is important for her, especially considering his relative power in the organization, to retain a positive image of Howard and to communicate that to him. She will not be able to do this if she is hooked by some of his nonassertive behavior.

Two areas deserve attention.

- Communicating feelings clearly
- Saying what you want

These are the two areas where Rachel feels she has had least opportunity to be heard.

I–You Messages

One basic premise of assertiveness is to develop behaviors that communicate clearly what you feel without blaming others. I–You messages do this effectively.

A nonassertive response would be one giving the responsibility for your feelings to someone else. It would not be useful for Rachel to say to Howard:

Do not off-load responsibility

"You make me feel unimportant because you give me so little time."

This suggests that Howard is the one who causes her to feel bad and that she has no control over this. It puts him in the position of having to defend his actions. He will hear this as, "Howard, you are an insensitive person (or even a bad manager)."

Examples of assertive responses:

"Howard, I am beginning to feel frustrated that we have spent so little time talking about my work."

"Howard, I am disappointed that you cannot spend more time with me today."

Both of these sentences say to Howard, when you do this, I feel this, and are less likely to put him on the defensive.

Being assertive does not guarantee that you get what you want, but if you want your feelings acknowledged there is more chance if you use I–You messages.

Don't Exaggerate or Overdramatize

"The power of assertion lies in its simplicity. It is a statement of genuine concern from one person to another" (Lawyer et al. 1985). If you feel very strongly about something, then you need to find a word that expresses that level of feeling accurately, but if not, then exaggerated language will make it more difficult for others to believe you.

Rachel feels frustrated, but no more. If she were to say "Look, Howard. I'm furious/really upset/very disappointed," she is not going to be convincing unless that is really how strongly she feels. People exaggerate because they believe they will be heard, but turning up the emotional volume often has the opposite effect, especially in the workplace, where people may well ignore or avoid your feelings if you express them in an exaggerated way.

Don't exaggerate

It is not always easy to describe your feelings accurately, and you may find it useful to build up a store of words that correctly describe the degrees of feeling connected with a variety of situations.

Overdramatization is equally difficult for others to acknowledge and respond to in a positive way. Exaggerated body language, such as handwaving, pointing, shaking of the head, turning quickly away, or moving suddenly closer, prevents others from focusing on what you want. Bashing desks, throwing down files, and slamming doors are common signs of emotion at times of conflict, but they arouse only hostility or defensiveness.

Rachel is in control of her adjectives and her body language. As she describes her feelings to Howard she addresses him with an open body position, keeping her head quite still and looking directly at him. Her tone of voice is relaxed, but firm, and she communicates her own frustration without inviting frustration back from the listener.

Give Examples

Rachel wants Howard to hear how she feels, and simple examples will help put the situation in perspective.

Give examples

"Howard, I feel frustrated when I think you do not have enough time for me to discuss my work with you. For example two weeks ago, we agreed to meet, but you canceled the meeting."

Refer to Previous Incidents or Agreements

Rachel has every right to remind Howard tactfully of previous incidents that relate to the present situation in order to consolidate and clarify what she feels. For example:

Refer back

"Thanks for agreeing to see me, Howard, although I'm disappointed we will not have much time together, especially as our last meeting three weeks ago was cut short."

Having feelings acknowledged is very important, but no matter how assertive one is this is not always possible. Another aspect of assertiveness is the ability to say clearly what you want.

Say What You Want

Six Strategies to Help You Say What You Want

1. Be clear about what you want to change.
2. Choose the issues you want to deal with carefully.
3. Be specific.
4. Avoid vague adjectives and adverbs.
5. Choose language that will not make the situation worse.
6. Use questions to check that you are being heard and understood.

Be Clear About What You Want to Change

Rachel wants more time to discuss her work with Howard. She may feel that he is not being positive enough in his attitude toward her, but her current concern is to get immediate or rapid feedback on the work she has done so far. This is what she should communicate to him.

Be clear

"Howard, I feel frustrated because we are not able to spend much time discussing my work. I would like to consult with you fully about your ideas, and what you think about what I am doing."

Choose the Issues You Want to Deal With Carefully

As Rachel has so little time, she is concentrating on one issue—the need to spend more time together that day, or to arrange another meeting soon. This is her most pressing need and she believes that once she has started the process of more extended meetings with Howard, she can begin to address other current issues, and also fresh ones as they materialize.

Choose issues carefully

Choosing to address the issue that is most pressing first may not always be best, and there are several considerations when selecting issues to deal with.

- Is this an issue in which I have a real chance of success?

- How complex are the issues? Are there some that are more manageable than others?

- Too many issues blur the picture. How many can realistically be addressed in the time available? What other time is there?

- Take one issue at a time. Do not confuse the issues.

- Separate practical issues from those connected to attitudes and beliefs wherever possible.

- Consider the issues in relation to yourself, the others, and the situation.

Be Specific

Be as specific as possible so that others understand exactly what is required of them. Rachel wants to encourage Howard to make a specific time for the next meeting. She restates her basic complaint, then narrows it down with a very specific request.

Make specific requests

"Howard, I think I've made it clear that I am not happy about the lack of time spent with you discussing my work. I would like to meet with you for at least an hour some time in the next two weeks."

Avoid Vague Adjectives and Adverbs

Rachel's statement above avoids using vague adjectives and adverbs, which only serve to confuse the listener. Had she been vague, she might have said

"I would prefer it if we could meet more often and for longer."

There is also a suggestion of blame here as these words suggest that contact has been insufficiently often and not long enough in the past. Rachel has already asserted that she is not happy and does not need to emphasize this with these adjectives and adverbs.

Choose Language That Will Not Make the Situation Worse

When describing the behavior you want changed and stating what you want, you need to realize that the other person may not necessarily be ready to hear what you are saying. If you choose your language carelessly you may lose any chance of being heard at all. For example:

Choose language carefully

"Last time you failed to let me know the meeting was canceled I was a bit annoyed; I am beginning to think that we will never get to meet."

("Failed" is loaded with blame, and "never" is an exaggeration that will not encourage the listener to take you seriously.)

"I am frustrated by the lack of time we have had up to now to discuss my work. I think it's about time you took my work more seriously."

(Ultimatum followed by an assumption about his attitude)

"I would have thought it would be clear to anyone that I'm disappointed. Surely you realize that I need to talk to you by now?"

(Negative criticism that gives the listener no information about what exactly is wrong, followed by manipulation, appealing to guilt)

Use Questions to Check That You Are Being Heard and Understood

After Rachel has made it clear what she wants, she may need to check with Howard that he understands.

Check understanding

"Howard, I know you have to leave quite soon, so can I just check that you are clear what I want—a meeting with you for at least an hour in the next two weeks?"

"Thanks for listening, Howard. Can you understand now what I'm frustrated about?"

"I wonder if you are surprised that I am frustrated, Howard?"

All three of these questions give Howard a chance to register with Rachel that he has heard and understood, and the last one also gives him a chance to say how he feels about her behavior.

"INFLUENCING-UP"

Three Reminders Before You Try to Get Something From Your Boss

- Separate the person from the issues. You will not change the person, but you may be able to achieve some resolution on the issues.

- Acknowledge the limitations of the manager's role. Assumptions, expectations, policies, and resources affect what attitude your manager takes.

- Focus on what you believe you can change. If you can get your manager to listen and understand on one subject, then you and your manager will feel more positive. If you try to solve several problems at once you may end up with nothing.

"Hellos," "Goodbyes," and "Thank Yous"

"Hellos," "goodbyes," and "thank yous" are clear, often powerful ways of communicating respect, openness, and a willingness to be positive. How many times have you noticed when you are not greeted? Are you often thanked when you have managed someone or a situation well? How did you feel? How did this influence the interaction, or future contact? People often forget these basic civilities with relation to their superiors.

Greetings, the expression of gratitude, and farewells are not uniform across cultures, but there are some basic guidelines. They should be

- Simple—you do not need a four-page speech.

- Genuine—do not exaggerate or pretend. You do not have to like someone to be able to welcome them warmly. You will not suffer by greeting someone you have a conflict with.

- Warm—you can communicate this with a smile, relaxed open body posture, handshake, embrace, or whatever seems appropriate.

Take responsibility for your own behavior, but also try to judge what suits the situation and person you are addressing.

Such open, positive behavior is useful in all conflicts. It is a very effective way of registering to your boss that you are focused on the present and prepared to engage in a positive dialogue.

Rachel thanks and welcomes Howard as soon as he enters the office.

"Hello, Howard, how are you? Thanks for finding the time to see me."

Communicate respect

He feels harassed and limited for time, and Rachel's positive attitude will help him relax. Even if he leaves after only a few minutes, she will hopefully have achieved her aim of gaining Howard's agreement for a further meeting. Once again, Rachel expresses her gratitude, and also makes a positive parting remark.

"I'm glad that we've managed to find a time to meet, Howard. Thanks. I look forward to discussing my work with you then."

Influencing-up is not just another phrase for "crawling," "kowtowing," or cooking up a pattern of behavior that will please, impress, or flatter others. It is about being genuine, using positive interacting skills, and having a realistic sense of outcomes. Influencing-up is the process

Be Straight, But Remember Who You Are Talking To

of developing a set of affirmative responses to our bosses as they present themselves in their role, and also trying to make contact with the person behind the role.

Here are some examples of this approach.

- Acknowledging and affirming statements, especially those which are supportive of one's positive qualities
- Positive body language and tone
- Showing interest in the person

Acknowledging and Affirming Statements

Rachel frequently reflects back to Howard what he is saying so that she can check she understands. This also tells him he is being acknowledged. She often prefixes a request with an affirmation to keep Howard in a positive frame of mind.

Reflect concerns back

"I can see that you are very busy, Howard, I know you work extremely hard. I would like to meet with you for an hour sometime in the next two weeks."

Acknowledge positive steps

Rachel also acknowledges positive steps that Howard takes, once again often as a prelude to saying what she wants or how she feels. This shows she is balancing his needs and hers.

"Thanks for taking the time to see me today. I really find these meetings useful. It is frustrating for me that we have only met for half an hour in the last two weeks. I would appreciate it if we could meet for an hour...."

Acknowledgment and affirmation communicate Rachel's respect for his authority and also demonstrate an interest in him as a person.

Positive Body Language and Tone

Aggressive or agitated movements will cut across any attempts you make to be positive. Throughout this interaction Rachel aims to have a relaxed body position, good (though not constant) eye contact, and to avoid sudden gestures, fidgeting, twisting in her chair, or sudden changes in the volume and tone of her voice. Positive body language depends on being in control of emotions, which will be easier if you

- Get comfortable physically. Avoid feeling cramped or stretched and try to balance your weight evenly, whether you are seated or standing.
- Breathe slowly and with a regular rhythm.
- Use listening spaces to stay calm.
- Listen actively—do not make assumptions or interpret as this is likely to make you less relaxed.

Showing an Interest in the Person

There is no need to relate to managers as though they are nonpeople. People in authority have a great need for basic human interaction. As they climb the ladder of authority they grow uncertain about the sincerity of positive remarks, aware that they have power over people. It is important to respond to managers as they are, while also acknowledging what they represent.

Respond to the person

A manager of a large community mediation program was relieved when people peeled off the manager mask from their perception and took an interest in his concerns and welfare. Other managers have echoed this sentiment.

Rachel knows how hard Howard works, and she notices that he often looks harassed and tired. She has no doubts, however, about his value to the organization, and his commitment to it. She decides to work with his lack of time rather than against it.

"You really work hard, Howard. The company must take up an awful lot of your time. Are you always as busy as this?"	(Responding to his work ethic, and showing concern)
"Have you always been at the center of so much of the company's activities, Howard? I would like to find out much more about how you view the current state of things."	(Giving him space to use his experience)

She could if she wishes also respond to his earlier remark about "computer stuff," once she has gained his agreement for a meeting. He seems to have made an issue about computers, so Rachel could explore that a little now in preparation for the meeting. "Howard, is there anything I can get to you in advance of the meeting that might make it clearer how we are planning to use computers in the future? I would be happy to prepare a brief paper for you."

At the time his "computer stuff" remark was made, it would have been counterproductive to address the issue. Five minutes later, however, she is demonstrating that she has heard that he has feelings about the issue and is concerned to make things easier for him.

Through a combination of assertiveness, active listening, and influencing-up, Rachel is able to arrange a meeting with Howard. She had just a fragment of time, but turned it to her advantage. The benefit of this three-way approach to getting the best from your boss is that it works, whether or not you are in conflict. If, however, problems recur, you may wish to adopt a more structured problem-solving method, which is covered in Chapter 23. There is also another assertion sequence in Chapter 9.

SUMMARY

Advantages

- Listen actively.
  - —meaning check
  - —reflecting content and feeling
  - —specifying questions
  - —focused question
  - —paraphrasing

- Be assertive.
  - —know your strengths and limitations
  - —choose to manage your feelings and those of others
  - —avoid being hooked by others' nonassertive behavior

- Respond assertively.
- Communicate feelings.
  - —I–You messages
  - —don't exaggerate or overdramatize
  - —give examples
  - —tactfully refer to previous incidents or agreements
- Say what you want.
  - —be clear what you want to change
  - —choose the issues you want to deal with carefully
  - —be specific
  - —avoid vague adjectives and adverbs
  - —choose language that will not make the situation worse
  - —use questions to check you are being heard and understood
- Influence-up.
  - —"hellos," "goodbyes," and "thank yous"
  - —acknowledging and affirming
  - —positive body language and tone
  - —show an interest in the person

Limitations

- Bosses have authority, of course, and their wishes and interests may not coincide with yours. You need to have contingency plans and alternatives if you cannot get what you really want.
- Even with people who are not accustomed to an enabling, empowering approach to conflict, this approach is powerful.
- All good managers are students of behavior and may well be impressed by your composure, control, and respectful assertiveness. They may even copy your methods of responding, because senior managers are always looking for ways to influence and motivate others. They may not, however, respond favorably to you at the first time of

asking. This approach may take some considerable time to really come to fruition, before you get what you want from your bosses.

Conflicts in Groups 10

*S*o far the focus has been on examples of conflicts between two parties: either yourself and one other or two others. The styles of interaction and skills covered are equally useful for group conflicts. Whether you are dealing with conflict between group members, between different groups, or between a group and yourself, you still need to operate on the principles of self-control, positive interaction between the parties, and aiming for the best possible outcome considering all the factors involved.

Groups can be wonderful things. You get the benefit of other people's ideas, skills, and experience as well as your own. Being responsible for a successful team, a flourishing department, or an effective meeting brings a manager great satisfaction. In a group that is really working well, the combined energy, effort, inspiration, and effect is greater than that of the individuals involved.

The expectations on any work group are high, yet groups also bring with them the risks of coalescing different people in one group. As well as their strengths, common aims, and characteristics, they bring their contrasting experience, ideas, and feelings. In a group, an individual has a problem of identity. How do I achieve what I want, express and experience my value, and get my needs met? This problem expresses itself in a variety of behaviors that an effective facilitator needs to deal with if the group is going to achieve its aims or perform its tasks.

Managers, who are often responsible for groups, need a good grounding in group theory, including purposes of groups, stages of the life of a group, roles and styles, and patterns of group behavior. Charles Handy provides a brief, stimulating introduction to the "Ways of Groups" in *Understanding Organizations* (Handy 1988). Managers also have to effectively deal with behavior as it happens, unlock tensions, and balance individual and group needs. There will be times when their own perspective is at odds with the others in the group. This chapter looks at ways of improving your ability to understand and respond to people problems in groups. Chapter 11 provides a workshop design for a group-building session when your department, team, or organization is in conflict or cannot function. Finally, Chapter 12 considers an assertion sequence for the odd-one-out in a group.

IMPROVING YOUR ABILITY TO UNDERSTAND AND RESPOND TO PEOPLE PROBLEMS IN GROUPS

Situation

The heads of department at Troubled Associates Ltd. are David, Surinder, Rachel, and Patricia. Helen and Phillip also attend the bimonthly heads of department meetings as they have responsibility for sections. Howard, the director, is satisfied that they work quite well individually, but conflicts occur when they meet as a team. In their separate meetings with him, they also speak about one another's departments with derision and applaud their own successes at the expense of their peers.

One particular meeting broke down in a huge argument with individuals accusing one another of conspiracy, uncooperativeness, and ignorance of one another's work. The issue involved a huge promotional campaign started by the customer relations officer, Phillip, in conjunction with his head of department, Patricia. They believed that the other heads had been made aware of the program and would be prepared for a huge response from the public. David, Surinder, and Rachel found that incoming phone lines were locked up by the general public with the result that they could not receive important calls for a couple of days. They claimed this severely disrupted their work and they were not consulted sufficiently.

In subsequent meetings, small-scale arguments occurred and never seemed to get resolved satisfactorily. The agenda was very rarely completed. Only cursory attention was paid to allocating tasks and reviewing work. This means that Howard had to spend a great deal of time on individual supervision and had little left for more strategic planning. This is one of the reasons he is always so busy.

As the person responsible for this group, he feels as though he is walking on eggshells. This is a group that is fearful of conflict and has not yet recovered from past disputes.

Dealing With Group Conflict

Step back and take a good look at behavior in the group.

↓

Develop a variety of instant and long-term responses.

↓

Deal with difficult behavior in and out of the group meetings.

GENERAL HINTS

One of the popular misconceptions about managers, which they often do much to perpetuate, is that they can manage all alone. Male and female managers fall into this same trap, determined to go it alone and find an answer to all problems, the right approach for all situations, the correct resolution to every conflict with no

**Do Not
"Go It Alone"**

help from anyone else. Why is this so? Is consultation or asking for advice a sign of weakness? Are managers so distrustful of their colleagues that they think there is no advantage in eliciting their support? Do they think they have nothing to learn from others? Or is it simply the power of the myth that the manager is always mightier than the situation, and that he or she is not fit to manage if asking frequently for help or support?

Ask for help

Certainly a manager must be expected to take responsibility, make tough instant decisions, and have faith in his or her own resources and abilities. But a manager can also gain strength from others, maximize human resources, and be open to difference.

The Advisory Conciliation and Arbitration Service (ACAS) conciliators often work in pairs, as do family mediators trained by the National Family Conciliation Council, and international negotiators often have a complete support team assisting them during, before, and after meeting with their clients. They realize how helpful carefully-planned, coordinated coworking is, both for the parties and the conflict managers, since they both benefit from the variety of skills, experience, and personal characteristics that can be brought to play on the situation.

Coworking

Coworkers are valuable

Coworking is not the same as delegation. It is a partnership aimed at utilizing the different faculties and skills in a pair or small team. Howard could arrange a program of coworking including each of his heads in turn. There are several conditions for effective coworking.

Howard could enlist the support of Patricia or another senior colleague, but he must ensure that her role and his reasons for selection are made clear to the group.

Allocating Specific Roles to People

Allocate roles

In the head of departments group, Howard could enlist one of the group in rotation each week as an observer, from which he will be able to build up a thorough picture of the behavior in the group. This is one example of clearly delineated role allocation.

CHECKLIST

Conditions for Effective Coworking

■ Clarity about personal specifications. What skills and experience are needed?

■ Careful planning about who does what. For example, one may take an active role, one more passive, observing, and taking notes. Plan how you will interact. If you have extra information to impart while your coworker is speaking, what will you do?

■ Creative thinking about combinations of skills, characteristics, and experience, and how they will affect people and situations. Do you need one "good cop" who will be friendly and encouraging and ask polite questions, and one "bad cop" who is tough and uncompromising?

■ Considering whether your partnership or team should reflect the group you are working with. For example, assign a male and female pair to a mixed male and female group.

■ Ensuring prompt and thorough debriefing and feedback so that partnerships can be evaluated and built upon.

■ Communicating clearly to the group how coworkers will function and what their expectations are.

Shedding Basic Group Maintenance Roles

Rotating the chairperson is not useful in meetings unless one aim of the meetings is to provide varied experiences of facilitation for the members. It is Howard's responsibility to chair; his task is to ensure that group maintenance and task-orientated behavior predominates and that self-orientated behavior is dealt with positively. Consistent and effective chairing will

- Enable differences to be expressed.
- Facilitate the management of conflicts.
- Move the group toward consensus.
- Get the work of the group done.

The most basic maintenance activities, such as timekeeping, minute-taking, and noticing who wishes to speak can be delegated. This frees the chair to facilitate group

Share out tasks

process and focus on the actions and interactions of its members. Howard often feels he has too much to do, so delegating these basic roles would be a useful exercise for him. Effective delegation requires clear instructions and carefully considered selection, support, and monitoring. It is useful to have a group secretary who is not directly involved and performs all three roles of timekeeping, minute-taking, and noticing who wishes to speak. There are times when delegating tasks can also be a way of counteracting difficult behavior, as is demonstrated later in this chapter.

Do Not Deal With Everything in the Whole Group

Some people are comfortable and function well working in very large groups. Others like to work individually or prefer the intimacy of small two- or three-person teams. Problems that are difficult to manage in the setting of the whole group are often more easily addressed outside that setting. Why not break up the numbers in your group occasionally? Splitting into pairs or smaller groups provides variation in the group dynamic and can be very effective for

Break up the large group

- Brainstorming individual problems with a smaller audience.
- Discussing individual problems with a smaller audience.
- Looking at what is happening in the larger group.
- Doing small projects for general consideration.
- Preparation on specific issues.
- Relaxing the group.
- Getting to know more about individual differences, strengths, and weaknesses.

Consistency

Managers who have regular access to their staff outside group meetings should be consistent in their behavior. Avoid saying or doing one thing in private and the opposite in public. Managers should not

- Say one thing in meetings and something different in individual sessions.

- Promise action and not follow it up.
- Express satisfaction in one-to-ones, then publicly criticize on the same issue.
- Disclose in whole-group settings information which was given in confidence.
- Support individuals when they are present and criticize them behind their backs.

If you adopt a consistently positive, open approach, even when you need to criticize or discipline staff, you are far less likely to provoke conflict in the group.

SUGGESTED RESPONSES TO PARTICULAR BEHAVIOR

Three assumptions are made in this section.

- You will be open and reasonable, and not make assumptions about or unchecked interpretations of behavior.
- You will frame your responses positively.
- Behavior is either very obvious and you decide it needs to be dealt with immediately, or it persists even after you have made it clear to the person that it is not in the best interests of the group.

Short scenarios focusing on individuals with different behavior problems, and several solutions to the problems follow.

Dominating Coworkers

Frequently a group is dominated by one individual, such as David. David considers that he is the whiz kid of the organization, so he does not listen to others, interrupting and blocking them. When he comes up with an idea, or is speaking in general, he says, "Just let me finish," and frequently speaks for a long time. Although some of his ideas are good, David is taking up so much of the group's space that other people, including Howard, are getting frustrated.

Suggestions

- Develop clear guidelines for how much time each person can take, and delegate someone to monitor and give feedback on the outcome.

- Give the dominator a specific task in the group to reduce opportunities for domination. For example, the timekeeper's role is ensuring that agenda items do not overrun and giving frequent time checks.

- Appoint someone to observe the group and to give feedback. Consider and discuss the impact of dominant and pliant behavior in the group, and follow up one-to-one.

- Ask focused questions to clarify and encourage specific, concise communication. For example:

  "David, I can hear that you have a lot of ideas on this subject. It will help me understand them if I summarize what you have said so far . . . ."

- Bring the group in.

  "What do you think about David's point?"

  "How do you think we would be able to do . . . ?"

- Be clear about your own feelings. How is your experience of this person affecting your behavior?

- Reframe dominant responses so that their positive content is emphasized and the negative minimized. For example, David is suspicious of the new computer setup. He talks about it at length, admitting that Rachel has done a good, professional job, but is worried about the cost and the long-term impact on his own department.

  "So you like the way Rachel has set up the computer system. Would you like to be more specific about what impressed you? What do you think we can learn from Rachel's work?"

- Address any concerns that do emerge from what the dominator says. For example:

"Thanks for being so positive about Rachel's work, David. First, I can assure you that I have no intention of putting more resources into computers without consulting you."

- Encourage other members to join in by brainstorming, splitting into small groups, and rejoining, with individual preparation followed by going around the room.
- Control the agenda items so that different specialists have the chance to contribute.

Phillip has a quick temper and has been attacking other group members verbally. He contradicts suggestions made by the group and is often negative and insensitive. Sometimes he is stubborn beyond the bounds of what is reasonable. He often is at the center of arguments both in and out of meetings.

Aggressive Coworkers

Suggestions

- Explore the feelings motivating the behavior by using neutral questions.

  "When I hear you speak in such an aggressive tone of voice, Phillip, I wonder what upsets you so much."

- Confront the aggressor's behavior without blaming. "One outcome of confrontation can be to release energy and good feelings toward the other and yourself. But it takes two to tango. If the other person will not respond openly, you are not likely to get closer. However, you will have said where you stand and what you want. You will be clearer about your own position" (Huston 1984). Use a three-part assertion message (see Chapter 12). For example:

  "When I hear you challenge others in such an aggressive tone of voice, Phillip, I feel apprehensive, and that means that I can never actually get the point you are putting across."

- Answer aggression with calm. "Picture your role as that of a peacemaker who is above the fray. Meet the person's fury with your own inner serenity and calm: this will help the other person put aside his or her aggression, and you can work things out from there" (Scott 1990).

- Suggest alternative behaviors.

"Phillip, would you like to frame that more positively so that we can understand exactly what you object to, and what you would like to do about it?"

This is reframing.

"People will hear what you are saying more clearly if you say something you like before moving on to what you do not like."

Howard is acknowledging and being constructive.

- Refer to and apply the ground rules.

- Follow up one-to-one.

- Avoid spiraling of conflict by using conflict management techniques, for example, by ensuring listening and equal space.

Paraphrasing

"Okay, stop there for a second, Phillip. Do I understand that what you're saying to Patricia is…. Okay, now Patricia, I will ask you to answer Phillip's point shortly, but first, how do you feel right now?"

This gives her a chance to vent her feelings so that Phillip can see the effect his behavior has. Patricia replies

Reflecting meaning

"It sounds as though you feel…when you speak in such an aggressive tone."

- Let the aggression burn out, then move on. Sometimes a person will explode with spontaneous anger. It is not easy for group members to hear, particularly if the anger is directed at them.

When someone really explodes, and is yelling and screaming, the main priority is to stop escalation. Use an incremental approach of listening, calming, and containing, and then move on to deal with the problem. Work in the following stages:

> Listen until the burst of emotion is ended.
>
> ↓
>
> Encourage the rest of the group to listen and stop them from interrupting.
>
> ↓
>
> Begin calming by acknowledging that you have heard and recognize the feelings of anger.
>
> ↓
>
> When the person has calmed down, treat him or her calmly and respectfully, and begin to deal with the problem.
>
> ↓
>
> Shift the focus away from the actual outburst; often the person concerned will acknowledge that the anger was exaggerated and will be embarrassed, even apologetic.
>
> ↓
>
> Acknowledge and contain the response of the group.

Deal with the issues

- Exclude the aggressor from the group or warn the aggressor that he or she will only be allowed to participate if he or she abides by the ground rules. As you really want all the available human resources in your group, this is a last resort. Follow up with intensive one-to-one.

Manipulative Coworkers

Surinder is normally very reasonable, but on some issues he tries to manipulate group behavior and opinion, both in and out of the meetings. He builds close relationships to get people on his side and discloses or withholds important information. Tension in the group is increasing as a result of this behavior and Howard is losing respect for Surinder, formerly one of his most trusted staff.

Suggestions

- Check the needs behind the behavior on a one-to-one basis.

  "Surinder, why did you feel it was necessary to...?"

  "I have noticed that sometimes you put other people in difficult situations. Are you aware of that? How would you describe what you did? So what were you hoping to achieve?"

- Address the behavior in the group, describe its effect on you, and ask for feedback.

  "I think that we would have been able to make a decision a lot earlier if we had had that information sooner. How do the rest of you think we can make life easier for decision making in the future?"

  "It is very difficult to judge what the consensus in the group is when people form alliances and battle with one another. Could I just check what you each think about this individually?"

- Challenge manipulative behavior as it happens.

  "I would rather have Rachel choose her time to speak, rather than have you put her in a position where she has no choice."

- Check what is going on.

  "It looks to me as though you have come to some sort of agreement with...that we do not know about. Could you tell us about the situation regarding...?"

Nonparticipative Coworkers (Silent in Group)

Rachel often says very little in groups. She says she would like to, but finds it difficult. How can Howard draw her out of her shell? She is creative and resourceful on her own territory, and has often come up with imaginative resolutions for difficult situations. Howard would welcome her also exercising this positive influence in the group.

Suggestions

- Pair or group the person with similar types. In meetings, organize pairs discussing ideas about items and feeding back to the main group or discussing their experience of being in the meetings. This sharing and comparing of feelings is affirming and builds confidence. Outside meetings, get quiet types to work together on some projects.

- Design a variety of structures encouraging contributions (see also Dominating Coworkers).

- Support any contribution and use questions to quietly and nonthreateningly elicit more information and ideas.

  "That's an interesting point, Rachel. How do you think your department would view...?"

  "Do you agree with David when he says...?"

  "Could you say a little more about that?"

- Elicit contributions in areas where you know this person has special expertise.

- Encourage questioning and interaction by group members. For example:

  "What do you think about Surinder's ideas, Rachel? I think they affect your department. Is there anything you would like to ask him?"

  "Just spend a minute or two discussing the pros and cons of this issue with the person next to you, then we can all discuss it together."

  "I am not the right person to answer that question. Who else do you think could give you the information you need? Check what you want to know with them, now, I think it would be useful for us all to hear each other's ideas."

Other ways of bringing in quieter members of the group include:

- Sharing talking time evenly.
- Giving a particular task.

- Allowing time for preparation. Some people will only speak in front of a large group if they feel adequately prepared.

Nonparticipative Coworkers (Do Not Attend Group)

Phillip misses one or two meetings a month, and although he seems to have a good reason each time, Howard would rather he attend more often. One of the reasons he may not be attending is to avoid the group's reactions to his aggressive behavior. Howard feels that if he can deal with the nonattendance it may be less easy for Phillip to be so aggressive. Also, he may feel less inclined to be so. Other heads of department are growing angry with Phillip, as they think he is not contributing equally to the group.

Suggestions

- Check out, one-to-one, whether this person is getting what he or she needs from the meeting and where his or her energies may be effectively directed.
- Give a task which means that he or she has to attend. For example, ask the person to prepare a report for the meeting, research some information, or cofacilitate the meeting with Howard.
- Give a choice of topic and provide support in preparation and presentation. Phillip's aggression and reluctance to attend may be a consequence of his insecurity. Give him the opportunity to develop a project he is interested in, and provide support, either by yourself or with another staff member, to ensure that he does himself justice. Then ensure that the group feedback is constructive.
- Make the meetings a positive experience.
  - Create a positive and efficient, but relaxed, atmosphere.
  - Use a variety of methods of presentation and discussion.
  - Encourage positive interaction among group members.

- Encourage individual members to express their feelings outside meetings about his nonattendance (assertively but without hostility).

David

"Phillip, I know that we sometimes have arguments in meetings, but I always miss your suggestions and opinions when you're not there."

Helen

"Phillip, I and the rest of the group have noticed that you are having difficulty attending meetings. I feel frustrated that we cannot communicate and would like to have the chance to work that out in the meetings with you there."

- Involve the nonattender in joint work with other group members to develop a sense of shared responsibility.

Complaining Coworkers

Patricia is normally quite assertive, but is still inclined to complain about a variety of things, some of which are realistic. Other complaints are linked to her feeling that on some issues people do not really take any notice of what she has to say. Under these circumstances, she blames other people in the group, or sometimes just the world in general. Her complaints are taking up a lot of time so that other issues are not being dealt with, and people are getting frustrated.

Suggestions

- Begin by listening actively, regardless of whether the complaint is true or unfounded. Make it clear that you have heard and understood. For example:

  "I can see that you're angry about...."

  "So you feel that...."

- Move toward closure, either by suggesting action or by inviting suggestions, and make a decision about what is next.

  "What I think we can do is...."

"What would you like to happen now...what would you like us to do?"

- If the complainer just returns to the original complaint, then respectfully interrupt, and focus on the suggestions. For example:

"Could I just ask you to pause a minute, Patricia. I believe we have dealt with that point."

Follow this with a brief summary of action or decisions.

"I can understand that you are upset about this, but I believe we have covered your point. Is there anything we have not dealt with, in your opinion?"

- If this does not work, move into problem-solving mode. What does the person want to do, or what can you both do to find a resolution, or is there anyone else who can help? Hopefully this approach will give the complainant the attention he or she needs, and eventually you will be able to encourage him or her more quickly into problem solving until the complainant can do it for himself or herself.

- Follow up one-to-one.

CONCLUSION

Step back when in deadlock

Even the most versatile and resourceful group leader or manager will experience disabling times when none of the familiar responses or skills work. Sometimes groups will simply cease to work because the dynamics between the members, including the leader, are locked. It is as though the effective life of this group has ceased. No one person from within the group will be able to break this deadlock in the normal setting of the group. Instead it can be very productive to step back, examine what is happening, effectively go back to basics and rebuild the group. The next chapter contains a workshop model for such a situation.

There are also conflicts between groups, such as departmental clashes, or disputes between interest groups, staff and management groups, and work teams. Often they hinge on the relationships between key individuals within each camp and are amplified and made more complex by the surrounding structures. The whole subject of group and intergroup conflict is a huge one, and not part of this book. The skills demonstrated in it can also be extremely effective in intergroup disputes. An experienced consultant or trainer will help your organization develop dispute resolution systems for such conflict.

SUMMARY

Useful Circumstances

- Do not "go it alone"
    - coworking
    - allocating specific roles
    - shedding basic group maintenance roles

- Do not deal with everything in the whole group
- Consistency
- Dominating coworkers
    - provide time guidelines, give tasks, and appoint
      observers
    - focus questions to encourage specific and concise communication
    - bring the group in
    - clarify your feelings
    - seek out and transmit constructive, useful material
    - address any concerns
    - redirect into positive role
    - encourage other members to join in
    - control agenda

- Aggressive coworkers
    - explore feelings behind behavior

— confront the aggressor's behavior without blaming

— answer aggression with calm

— suggest alternative behaviors

— refer to ground rules

— follow up one-to-one

— avoid spiraling of conflict by using conflict management techniques

— let the aggression burn out, using an incremental approach from listening and calming to containment and dealing with the problem

— exclude the aggressor from group or warn of consequences of behavior

- Manipulative coworkers

    — check the needs behind the behavior one-to-one

    — check what is going on

    — address the behavior in the group, describe itseffect on you, and ask for feedback

    — challenge manipulative behavior when it happens

    — check what is going on

- Nonparticipative coworkers (silent in group)

    — pair or group in small group with similar types

    — structure groups encouraging contributions

    — support any contribution

    — elicit contributions where person has special expertise

    — encourage questioning and interaction by group members

    — share talking time evenly

    — give a particular task

    — allow time for preparation

- Nonparticipative coworkers (do not attend group)
    - check out one-to-one whether this person is getting what he or she needs from the meeting and where energies may be effectively directed
    - give a task
    - give choice of topic and support in preparation and presentation
    - make the meetings a positive experience
    - encourage the individual members to express their feelings about his non-attendance outside meetings
    - involve in joint work projects with other group members
- Complaining coworkers
    - listen actively
    - move toward closure
    - focus on suggestions
    - use problem solving
    - follow up one-to-one

Limitations

- Running groups of any kind is not an easy business. These suggestions are not intended as easy fixes and should be used in the context of active positive facilitation, clear group guidelines, and clarification of goals, tasks, and roles. (See Chapter 11 for a series of exercises to clarify roles, goals, and tasks.)

A Group-Building Workshop for a Group Experiencing Conflict or Dysfunction **11**

*T*his is an alternative approach to prolonged group conflict or dysfunction. These exercises can be used either separately or as a whole workshop unit.

The main aims of this set of exercises are to

- Facilitate communication about the group by its members.

- Model constructive group behavior, that which helps the maintenance of the group and is not self-oriented.

- Demonstrate conflict resolution skills.
- Enhance individual and group effectiveness.

The facilitator of such events should have

- Good interpersonal skills.
- Understanding of conflict management skills.
- Interest in encouraging group learning by experience and discovery.
- Ability to take an impartial stance.
- Ability to notice and discuss different kinds of group and individual behavior and its effect.

If you believe you fit these specifications, then you may wish to run this whole workshop yourself or in conjunction with a colleague. You can also use the separate exercises over a period of time as they each have a specific task. Do not double up as participant and facilitator. These are two quite separate roles that will be difficult for you to manage together and for the group to comprehend. If you wish to join in, you could enlist someone else from inside or outside of your organization as facilitator.

ATTENDANCE

Whole group must attend

Patricia and Howard make it clear to the heads of department that attendance at this session is mandatory, and Howard too will be there. Try as hard as you can to ensure that all members of the group attend. Absent members have quite an effect. The "empty-chair syndrome" is a common occurrence; individuals present at a meeting, workshop, or planning session look at the empty chairs of absent members with an expression of horror, disappointment, or glee. These reactions reveal a great deal about the issues and individual dynamics in a group, and it is far more satisfactory to deal with those issues when all are present. If this is not possible, however, there will be plenty of value for those who do attend, and you can set up structures to communicate the content and spirit of what happened to those who genuinely cannot make it.

EQUALIZING

When you run group-building sessions, your aim should be to encourage participation on as equal a level as possible, regardless of status or length of time in the organization. You will achieve this by ensuring that

- Aims of the sessions are clear and understood by all.
- Tasks do not require specialist knowledge.
- Structure encourages people to take part; for example, by not doing everything in a full-group setting.
- There are clearly established ground rules.

Everyone is equal

NUMBERS AND TIMINGS

This session will work for up to twenty people. As there is a lot of work done in small groups, you will need more time for increased feedback as the numbers go up. With twenty people, you really need a full-day session of at least eight hours. Timings given here are approximate and are based on a group of twelve people.

PROGRAM

1. Introduction
2. Warmup
3. Negotiating ground rules—an early chance for the group to look at itself
4. Comparing and aligning the aims of the group and the individuals
5. Self-evaluation of behavior
6. Action plans for individuals and the group—behavior and tasks
7. Conclusion

MATERIALS

Plenty of paper, pens, and clipboards are required for individual and pair exercises. Each person will need up to ten sheets of paper. Ten sheets of flip chart paper per four people for small group recording and feedback are also needed.

FURNITURE AND SPACE

Use chairs that are comfortable enough for people to feel at ease, but not so comfortable that they might encourage people to curl up, relax too much, and avoid the session by dozing.

The space should be sufficient to accommodate a circle of chairs with an open end facing a wall or series of flip chart easels. It will also help if chairs can be moved into different areas of the room for small-group exercises. If you do not have such a room on your site, and if you have the resources, there are often rooms available for hire at local conference centers, community halls, libraries, or training and enterprise centers. Well-organized, adequately equipped, comfortable physical space contributes significantly to a constructive mental and emotional attitude. Always try to get to your venue early to ensure that the furniture, equipment, and materials are in order.

THE WORKSHOP CONTENT

**Introduction
(15 minutes)**

Introduction to the Session

In your introduction, include a concise reminder of the purpose of the meeting and briefly run through the program. Any practical issues, such as timing of breaks and provision of food or drinks, should be dealt with here.

Personal Introductions—Re-forming the Group

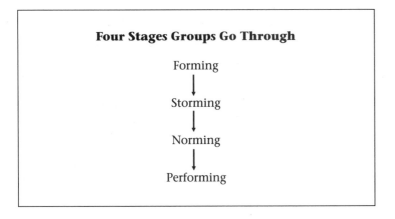

Four Stages Groups Go Through

Forming

↓

Storming

↓

Norming

↓

Performing

People do seem to need to know a little bit about each other before they can get on with the business of working out how to function together. This forming should be done in the introductory stages of any group or meeting, especially when there are significant changes in the group membership or, in the case of Troubled Associates Ltd., when the group is not functioning adequately.

Whether the people in the group know one another or not, get them to check in by saying their name plus another relevant but low-risk piece of information; that is, one that is not likely to embarrass or threaten the individual. For example:

Forming

- "Summarize your feelings about this session in two or three words, or describe an image that represents how you feel."

- "Briefly say one thing you like about yourself." This is not risky; just unfamiliar to many people, who are not encouraged to publicly take credit for their own good points. "Briefly describe one thing you are pleased with yourself for doing at work."

It useful to ask people to check names, if they cannot remember them as the session progresses, when they wish to refer to something someone else has said, or address another group member directly. This is a simple act of acknowledgment that builds up individual comfort levels in the group.

Clarifying Basic Behavioral Ground Rules

Some ground rules are not negotiable. These should be written on a large sheet of paper for everyone to see. Go through them with the group, giving examples and gaining consent.

Respect

Respect

No verbal or physical abuse; no discriminatory language or behavior is acceptable.

Space

Space

People should have time and space to say what they need to, which means no interrupting, arguing, or monopolizing attention.

Care

Care

People should do their best to be sensitive to the needs of the other members of the group; for example, listen quietly when difficult issues are being spoken about, be encouraging and positive, and frame critical remarks constructively.

Confidentiality

Confidentiality

People should be free to say things that they wish to remain confidential and would say if that were the case. Others should respect that wish.

These ground rules are universally useful for all kind of meetings. Referring to ground rules when challenging behavior is a way of depersonalizing the control and discipline element required in all groups. People whose behavior is challenged on the basis of previously agreed upon rules are less likely to feel personally threatened or blamed. Individual members are also empowered when given joint responsibility for group maintenance.

Warmup Exercise (15 minutes)

Time spent giving group members chances to learn about themselves and how they interact is well invested. Understanding reduces the chances of high-risk, damaging conflicts, so time spent early on with warmup exercises is extremely constructive providing they are

- Nonthreatening and light.
- Informal and relaxed.
- Inviting and enjoyable.
- Useful to the group because they have a skill element.

Here are a couple of ideas for warmup exercises.

Exercise: A Couple of Things You Don't Know About Me (15 minutes)

1. Each member thinks of two things he or she is prepared to disclose about himself or herself that the others do not know. They could be hobbies, interests, skills, or fragments of personal history.
2. Pair up. The facilitator can be the extra one for a pair if numbers are odd. Each person has five minutes to share.
3. One person discloses the two pieces of information and the other listens in silence.
4. The listener reports to the speaker what he or she has heard.
5. The listener gains feedback on the accuracy of the report and briefly asks questions to discover more about the information.
6. Switch roles.
7. Each pair joins up with another pair.
8. Each person should report briefly to the small group what his or her partner has disclosed. A total of five minutes is allowed for this feedback.

Teaching point: Outline the benefits of active listening, such as gaining information and giving the other person positive attention.

This exercise is useful for promoting active listening and helps create a relaxed atmosphere by encouraging low-risk self disclosure. Very formal meetings, workshops, training courses, and conferences can be opened with a version of this exercise.

People who feel threatened by groups are given an immediate chance to focus on themselves and take account of others. Diving straight into group process can sometimes create a feeling of engulfment for some individuals, which such warmup exercises counteract.

Exercise: Autobiographies (10 minutes)

1. Each member is asked to think of the title he or she would like for his or her autobiography, and what kind of picture he or she would like on the cover.

2. In pairs they describe, discuss, and explain their titles.

3. Each then tries to visualize the other's cover and describes what he or she thinks it would be like.

4. Each person then discloses his or her ideas about the covers. At the beginning, tell people that they have ten minutes for the exercise and that it is their responsibility to manage the time fairly.

5. Ask each person separately to say what percentage of the time they thought they had with their partner.

Teaching point: People verbalize and visualize their experience differently. Emphasize the need for good observation and checking.

Register any significant imbalances in timesharing, and ask the groups to continue to be aware of how much time they claim. It is their responsibility to claim enough time and work out ways of dealing with those who dominate the time.

Negotiating the Ground Rules— Giving the Group an Early Opportunity to Look at Itself

There are certain behavioral issues which invariably seem to provoke heated discussion. Managers recall groups where often long minutes, even hours, have been spent arguing over whether to smoke or not, when to start sessions if not all participants are present, and how to deal with people who break ground rules.

Groups go through different stages when working together; these are the stages of forming, norming, storming, and performing, common to all groups. All group leaders would like their groups to start performing right away, but people do seem to need time to get to know one another and to make an impression on one another (forming). The storming stage, when people rise up and challenge the leader, organization, or one another, is uncomfortable, but has to happen if a group is to come to terms with how it is going to work (norming).

Storming

The following exercise permits early storming and yields a lot of information about behavior in the group.

Exercise: Negotiating Ground Rules (30 minutes)

The aims of the exercise are to

- Provide the group with an early chance to storm or at least express opinions within a limited framework.

- Focus on and collect information about how individuals in the group behave that can be used as learning material.

1. Briefing an observer (5 minutes)
   Appoint an observer (or perform this role yourself if you have a small group). The observer's tasks are to

   a. Look at the kind of interactions that occur in general.

   Instructions to the observer:

   "Write down what you notice about how people behave, and pay particular attention to the order in which things happen. Are questions asked? Do people appear to be listening? What kind of words, tone of voice, and gestures are used? Do you notice anything specific about body language? Do people listen carefully before responding, or do they interrupt? Is there anything else you notice? Do not record any names. We do not need to know who does what, but be as specific as you can about what people do."

   b. Notice and record how decisions are made.

   Instructions to the observer:

   "Were any decisions made? How did they come about? Describe the process, but do not use names."

   Reassure the group that this information will be collected and reported in a non-critical, neutral manner, without naming specific people, and that they will be given a chance to add their own observations.

2. Group task (10 minutes)

Instructions to the group:

"You have ten minutes to decide what you are going to do about the following issues. I will rule on any unresolved issues: smoking, starting sessions regardless of who is present, leaving the group room during sessions for any reason, and any other important issues. I have asked the observer to write down what he or she sees happening, and will ask for feedback in ten minutes."

3. Recording decisions

At the end of ten minutes, ask one member of the group to report the decisions only, and write them on the sheet containing the other ground rules.

4. Feedback from the observer (5 minutes)

Instructions to the observer:

"Tell us what you noticed, and remember not to mention any names. I will record the key words on the sheet."

Instructions to the group:

"Listen to the observer, and then I will spend a few minutes collecting your own observations."

Refer to the mapping examples that follow for recording feedback.

Mapping

Mapping is a word used by mediators, negotiators, and arbitrators. It refers to the practice of depicting part of a conflict—the structure, arguments, interests, positions, and even feelings—through simple graphic representation. It works the same way a map does. The mapper devises a system of arranging words and symbols to depict the real world. For instance, a blue line represents a river, or on English maps, the letters PO stand for a post office.

Mapping: Example One

Observer says

"A lot of questions and suggestions came in very quickly, with everyone trying to outshout one another. Then someone started writing them down and asked individuals to repeat their points. Finally, a vote was taken on each issue. The initial noise eventually calmed down and people seemed quite relaxed by the end."

How would you record this? The following illustration shows one alternative that depicts the movement from competition to participation and joint decision making.

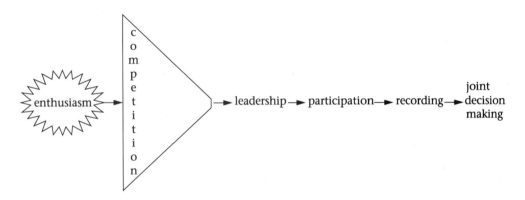

Mapping: Example Two

Observer says

"One person said what he wanted about one issue in a very aggressive way, and, since there was little disagreement from the others, he said that as far as he was concerned the matter was resolved. One other person started to speak, but he stopped her, suggesting that the group had very little time and should move on to the other issues. He was very persuasive and powerful and very few other people really got the chance to speak on any of the issues, which were all resolved the way he suggested."

How would you record this observation? One suggestion is power play group allows itself to be dominated—

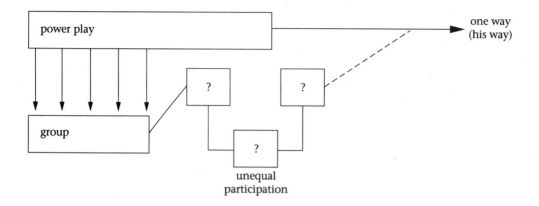

unequal participation—one direction (his way). You could depict this in a way that contrasts the process with the task, as shown above.

Mapping provides another way of looking at and understanding behavior, and can be particularly useful if people are having trouble expressing themselves or getting a clear overall view of their situation. When words fail, a map can sometimes work very effectively. When you have no common language in a group, or great disparity in levels of linguistic competence, mapping may in fact be the most appropriate form of representation.

Using the observer's feedback, begin a preliminary mapping of the group behavior. You need one large sheet of paper. Summarize the feedback into key words first at the top of the sheet. Then look at what you have and see if there is any way you can depict graphically what is going on.

Mapping: Example Three

Observer says

"No one spoke initially. One person started the process by making a suggestion. Still no one else spoke; then the same person made another suggestion. A counter suggestion was made in a louder voice, and the group went quiet again. One other person then complained that the group was always arguing and could never make decisions."

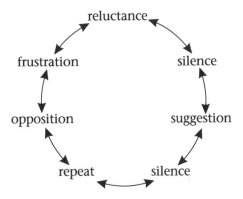

How would you record the key elements of this example? The sequence, reluctance—silence—suggestion—silence—repeat—opposition—frustration, records the key elements. If you wanted to make a point about the circular nature of this process, you could write it up.

5. Feedback from the group (10 minutes)

The aim is to collect more opinions, not to decide what is right or wrong.

Instructions to the group:

"What is your reaction to these depictions? Is this how you understood what went on? Would you suggest another way of describing what went on? Either come and draw it for us, or tell me how to. We have a maximum of ten minutes to collect your ideas."

6. Conclusion

Leave the sheet on the wall as information and move on to the next stage. Tell the group members they will have a further chance to concentrate on, and evaluate, behavior in the group. Remind them of the ground rules they have agreed upon.

Exercise: Stage One—Consensus Building (45 minutes)

Comparing and Aligning Aims of the Individuals (90 minutes)

1. Get into groups of three or four. It is helpful if people get into a group with someone with whom they do not often work.

2. Individually write up to five of the aims or purposes of the group, organization, team or, in this case, heads of department, as a group. Individuals have five minutes to think about this and write something down.

Note

As people often get confused by aims, here are some clarifications. An aim is the

- Reason for something being there. For example, the aim of a doctor's office is to provide care for the patients.

- Answer to the question "Why does it exist?" not "What is it?" For example, the answer to "Why does a restaurant exist?" is, "to provide an alternative environment for eating where the customer is served, is comfortable, and has no responsibility for preparation or cleaning up, and to make a profit in the process." Whereas, the answer to "What is a restaurant?" is, "a place where people go to eat food cooked by someone else and pay for it."

Another helpful question to clarify aims is "Why this and not that?" For example, "Why go to a restaurant and not stay in and cook at home?" The answer points to the aims of the restaurant: because someone else is doing the cooking and cleaning up, and you will eat in a different environment.

Some examples of aims for teams, such as the heads of department, would be to

- Monitor and evaluate work done across the whole organization.

- Enable public sharing of information.

- Keep the director in regular contact with his or her managers.

- Provide opportunities for feedback, constructive criticism, and appreciation.

- Plan strategically.

- Allocate special projects and tasks.

3. When each has finished, read the ideas to the small group in turn.

4. Identify those aims on which all in the small group agree, and write them on a piece of flip chart paper. Think carefully about the use of words and be as specific as possible. Allow thirty minutes.

   One person will then report the findings to the whole group. Only write down those aims on which all agree can be written down.

5. Each small group provides feedback from its flip chart to the whole group. Questions can be asked for clarification only.

6. The facilitator highlights those aims on which both groups agree. Allow ten minutes.

Remember, all the aims on the flip charts have been agreed on by at least three people in the small groups. If there is complete agreement on any of the group aims, that is, they appear on every flip chart, then there is a consensus—an agreement of opinion by all concerned.

All effective groups must contain some measure of consensus about aims. In all groups there is some degree of pressure to agree or conform. This exercise reduces that pressure, starting as it does with the individual perspective, and then utilizing small-group discussions where there are plenty of opportunities to discuss, question, and reach compromises. However, as with most experiential training exercises, this is a condensed version of the real thing. There are many possible outcomes which will dictate what you ask the group to do next.

Norming

Exercise: Stage Two—Identifying and Working Through Differences (45 minutes)

There are three possible outcomes to the small group feedback.

1. There is complete agreement. The same aims appear on all the flip charts.

2. There is no agreement. None of the aims appears more than once.

3. There is some measure of agreement and disagreement. Only some of the aims appear on all of the charts.

The next stage is to identify and work through differences. If you have arrived at the first outcome, or there is a substantial measure of consensus, then use option one below. If there is still some degree of strong disagreement in the group, use option two below. Both options are designed to model conflict management techniques and to promote group maintenance behavior.

Option One (45 minutes)

The group has already reached a substantial measure of consensus on aims, but how does it handle differences?

1. Split into new groups of three or four.

2. Individually, members should write up to five things they hope to achieve as head of the department. Allow five minutes. Some examples are to

   - Secure sufficient resources to run the department effectively.

   - Present the department well to the general public and to the rest of the organization.

   - Establish the status and importance of the department.

   - Create structures that motivate staff.

   - Re-equip the office.

   - Create pay incentives for staff.

   - Stop racial and sexual harassment by introducing severe penalties.

   - Recruit an extra staff member.

   - Be the best manager in the organization.

   - Provide a service to the other departments.

   - Prevent a decline in standards of work.

3. When finished, take turns reading them to the small group.

4. The next step is to spend forty minutes working through member differences in the small groups

and to find out more about one another's ideas. Do not try to destroy them, but test, explore, and work toward understanding. See how they relate to group aims using these four categories to help.

- Legitimate individual aim but not appropriate for whole group

- Legitimate for individual and whole group

- Inappropriate individual aim which contradicts group aims

- Need more information or discussion to decide

Use the following guidelines to help achieve this task.

- If a person disagrees with, wants to challenge, or simply wants to find out more about someone's aims, he or she can only do so by questioning. For example:

"How exactly will you get a budget to create pay incentives for staff?"	(Specifying)
"What do you mean by being the best manager?"	(Focused)
"Can you help me understand how you can be sure that you can stop racial harassment by introducing severe penalties?"	(Challenging)
"Am I right in thinking that you have not considered the effect of this on the other departments?"	(Clarifying)

- When explaining ideas, frame them in a way that will increase the likelihood of their being heard and understood. For example, do not say

"Of course I have
thought about the
implications of this. Do
you think I am stupid?'

or

"This is the only way you   (Vague and unhelpful)
can possibly make the
situation better, and stop
the harassment."

Instead, frame your ideas
usefully.

or

"I am glad that you are   (Acknowledging and
concerned about the   specific)
issue of harassment as
well. I have spoken to
experts about this, and
they see harsh penalties
as one of a variety of
measures that do work."

- Remember the ground rules.
- When an item has been discussed fully, write the key words from it on the flip chart. Each person should rate it individually as one of the four categories above. Write these on the paper.
- Move on to another item. Make sure the roles of questioner and defender are shared equally.
- If you run out of items, try to think of other opinions about individual and group aims that you would like discussed by the same process.

Option Two (45 minutes)

Go back to the flip charts from the exercise on consensus building. There will be some group aims on which everyone did not agree. Use these as the material to work through differences.

1. Each small group of three or four combines with another.

2. Using the flip charts, identify the differences between the two halves of this new group. What are the aims disagreed on? (five minutes)

3. The groups are to spend forty minutes

   • Finding out more about the divergent opinions. Do not try to destroy one another's ideas, but test, explore, and try to understand them.

   • Rating the levels of agreement after you have discussed each item.

There are four categories to help group members do this.

1. You understand and respect the opinion, but do not think it is appropriate for the whole group.

2. You agree and think it should be added to the group aims as it is legitimate for both the individual and the whole group.

3. You disagree strongly with the opinion.

4. You need more information or discussion to decide.

Use the first three guidelines from Option One, plus the three below.

   • When an item has been discussed fully, rate the individual levels of agreement of the questioners according to the four categories above. Write these on the paper alongside the correct item.

   • Discuss as many aims as possible. Try to switch roles in the group so that each person gets the chance to question and to explain an issue.

   • If there are not enough items to discuss, think of any other group aims so far not covered that would be interesting to discuss using the same process.

Feedback (This is the same for Options One and Two.) (10 minutes)

Ask each group to summarize only those items which were placed into categories 1 or 2. These are those that were appropriate for individuals but not for the group or that were generally agreed upon. Briefly discuss the findings.

Teaching points: You may wish to emphasize and summarize the conflict management skills that have been included in the exercise.

- Consensus building, concentrating on where there is agreement
- Constructive questioning
- Positive framing of responses
- Separating what is appropriate for the individual and the group

Self Evaluation of Behavior (90 minutes)

Introduction (10 minutes)

This section provides some teaching and exercises about self-oriented and group maintenance behavior. Begin by giving some examples of both behaviors.

Self-Oriented Behavior

Self-oriented behavior is characterized as being blocking, aggressive, special-interest pleading, withdrawing, and seeking diversion.

Group Maintenance Behavior

Group maintenance behavior is characterized as being encouraging, standard setting, harmonizing, and standard testing, and uses conflict management techniques.

Individual Exercise: To Evaluate One's Own Behavior and Its Effect on the Group (20 minutes)

1. Instruct group members to write up to three examples of their behavior that they think have made a positive contribution to the group (five to ten minutes). For example:

- Backing down on what was an important issue
- Giving positive strokes and encouragement
- Working out guidelines for recording phone calls
- Arriving on time

- Giving advance notice for absence or lateness
- Preparing a paper for consideration
- Postponing an urgent agenda item because another took precedence

2. Have group members write down up to three examples when they would have liked to change their behavior as it had a negative impact on the group (five to ten minutes). For example:

- Interrupting other people
- Not listening
- Bringing in outside issues which were not relevant
- Making personal remarks or accusations
- Misunderstanding someone else's opinion
- Making assumptions
- Overreacting
- Omitting important information to make their case look better
- Obstructing decision making

Exercise: Affirmation—"Positive Strokes" (20 to 30 minutes)

This exercise can be used to affirm positive behavior and to use clarification and reflection to help self-evaluation.

1. Get into pairs.
2. Each person reads examples of positive behavior, while the partner tries out various kinds of affirmative behavior to see what feels comfortable. For example:

- Nodding and smiling
- Maintaining steady eye contact and an open, relaxed body posture
- Giving verbal affirmation: "I liked this.... " "I didn't realize that. Thanks for telling me." "Well done." "Great." "That was clever of you."

3. Check how the partner felt about the responses. What was helpful and positive? What was not?

Note: Giving Strokes

Some people find it easier than others to give positive strokes. These are appreciative words and gestures, and genuine expressions of congratulation and affirmation. Many times, powerful, confident people struggle to express appreciation as though it is somehow socially unacceptable, or not appropriate for someone of their status. Conversely, gushing, transparently dishonest compliments are often rained on these powerful people by their underlings.

Give positive strokes

A positive stroke is a simple, spontaneous expression of recognition, and as such is a selfless gift from you to the recipient. It costs you nothing. Such strokes should not be saved only for moments of excellence. Keep a lookout for the times when you

- Admire someone's skill.
- See an improvement in someone's behavior, attitude, or performance.
- Are stimulated mentally.
- Enjoy working with a colleague or member of staff
- Appreciate extra effort.
- See a characteristic you like.
- Have been helped by someone else.
- Feel positively about someone, their ideas or efforts.

Practice different kinds of words, phrases, and gestures. You will find what is congruent with your own sentiments. Do not exaggerate or understate, but match the positive stroke to your feelings and the situation.

Avoid negative strokes

Negative strokes, responses that focus on what is not okay about a person, are all too familiar: school reports that constantly say "could do better," in the misguided notion that this will help students be better; parents who say "naughty girl," when what they are experiencing is their own anger and embarrassment because they do not know how to control their child. Such responses are learned from our peers, parents, and from the many examples of negative behavior seen on TV. People confuse our disapproval or disappointment of what our colleagues or staff have done with disapproval of who they are. Negative strokes embody this confusion.

"This is no good."	(Implying you are no good)
"You always do this when you're under pressure."	(Focusing only on the bad)
"You've really let me down."	(Putting down)
"Are you stupid or something?"	(Implying you are stupid)

These words are often used in conjunction with gestures like pointing, turning away, rolling or raising eyes, or shaking of the head. Although psychologists say that some attention is better than none, when individuals consistently receive this kind of negative attention, they may feel angry, sad, defiant, or compliant. People who use negative strokes do not encourage or nurture, nor do they provide adequate constraints or boundaries, although they often pose in the guise of disciplinarians.

The skills in this book are designed to interrupt the unconscious processes and influences which make people react in a negative fashion. If you listen actively, stand back emotionally from what you see, and are a skillful, balanced observer, you will be able to mediate your own inclination to give negative strokes and will frame your criticism more positively. How would you reframe the four examples above?

Note: Receiving Strokes

How do you react when people make remarks about you? Do you flush with embarrassment and change the subject when given a positive stroke? Or do you burn with anger when criticized negatively, and not really hear what is said next? People all have their own "stroke economy" that governs how much positive or negative currency they can take in. As a manager, you need to develop your own style of positive stroking. It will work for you, but do not expect people always to react in the way you expect. Some may find it very difficult to hear good things about themselves or trust positive behavior of any kind. As you begin to interact with people more positively, you will get to understand their characteristics, boundaries, and preferences, and you will be able to tailor your responses to them.

Exercise: Active Listening (20 minutes)

1. After having spent some time affirming positive behavior, one person reads the behavior he or she would like to change. The partner's task is to use reflection and feedback to initiate discussion and help the speaker clarify what he or she wants to do.

2. The listener listens without interrupting. When the speaker has finished, the listener should report the key points of what has been said, reflecting the content (ideas, facts, beliefs, and thoughts) and feelings. The aim is to help the speaker clarify what is being said for himself or herself. The listener is not there to challenge or offer interpretations.

3. After ten minutes partners switch roles and repeat the process.

Feedback (15 minutes)

Concentrate on the skills, rather than the content, of exercises. The behavioral reminders which the members have drawn up are for their individual guidance and need not be shared with the whole group.

1. Get some brief verbal feedback on identifying individual strengths and positive stroking. How did it feel? Was it helpful?

2. Ask the group what the benefits are of active listening and write these on a flip chart as a reminder. Here is a checklist to help.

CHECKLIST
Benefits of Active Listening
■ Lets other know he or she has been heard and understood
■ Gives feedback on how he or she came across
■ Enables accuracy checking for hearer
■ Avoids illusion of understanding
■ Helps other to focus on self, sort out issues, and deal more effectively with emotions
■ Helps other arrive at solution to his or her own problem
■ Helps you clarify what you need to do
■ Helps you deal effectively with problem and issues raised (Lawyer et al. 1985)

Action Plans for Individuals and the Group (90 minutes or more)

If you have used all these exercises and the groups have responded well, they have worked very hard, with the emphasis mainly on behavior and process. In the final exercise, there is a switch to a task-oriented exercise. Having passed through the forming, storming, and norming stages, they now have a chance to perform. The process and structure of this segment reflects and models types of behavior that are relevant to the group's fulfillment of its task. These task-oriented behaviors are as follows:

Performing

- Initiating
- Seeking information or opinions
- Giving information or opinions
- Clarifying and elaborating
- Summarizing
- Listening actively
- Seeking decisions
- Taking decisions

The original task of this workshop, or series of exercises, was to get more out of the group and to unlock dysfunction; and it is to that task that we now return.

The specific aim of this section is to develop a set of suggestions for a six-month action plan. It is designed to foster constructive task-oriented working, and to provide an agenda to continue the positive momentum generated in the group.

Introduction (15 minutes)

Take the group through the eight task-oriented behaviors listed above, giving examples, asking for questions, and offering clarification where necessary.

Exercise: Task-Oriented Behavior (75 minutes)

1. Instruct group members to individually write three things they think the group needs to do in the next six months (10 minutes).

2. When writing down these three tasks, remind them to consider

   - Are there the resources to do it (time, money, staff, current workloads)?

   - Who will do it?

   - By when?

   - How will you know it is completed?

   - How will it be evaluated?

   For example, it would not be useful to write "Be more organized about decision making and following up decisions."

   This task is more helpfully phrased in the following manner:

   "Spend half an hour in a full meeting within the next month to discuss ideas about decision making. Set up a working party to devise practical suggestions and bring them back to this meeting within four weeks."

3. Get into small groups of three or four. Discuss one another's ideas, and decide how to present suggestions back to the whole group (45 to 80 minutes).

4. Begin by each reading one idea.

5. Concentrating on task-oriented behavior (referring to the above eight task-oriented behaviors), use the small group to test validity, to clarify, to finalize and, if necessary, to change your ideas, and decide what to present to the whole group. Summarize the suggestions on a flip chart.

The following are suggestions for decision making. They should be written down.

- Ideas all agree on
- Ideas a majority agrees on
- Ideas to which there are no strong objectors
- Everything, that indicates the levels of agreement in the group

Feedback (1 to 15 minutes)

Invite each group in turn to present its suggestions. Permit questions for clarification only.

Conclusion (60 to 90 minutes)

This session usually generates a lot of energy in terms of controversy, enthusiasm, hopes, and fears. The energy levels will almost certainly be lower next time the group meets in its normal work context. The main purpose of this concluding element is to ensure there is a constructive link between the group-building exercise and the normal workplace.

1. Summarize areas of agreement. Begin by offering a brief summary of the action plans concentrating on areas of agreement. If you notice something which is insufficiently clear or specific, check with the group. Ideas should be workable and measurable. Identify other individual ideas and check what is going to happen to them.

    Action plan

2. Assess priorities and be realistic. Priorities are not easy to measure. Extensive analysis of resources and other commitments will be needed before the action points can be realistically prioritized. Gain an initial impression of what people's priorities

    Priorities

are, either by voting on ideas or rating them
numerically.

Assign tasks

3. Assign immediate tasks. The group has usually
created a lot of material. Decide how it will be used
in the future.

Ensure a framework is provided to continue
this work. Who will take responsibility for particular tasks, such as compiling material, and evaluating ideas? How will a collective action plan be
devised?

Facilitate then retreat

4. Facilitate. Once a group has developed its own
momentum and is beginning to perform to some-
where near its potential, then it is best left to apply
itself to its task without too much outside facilitation. Dependence on a facilitator develops quickly,
although it is often useful to have a follow-up session with an outside facilitator by way of evaluating progress and monitoring change. The group
needs now to find its own functioning level, including all the decisions about leadership, decision making, and evaluation, which it will now be
much more ready to face.

Conclusion

Debrief

An intensive, challenging session like this passes very
quickly when people are positive in their approach to
their tasks. The conclusion provides a space where individuals can step back and register their thoughts and
emotions briefly, before leaving the group. It is a useful
time for evaluation. Exit questionnaires about the content, style, quality and practicality of the session are best
done here, before people depart.

To conclude, you may wish to use one of the following
suggestions.

- Go around the whole group asking each person to
comment on

— How he or she is feeling in three or four words.

— What he or she has learned.

— His or her expectations for the group in the
future.

- — Something different he or she has tried that worked.

- Invite contributions from individuals who wish to speak using any of the above questions.

- Conclude with some of the positive behaviors, ideas, and efforts you have witnessed as facilitator.

SUMMARY

Useful Circumstances

- Facilitate, don't participate
- Make sure everyone attends
- Equalize
- Respect comfort and space
- Forming, storming, norming, and performing
- Begin with introductions and warmups
- Clarify ground rules
  - — Provide an early chance for the group to look at itself
- Brief and gain feedback from an observer
  - — Depict conflict by mapping
- Build consensus
  - — Clarify aims
- Identify and work through differences
  - — Frame ideas usefully
  - — Develop questioning techniques
- Self-evaluate behavior
  - — Give and receive positive strokes and affirmation
  - — Listen actively
- Organize action plans for individuals and the group
  - — Use task-oriented behavior

— Link the workshop and the workplace

- Conclude on a positive note

Limitations

- Renovating a dysfunctional group may take a long time. This workshop will help you to identify key issues, repair lost trust, and identify the way ahead. It will not turn an ineffective team into a mercurial, dynamic unit overnight.

- The timings in the workshop are approximations. You may need much more time to identify an action plan or even to agree on your ground rules. If a group is worth repairing, then it is worth repairing well, so take all the time you need.

- Differences raised in such a workshop can generate a considerable amount of emotion. The facilitator should be sensitive to feelings, while ever conscious of the need to achieve the task of creating an effective work group. This balance between the needs of the group and the needs of the individual is at the heart of group problems. The facilitator, if he or she handles it well, can provide a positive model for the whole team.

The Odd-One-Out in a Group— Being Assertive in a Defensive Situation 12

Situation

The four senior managers in the organization and the two section heads are meeting—Howard, the director; Surinder, head of personnel; David, head of finance; Rachel, head of computing; Patricia, head of customer services; Helen, quality control manager; and Phillip, the customer relations officer. Howard chairs and convenes these meetings. The main item on the agenda is staff salaries for the next year. Normally these are done between individual managers and the director, but finances are tight and Howard wants to discuss the situation openly. This is the first time all the information about salaries has been shared.

Helen discovers that her budget is substantially lower than what she expected, and that it does not compare favorably with those allotted to the other heads. Even the allocation for her own salary is inadequate to keep her in line with the pay of the other managers.

She is frustrated, and wants to state her case while all the managers are present. Others in the meeting are frustrated too, as they do not believe this is the purpose of the meeting. Helen believes her rights as a manager have been infringed, and is in a tight, defensive situation.

Dealing With a Defensive Situation

Overcome the hostility of the group.

↓

Communicate clearly what you feel and what you want.

↓

Maintain your position in the group, and do not disrupt its overall effectiveness.

CHOICES WHEN YOU ARE IN DEFENSIVE SITUATIONS

Helen has five choices:

1. *Change Herself.* One could stay quiet or lessen the anxiety, and hope to overcome the wrong one believes is being committed. Helen could say nothing and hope that she will get another chance or that others will take up her case.

2. *Change the Environment.* Modify the immediate surroundings so that the effects of the problem are minimized. It is difficult to see what Helen could do here other than ask for other people's budgets to be reduced to the same level as hers.

3. *Withdraw.* Get out of the situation and find a more acceptable one. In the meeting, Helen could choose to say nothing, and ultimately she could leave the organization.

4. *Be Aggressive.* One could confront those felt to be in the wrong in a way unlikely to help one's case (see the section on "Avoiding Responses That Are

Likely to Make the Situation Worse"), such as threatening, moralizing, or name calling. Helen could complain angrily, or moan constantly, disrupting the meeting.

5. *Assert With Skill.* Use assertion skills which clearly communicate your position, your feelings, and what you want changed. This choice is likely to produce the most positive outcome for both Helen and the group, and deserves closer attention.

ASSERTING WITH SKILL

Helen has a conflict with the group that could seriously damage the group if not managed in a positive way. The fifth choice above, assert with skill, is the choice most likely to have a positive effect on the group and eventually get Helen what she wants. She would be unrealistic, of course, to expect to get instant success there and then. Chapter 23 examines a five-part assertion sequence of which this method is the first stage.

Three Key Components of the Asserting With Skill Method

1. Communicate the problem, how you feel about it, and its tangible effect on you.
2. Listen actively.
3. Avoid responses which are likely to make the situation worse.

This is called a Three-Part Assertion Message by Lawyer and Katz (1985), and overlaps with the assertion section in Chapter 9.

**Communicate the
Problem, How You
Feel About It, and
Its Tangible Effect
on You**

Communicate the Problem

Helen is frustrated for two reasons: first, the disparity in budgets, and second, the apparent concealment of the figures in the past. Communicating this involves describing the problem accurately and not inviting a defensive or aggressive response.

Offer a description, not an interpretation. Helen experiences what has happened as a failure of management, and a conspiracy of silence. Her interpretation of events is entirely subjective.

Don't interpret

"You are not taking your responsibility for managing me seriously."

or

"When you don't believe it is important for me to know what everybody else knows...."

Since these interpretations are full of her feelings, they will evoke emotional responses. The following statements would not be useful:

"When you keep me in the dark like this...."	(Too general and blaming)
"When you devalue my work by not allowing me sufficient money to do the job properly...."	(Focuses on another issue, the value of her work, as well as the budgets, which confuses the situation)
"If you neglect to tell me what other departments are allocated...."	(The word *neglect* is highly emotive and loaded with accusation.)
"If you don't ever tell me what is going on...."	(An exaggeration that is likely to encourage a defensive response.)

Describe

A description, on the other hand, contains clear, specific information, and avoids generalization or inflammatory language.

Useful, assertive descriptions would be more beneficial for Helen. For instance:

"When I find out for the first time, in a meeting with my peers, that I have received a budgetary allocation below an acceptable level, I feel...."

"I have not seen all the figures for budgets before, and I do not know whether any of you have either. If you have, when I have not, then that concerns me. I also notice that I am likely to end the year on a lower grade than...."

Both of these are neutral and nonblaming in tone, and contain accurate, specific information.

Communicate How You Feel About It

The guidelines for expressing how you feel from Chapter 9 apply here. Use words that accurately describe how you feel. Helen is frustrated, not furious; mildly annoyed and dismayed. This is the word closest to how she is feeling.

Don't exaggerate

She should not use stronger feelings to build her case; for example, "I am outraged that you have treated me this way." She does not need words this strong to get her message across.

Continuing from above, Helen could describe her feelings by saying

"When I find out for the first time, in a meeting with my peers, that I am on a lower grade and being paid less than them, I feel frustrated (or concerned)."

Communicate the Tangible Effect on You

Lawyer and Katz stress the importance of this, the third part of their Three-Part Assertion Message.

> Even when you describe the problem behavior itself accurately, if you don't communicate the problems that behavior is causing you in a way that helps the other person understand the negative impact the behavior has on your life, he or she is not likely to change the problem behavior.

The most effective method of communicating the negative effect is to focus on what is tangible and concrete, such as time, health, money, or other resources.

Include Other Examples

Give previous examples

Include examples of other times when you have experienced the same problem. Helen has previously found that information has not been forthcoming, and has also experienced occasions when she has not received credit for what she thought was good work. By referring to them now she will create a clear idea of what the effect of such behavior is on her.

- She is now suspicious regarding other information she may or may not have received, and feels she will have to spend much more time seeking information out.
- She questions how her work is valued.
- She is fearful, in general, for the long-term status of her department.

Helen combines the most concrete of these three effects into her assertion message.

"I feel frustrated. When I think that information is being withheld from me, as I have in the past.... (give example) I have to spend much more time seeking out and checking information. I would estimate about three or four hours of extra work a week."

Concentrate on the concrete

Often in work conflicts you need to concentrate on the concrete, and this requires tremendous self-discipline. If Helen had tried to deal with the issue of being undervalued in this particular group, she would almost certainly have not gotten what she wanted. This is an issue she should first bring up with her immediate supervisor.

Listen Actively

Once Helen has communicated the problem, she needs to concentrate on the response of the group, and can use any of the active listening techniques covered earlier to assess where the group members stand. Helen should not neglect to communicate to them that she is prepared to take their point of view into account.

"So Patricia, are you saying that you do not think we can discuss my point at all now?"

(Meaning check)

"I have heard three or four of you say that you think the issue of individual salaries should be on the agenda. What exactly do you want to discuss? How the salaries were assigned? What the gradings involve?"

(Focused questions)

"Howard, you said that you too were concerned about the inconsistency in the pay structure, unless I am mistaken."

(Reflecting feelings and meaning)

The process of dialogue that Helen has started need not get out of hand if she avoids certain dangerous responses. There are a variety of responses that, in any conflict, can inflame the situation. Although they are particularly dangerous, they are all too frequent in groups; for example, ordering people around.

Avoid Responses That Are Likely to Make the Situation Worse

"You must not do this to me."
"Don't talk like that."

Avoid ordering

This is probably one of the most commonly heard interventions in conflicts, especially with children who are in conflict with their parents. (Much of our conflict behavior is learned from our parents.) While, in some situations, it can create the desired effect and get things done, there are many times when an assertive statement will get your goals met more effectively. For example, Helen will not alienate the group if she uses an assertive statement rather than ordering them about.

"I would rather you did not do that."

or

"I am offended when you say...."

Don't threaten

It is not useful to threaten either.

"You had better listen to me or...."
"I'm warning you."

Assertion is again more effective than threatening statements.

Don't moralize

Moralizing also fails to encourage listening and understanding of problems.

"You really should not be talking like this."
"It's your duty to do this for me."

Imposing your values on another person will not help him or her understand you, nor vice versa. Active listening is more effective, as you will be able to check and compare values and take both sides into account.

Don't name-call

Name-calling should also be avoided since it makes others feel stupid, angry, or upset and is antagonistic and invites aggression.

"You're a hopeless manager."
"That was really stupid!"

Don't get diverted

The group may try to divert Helen from her budgetary concerns by responses such as

"Try not to worry about it too much."
"Phillip had a much lower budget than you last year."

These sorts of responses to Helen from the group try to push the problem away. Helen will need to control her emotions so that she is not sidetracked or convinced to withdraw by such responses.

Don't withdraw

"I might as well not bother then."
"I can't take any more of this."

People do have limits, and Helen or the group, for example, may not want to stay on this issue for too long.

It is better for Helen if she clearly accepts other people's boundaries when they need to stop, but does so in a positive way, securing an agreement about what will happen next.

"I agree we have spent a long time on this. Could I perhaps discuss this with you tomorrow at noon, Howard, or find a time by comparing day planners after this meeting?"

BE FLEXIBLE DURING THE ASSERTION WITH SKILL PROCESS

To be effectively assertive, you also have to be flexible. After your original three-part assertive message you may expect to

- Provide additional material.
- Express appreciation if you are offered an acceptable solution.
- Receive new information, in which case you can modify your own position or discuss solutions.
- Listen to topics which are irrelevant, then return to the original focus.
- Move to problem solving if the others will not change their behavior.

CONCLUSION

Helen must remember to continue being assertive throughout this process with the aim of being heard and changing the behavior that concerns her—the withholding of information and undervaluing of her work. At the beginning, she will be questioned and challenged, and may have to contend with the group colluding against her, strong attacks by individuals, or attempts to divert and sidetrack her. If she continues to assert, listen, and avoid high-risk responses, there is a good chance she will win the group over. Once the behavior of the group is positive towards her and her demands, then the facilitator or chair can simply invoke the decision-making procedure to gain an agreement on what to do with regard to those concerns. If not, then Helen need not give up, but can move on to the next stage in the five-part assertion sequence, which includes monitoring what happens next, confronting and trying to resolve the problem, and decision making. This is fully described in Chapter 23.

SUMMARY

Useful Circumstances

- Communicate the problem, how you feel about it, and its tangible effect on you
  - offer a description, not an interpretation.
  - use words that describe how you feel accurately.
  - don't use stronger feelings to build your case.
  - focus on tangible and concrete effects.
  - include examples of times you have experienced the same problem.
- Listen actively
- Avoid responses likely to make the situation worse, such as ordering, threatening, moralizing, name-calling, diverting, or withdrawing
- Be flexible

Limitations

- If the behavior of the group does not change for your benefit, and you still believe that your rights have been infringed, you will need to move into the next stage of the five-part assertion sequence described in Chapter 23.

Part Three

Conflict Management Procedures

INTRODUCTION

The majority of workplace disputes can be prevented, or resolved quickly after they surface, by using the skills and techniques already covered. If they persist, or are too severe or deep-seated, they may require a more structured, step-by-step process of management. The method that best combines the skills and approaches of positive conflict management is mediation, the use of an impartial third party to assist disputing parties to reach a settlement. Mediation is the focus of Part Three of the book. There is also an example of arbitration, the use of an impartial third party who is authorized to decide a settlement. Arbitration and mediation are useful for a wide variety of conflicts between people.

The Role of the Third Party

Edward De Bono (1990) is emphatic in his view that "disputants are the worst persons to solve their dispute." He cites a combination of reasons, including "tension of hostility," "secrecy, suspicion, and mistrust," "lack of communication," and the fact that for some conflict is "enjoyable" and to be prolonged, not resolved. Once the disputants are locked into combat, introducing a third party will enable a shift of focus: "The plain purpose of the third party is to convert a two-dimensional fight into a three-dimensional exploration leading to the design of an outcome." This succinctly describes how a mediation works.

Mediation 13

*M*uch of this book has to do with giving you the skills that can unlock conflicts. The process that puts all of these skills to use most effectively is mediation. Mediation involves a third party adopting a role between disputants—not getting directly involved, or taking sides—and helping them move out of conflict mode into a process of collaborative negotiation. It is a practical process through which the facilitator helps the parties themselves check facts, share feelings, exchange perceptions and ideas, and work toward agreements.

In the United States mediation is widely used in disputes between neighbors over domestic noise; clashes between environmentalists, developers, and communities; medical insurance award negotiations; disputes between employers and employees; and as an instrument of peacekeeping and education between students on campus, victims of crime and offenders, parents and children, and even artists and gallery owners.

The next several chapters contain a detailed, step-by-step demonstration of a mediation. As you will see, a mediator uses all the skills of constructive conflict management, and maintains a positive stance to the participants throughout.

SKILLS AND CHARACTERISTICS OF AN EFFECTIVE MEDIATOR

There have been many studies of mediators in the last ten years concentrating on qualities and skills, roles, and views of the parties mediated.

Qualities and Skills

A summary checklist based on Cohen, School Mediation Associates (1990) and Honeyman, lists the key elements of an effective mediator.

Roles

Moore's list of the mediator's roles (1986) includes eight functions.

- Opener of communication channels
- Process facilitator
- Trainer
- Resource expander
- Problem explorer
- Agent of reality
- Scapegoat
- Leader

Perceptions of the Involved Parties

Mediated parties focus on other aspects of the mediator's skills, including the mediator's.

- Ability to originate ideas.
- Unobtrusiveness.
- Managing his or her own feelings and those of the parties.
- Willingness to give sufficient time.
- Focus on problem solving in the present.
- Clear and effective communication skills

CHECKLIST

Qualities and Skills of an Effective Mediator

■ Impartiality—is concerned about the outcome on both sides and has the ability to demonstrate that to the parties.

■ Good listener—can empathize with the parties and listen actively.

■ Creates trust—makes the parties feel that their thoughts and feelings are understood; makes them feel comfortable; gives them a chance to make their own decisions whenever possible; is truly interested in helping parties resolve their dispute.

■ Persuasion and presentation skills—realizes the effectiveness of verbal expression, gesture, and body language in communicating with the parties and uses them appropriately.

■ Inventiveness and problem solving—demonstrates these qualities in the pursuit of collaborative solutions, and in the generation of ideas and proposals consistent with case facts which are workable for the opposing parties.

■ Management of the interaction—is effective in developing strategy, managing the process, and coping with conflicts between the parties.

■ Self-awareness—pays attention to own feelings and behavior so as not to treat the parties unfairly without realizing it.

■ Flexibility—is able to change process in order to meet the needs of each situation.

■ Understanding of situations and people—has experience with people, some understanding of various kinds of behavior, the necessary substantive knowledge, and a familiarity with relevant rules or guidelines.

■ Professionalism—takes work seriously; is prepared and on time; is respectful to parties at all times.

■ Balance—has the ability to be aware of own feelings, and balance them with the needs of the situation; can match the need for authority and control with a concern for the parties; has the analytical ability to assess realistic chances of change and agreement; knows when to stop and when to continue.

Are You Ready to Mediate?

As you can see, mediation is a complex, demanding task. Mediation training takes between forty and eighty hours of theoretical learning, practice, and discussion, followed by more practice and assessment. Then there is a period of working under close supervision with an experienced mediator.

Some people take to it like a fish to water, others spend years trying to stop making decisions for others or ordering people around, and finally decide that they simply prefer to use their own authority rather than a party-centered approach.

If you want to try to use these methods, first ask yourself the following questions:

- Are you comfortable giving other people the responsibility for finding their own solutions to conflicts, even if this may initially be a more lengthy process and be more frustrating than making decisions for them?

  Most of the time in mediation is spent in a confrontation phase, when parties continue to disagree, argue, and blame one another. In this phase the conflict may actually escalate, but genuine resolution usually requires a period of escalation. The parties will feel more able to negotiate, having let off steam and seen how their counterpart feels. After genuine, facilitated head-to-head confrontation the mediator can encourage conciliatory gestures and help the parties move toward the agreement phase.

- Do you consider yourself competent to handle the process?

  There are variations of structure from model to model and of practice from mediator to mediator, but all mediations contain the stages described in this section. You will almost certainly need extra training to manage the transitions and to make the most effective use of the whole process. There are many skills and techniques, however, which you can try out from within the process, such as fact-finding, option generation, and encouraging communication.

- Is there a way you can gain feedback and evaluate how effective you are?

  A colleague may observe or co-mediate, or you can use self-evaluation or consult the parties. Do not mediate without the opportunity for feedback and evaluation. You are in the middle and will need support.

- Do you have the backing of your organization in using this method?

  In the long term, mediation saves time, because it provides more lasting agreements and also teaches the parties how to resolve disputes. Be clear to your organization—bosses, colleagues, staff, and the parties themselves—what you are doing and what resources you need.

WHEN SHOULD YOU CONSIDER MEDIATION?

Andrew Floyer Acland, who worked with Terry Waite and also in the field of political mediation in South Africa, wrote the aptly titled *A Sudden Outbreak of Common Sense: Managing Conflict by Mediation* (1990). In it he lists several "circumstances favoring mediation," a few of which are on the following checklist.

CHECKLIST
Circumstances Favoring Mediation
■ Relationships are important.
■ Those involved want to retain control of the outcome.
■ Both sides have a good case.
■ There is no great disparity in power.
■ Speed is important.
■ Confidentiality is important.
■ Both sides need the opportunity to let off steam.
■ Neither side really wants to litigate.

Add to this from Karl Mackie (1991) some thoughts on "when a mediator is useful" as outlined below.

CHECKLIST
When a Mediator Is Useful
■ The parties have stopped (or never even started) communicating to each other.
■ The parties have neither the skill (negotiation skills) nor desire (lack of trust) to communicate effectively.
■ The parties cannot find a solution themselves.
■ The parties feel they may lose by changing their previous demands.
■ An impasse, or delay in negotiations, will have damaging effects on the parties, or their relations with other parties.
■ Mediation will be more efficient even if the parties could negotiate with some degree of success.
■ A private, (usually) voluntary, and nonbinding procedure is preferable to a procedure that does not have all or some of these characteristics.
■ There is an imbalance of power between the parties that can be effectively counterbalanced by use of an intermediary.
■ There is a need to influence the settlement terms in accordance with some external standards and the parties may need to be made more aware of these than they might otherwise be.

From the opposite perspective Acland (1990) suggests you should not use mediation under the following circumstances.

CHECKLIST
When Not to Use Mediation
■ If the jurisdiction of the court (or other authorities) is essential and paramount
■ If one side wants a punitive judgment
■ If at least one side wants a judicial decision to establish a precedent
■ If neither side is ready to consider settlement

The last three are situations that can be explored in mediation, but if these conditions persist then mediation should cease.

Finally, American professor and business consultant Dan Dana (1989) suggests asking four questions to find out whether the problem is "mediative." (See checklist on following page.)

Using a combination of these questions and bearing in mind the limitations of the approach will ensure that you do not use the process in situations where it does not work.

CHECKLIST
Is the Problem Mediative?
■ Is illegal or unethical behavior involved, as defined by law or by organizational policies and standards?
If so, disciplinary or corrective action should be taken before, or concurrently with, mediation. Do not count mediation out. It can be very useful if used in the framework of legitimate authority.
■ If the conflict has arisen from either party's failure to perform individual job duties, is the failure due to lack of job skills or knowledge?
If lack of skills or knowledge is the cause, training should be conducted prior to, or concurrently with, mediation.
■ If the conflict has arisen from either party's failure to perform individual job duties, is the failure due to personal factors, such as current personal crisis, drug or alcohol dependency, or emotional problems?
If personal factors are the cause, referral to a person in your organization who can help, for instance the staff counselor, or outside to a local advice and support agency, such as Alcoholics Anonymous, is recommended prior to mediation.
■ Is the conflict one that the parties, individually or jointly, have the authority to solve?

CHOOSING WHO MEDIATES

Mediators must be impartial

Mediators should be impartial, and the parties should be convinced that they are so. People who have some stake in the outcome, or a place in the history of a dispute, will only be effective if they have a proven capacity to remain impartial and deal evenly with each side, whatever the circumstances. Often it is better to enlist a manager from another department, or a freelance mediator, because the trust of the parties should not be sacrificed for the convenience of a mediator who may not be able to resist the temptation to get involved.

EXAMPLES OF SITUATIONS IN WHICH MEDIATION IS APPROPRIATE

Mediation most effectively resolves disputes in a variety of work situations, such as

- Disputes between coworkers or colleagues who are unable to function together.
- Interdepartmental squabbles.
- Long-running personality clashes or problems with working relationships.
- Communication breakdowns.
- Planning deadlocks.
- Negotiations of role redefinitions in the team.
- Conflicts over allocation of tasks.
- Conflicts over aims and objectives.
- Conflicts where there is a long history of bad feeling.

There are many more possibilities.

THE MEDIATION PROCESS

This book presents a work conflict by way of illustration, ideally suited to mediation. It fits many of the criteria presented in the previous chapter.

Situation

Surinder, head of personnel, interviewed and recruited Thomas nine months ago to the post of secretary to Patricia, head of customer relations. He is a twenty-three-year-old Afro-Caribbean man who had been working as a part-time temporary administrative assistant in the department for eighteen months.

Moira, a thirty-five-year-old white woman, is part-time bookkeeper in the finance department. She began working for the company two years ago after fifteen years off work to bring up her twins. She has a variety of secretarial and administrative skills, but only works twenty hours a week. She saw the post of Patricia's secretary as her chance for a full-time job. She applied for the job, was interviewed, but did not get it.

In the nine months since the appointment there has been a history of clashes between Moira and Thomas. They both say that they do not know what to say to the other and that it is the other's problem. There are tasks that depend on them working together across departmental boundaries. Patricia's monthly service reviews are dependent on financial reports that Moira compiles and Thomas types and copies. She has not been getting these on time.

Patricia has spoken to Thomas who says that he gets the reports very late, and often with several mistakes and confusing entries from Moira. Moira is not very obliging when he approaches her for help.

David, Moira's direct boss, has spoken to her, but she does not really acknowledge the problem, blaming Thomas for his offhand way of dealing with her.

THE STAGES OF MEDIATION

Different commentators describe these stages in various ways, but an effective mediation always has the eight stages shown in the following checklist.

CHECKLIST
Stages of Effective Mediation
1. Preparation
2. Opening
3. Parties' statements
4. Interchange
5. Seeking movement
6. Preparation for resolution
7. Closing
8. Follow-up

The stages may not be as distinct and separate in practice as they seem on paper, but they are always there. The following chapters will examine the example and the different approaches Patricia can take at each stage.

The Mediation Session: Stage 1— Preparation **14**

The preparation stage includes

- Preliminary meetings with the disputants.
- Selection of the mediator.
- Meeting with co-mediator (if applicable).
- Preparing the room.

PRELIMINARY MEETINGS WITH THE DISPUTANTS

Preliminary meetings can be conducted by the mediator or another person who is skilled in neutral questioning and empathetic responding (see Chapter 6) and who understands how mediation works. In these initial meetings there are two main tasks.

- Collecting basic details of the conflict
- Getting the parties to mediation

Collecting Details

Listen and question

Patricia already knows the basic details of this dispute. If this is your first contact with a conflict, use questioning skills and active listening to get some preliminary details. You only need the absolute basic facts. Do not get into identifying issues and positions. Once parties begin to fix themselves into positions it is far harder to get them to communicate and find common ground. Do only enough fact-taking to gain their trust, assuring them that they will have plenty of time in the mediation to state their case. For example:

"It will help me decide whether I can be of assistance if you briefly outline the dispute."	(Open question)
"Am I right in thinking then that you find it difficult to talk to...?"	(Focused question)
"Can you give me a specific example of...?"	(Specifying question)

Do not open the floodgates of the whole conflict. Instead, respectfully guide the parties to some brief facts. They can say more in the mediation.

Getting the Parties to Mediation

Voluntary attendance

Disputants should attend mediation because they want to. Some court-based mediation is mandatory, and the punishment for nonattendance is prosecution. Resolutions are achieved, but a considerable pressure is put on disputants by making the process mandatory. Some practitioners argue that this coerces agreements out of people, and that such agreements are less likely to reflect the true wants of the parties, or to be as long-lasting and effective as results achieved by voluntary mediation. Voluntary attendance should be encouraged, because it removes one level of resistance to the mediator, and may provide you with a useful impartial lever at a stage of impasse. You can remind both parties that they chose to be here and it is in their interests to use the space and time constructively.

There are several ways to get the parties to agree to mediation.

- Point out the benefits—equal time and space; opportunity to express feelings; neutral setting; chance to check out information; careful, professional facilitation; written agreements if required.

- Point out the dangers of alternative methods—loss of time; continuation of conflict; possibility of both parties losing rather than winning.

- Be clear about the mediator's role—to be impartial; able to control negative behavior; willing to hear feelings; facilitate communication.

- Be clear about your expectations of the parties—willingness to express feelings, ideas, and opinions, willingness to look for a solution and to clarify information.

- Point out the mutual benefit of contact.

Timing is important

The timing of the mediation is important and once you have gained the consent of the parties and gathered some basic details, the mediation session should take place as soon after the preliminary meetings as possible.

Selection of the Mediator

A mediator should possess the skills and characteristics mentioned in Chapter 13 and be able to manage the process effectively. This book will give you a good idea of the method, but mediation training is the ideal preparation.

Be impartial

He or she should also have no direct involvement in the background to the conflict, nor be closely identified with either of the parties. It is desirable to enlist the manager of another department to mediate disputes between your staff, unless you have a specialist, such as Patricia, who has had mediation training and has a long record of dealing with a variety of disputes and maintaining impartiality. She has gained respect within Troubled Associates Ltd. for this, so Thomas, Moira, and David are quite happy for her to handle this situation.

Consider an external mediator

There are a growing number of freelance mediators, who are particularly useful if you can find no one in your organization who will be sufficiently impartial or have the appropriate skills.

MEETING WITH CO-MEDIATOR

In Chapter 10, the advantages of working with a partner are described. If you and a colleague are sufficiently confident in one another's ability, you may well find that working in pairs is the most effective way to mediate. Immediately before the mediation, give yourselves time to talk over case details, allocate roles and tasks, and decide how you are going to work as a team. Cohen, School Mediation Associates (1990) lists three helpful things to do, and three that are not helpful.

Helpful Activities

- Share leadership and responsibilities.
- Do the things you are better at and let your co-mediator do the things that she or he is better at.
- Follow and build upon each other's questions.

Not Helpful Activities

- Interrupt each other unless you have to.
- Disagree with your co-mediator in front of the parties.
- Let your co-mediator do all the work.

Use these points to guide your premediation discussion. You will need less time to prepare as you get used to particular partners but, at first, allow at least thirty minutes of preparation together. As you develop your mediation skills you could also ask your co-mediator to give you specific feedback after the session in particular areas which you are trying to improve.

PREPARING THE ROOM

Neutral environment

A mediation room should suggest calm, space, and comfort, but it does not need to be luxurious. It should be neutral, offering no advantage to either person. Territorial instincts are at their fiercest at moments of conflict. If there is not an appropriate meeting room, use someone else's office or your own, or create a space in the main office where the parties can feel at home and away from one another's normal sphere of influence. You should endeavor to control interruptions, such as phone calls and other people coming in.

Arrange the furniture in a way which you believe encourages communication between you and the parties, and also enables them to establish communication when they wish. Some variations of mediation seating are shown in Figure 9.

Figure 9. Sample Seating Arrangements for Mediation

M = Mediator
P = Party

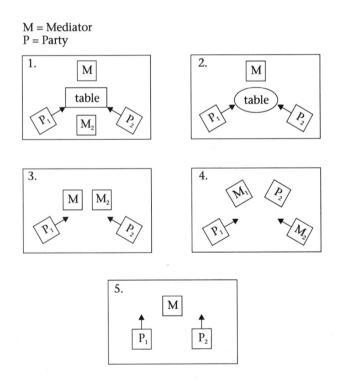

The Mediation Session: Stage 2— Opening 15

MEDIATOR'S OPENING STATEMENT

This is where a mediator often does his or her best work. This is almost the most important part of the whole process. The parties are tense and expectant. The mediator has to do enough to describe what is going to happen, without losing the interest of two disputants who are eager to get going and use the space and time. Opening statements are a challenge for mediators, demanding economy and precision, while also being settling and encouraging for the parties. Some mediators script it almost word for word, others rely on notes, others work from memory. Richard Cohen of School Mediation Associates even provides the school administrators, teachers, and students who are his trainee mediators with mediation checklist notepaper, topped with opening statement reminders. The Mediator's Opening Statement checklist lists the items useful to include in an opening statement.

Reassure; don't patronize   Choose your language carefully, avoiding jargon and long-winded theory. Use a warm tone and adjust your vision and body language to take both parties into account. For example, Patricia may open with

"Hello, Thomas and Moira, thanks for coming. We have up to an hour and a half, and I do not think we will need a break, but I will let you know if I think a break would be useful. You tell me, as well, if you would like a break. I am here to help you work out what you can do to improve the situation between you two, and I believe that you will be able to sort this out with my help."

CHECKLIST
Mediator's Opening Statement
■ Welcome parties.
■ Make personal introductions.
■ Address practical considerations like breaks.
■ Explain the purpose of the mediation.
■ Clarify the mediator's role.
■ Explain the value of mediation.
■ Describe expectations of the parties.
■ Encourage the parties to "give it a try."
■ Describe the structure.
■ Deal with questions.
■ Communicate and gain agreement on ground rules.

"First, I am going to ask you both to describe briefly how you feel about the situation and what has led up to it. Then we will discuss that, clarifying and questioning until we can get a better understanding of both your points of view.

"I hope we will then be able to work through some of the differences and find some common ground to help you work together more effectively in the future. This won't be easy, but I can assure you that I have used this method to resolve some very tricky disputes before. I will do my best to ensure you have equal time and space, and l think you will feel comfortable enough to say what you need to.

"Is that clear? Are there any questions you would like to ask?"

Even the most experienced mediators learn new ways of managing the introduction effectively: introducing phrases they have picked up from a colleague, refining their tone of voice so that it oozes reassurance without being patronizing, and quickly attending to signs of discomfort from the disputants.

People find the words and tone that work for them, and frequently check in with the disputants saying things like

"Do you understand?"
"Is that clear?"
"Do you have any questions?"

After dealing with questions Patricia moves on to ground rules.

Ground Rules

As discussed previously in the book, ground rules are very useful for maintaining certain standards of behavior. They are for the mutual benefit of the parties and the mediator. Any one of the parties should be able to object if he or she believes the others are breaking the ground rules, and the mediator will refer parties back to them if behavior strays beyond their bounds.

Almost all mediations and mediation services have a ground rule concerning verbal or physical abuse or other disrespectful behavior. Here are some examples of how this has been introduced.

No verbal or physical abuse

"In our experience people do get angry in these situations, but I will ask you to remain seated throughout."

"We would like your permission to restrain you if we think your language or behavior to one another is getting out of hand."

"Do your best not to interrupt one another, or use any words that you think the other might find abusive. In our experience this will enable you to get your feelings across and get them heard much more effectively."

"One of our aims here is to ensure that you get equal space and time, and I would like you to agree not to interrupt or dominate. Would you give me the authority to say 'stop' if I think it is appropriate?"

Mediation is off-the-record

Patricia then suggests that the meeting is confidential and off-the-record. By this she means that any personal comments made or details of behavior within the session are not to be shared with anyone else, nor would any written record be kept. What is said and what happens in the meeting is privileged information, that is, it cannot be used in any future formal hearings or procedures. An agreement about confidentiality often allows the parties to be a little more free with their comments than they otherwise would. If they work out an agreement, they can, however, have that in writing, and may decide to communicate this to their peers and superiors.

GETTING THE PARTIES TO TRUST YOU

Parties will not be open with you, take risks, be willing to express their feelings, or divulge information if they do not trust you. Throughout the process of mediation, from preliminary meetings to closing and following up, they need to believe that you will

- Explain what you are there for, defining your presence and role clearly, and doing what you say you are going to.
- Allow yourself to learn about the parties, and not give the impression that you know all about their problems or have formed opinions about the dispute.
- Listen to and understand what they need.
- Remain impartial.
- Behave consistently.
- Keep confidential what goes on in the session.

In order to win the parties' trust

- Listen actively.
- Be honest about your own feelings with the parties, and balance emotion and reason.
- Encourage the parties to make their own decisions about whether to speak about certain issues, which parts of an agreement will work for them, and whether they can continue in mediation.
- Control the process of communication so that emotions are acknowledged but not allowed to overrun the other parties', and so that no one dominates.
- Show respect for the parties.

To avoid losing trust, do not

- Use value-laden statements.
- Offer interpretations of behavior.
- Push the parties to talk about uncomfortable things before they are ready.
- Forget what people say and what is important to them.
- Adopt a superior approach (Cohen, School Mediation Associates 1990).

The Mediation Session: Stage 3— Parties' Statements 16

The parties' statement stage can be handled in two ways: either with the parties together or with them apart. Both methods are viable. In each the mediator helps each person to make an initial statement, which should contain the following:

- Important facts
- Background and history
- How each party feels
- What each party considers most important
- What they want to change

PARTIES MAKING THEIR INITIAL STATEMENTS SEPARATELY

The mediator's task is largely the same in both separate and open session, that is, to elicit from the parties a statement that contains the above five elements. This will be outlined in the section describing opening statements taken with both parties present.

Separate sessions can be structured as follows:

Summarize to check

1. One mediator sees each party separately for the same length of time as the other waits outside. The mediator will subsequently summarize what each party has said, having checked with the party if there is anything said in their private session that he or she is not willing to disclose in open session.

2. Two mediators see each party separately for the same length of time as the other party waits outside. One mediator will report what was disclosed in an open session, while the other adds or clarifies as necessary.

3. Two mediators each see a party separately for the same length of time. The mediators report their respective party's concerns in turn in the open session.

If you decide to use separate sessions, then select which of these three methods you prefer.

Some Important Considerations for Mediators Using Separate Sessions

Separate sessions are very useful to

- Encourage parties to introduce things to the mediation through you that they may not be prepared to say in open session.

- Remove the threat of confrontation with one another at the beginning of the mediation.

- Give each party an early taste of the mediator's even handed approach and trustworthy attributes, such as active listening and acknowledgment of feelings; the parties will notice the mediator more without the other party present initially.

However, mediators must make sure that they

- Allocate time evenly.
- Do not pressure the parties to disclose things that they are not yet ready to say in open session.
- Give the parties a chance to correct or modify their summary.
- Do not begin to take sides, especially if one party is more obviously likable, articulate, or apparently ready to change than the other.
- Do not become simply message carriers.

PARTIES MAKING THEIR INITIAL STATEMENTS IN OPEN SESSION

However you decide to structure the initial statements, the principle remains the same—the parties speak to you, not to one another. Through you they can say things they may otherwise not, and you can then get them heard by the other side. Dialogue will come later. If the nonspeaker attempts to confront, interrupt, or challenge, the mediator will respectfully maintain order, and remind both parties that they will have a chance to answer any challenges, correct any misperceptions, and ask questions in the next stage. Prepare for any shouting or other difficult behavior that emerges by reading the suggestions for handling difficult behavior at the end of this chapter.

Speak through the mediator

The three main tasks for the mediator at the initial statement stage are to
1. Get the parties started.
2. Get feelings heard by both sides.
3. Collect information and background, and get an initial idea about issues.

Get the Parties Started

The First Party

A warm, reassuring invitation to speak will usually encourage the first person to start.

Invitation to speak

"So could you tell us (the mediator/s) what you believe the problem is?"

"It will help us to understand the situation if you describe to us what is going on and how you feel about it."

These are open enough to give the party the chance to talk about facts and feelings.

Giving space to let off steam

Although the mediator does not want anger to overcome the proceedings, the expression of anger is a fundamental part of the movement toward resolution. The parties may ramble and repeat for a while, may say things that you want to question right away, or may go around in emotional circles, calming briefly then flaring up again. At the opening statement do not interrupt or begin to process the emotion too soon. Give the parties a chance to let off steam.

Encouraging parties who are quiet

Sometimes the presence of the other disputant, or the strength of emotion will cause one party to be very quiet. Do not push people into emotional or factual areas they do not wish to enter. Here are some hints for encouraging quiet parties to participate.

- Focus first on something they may be more comfortable with and then lead them up to the problem gently.

  "So, Moira, you have worked here for some time now. What do you like about your job? Is there anything which you dislike?"

  "Could you tell us more about that?"

- Use focused and specific questions to get more details.

  "What is it about that behavior that upsets you?"

- Arrange for a separate session with the agreement of the other party and feedback to the open session (if working with both together).

- Show patience and give people space.

  "You are very quiet. I'm really interested to hear what you're thinking."

- Support people when they begin to open up.

  "Thanks for saying that. That was very useful information. Was there anything else you wanted to say?"

Do not begin a detailed and lengthy interrogation of one person, before you have asked the other to speak. This will give the impression of bias. Giving each party a set time limit for their statement and keeping them to it is a useful way of remaining evenhanded in the eyes of all concerned.

The Second Party

The above techniques are equally applicable to the second party, but the mediator also has to contend with the second party's strong and understandable desire to respond to the other's statement. The mediator should gently redirect attempts to get hooked into a conflict dialogue at this point, reminding the second speaker that he or she will have plenty of time to respond and engage in discussion.

Direct the second party

At this early stage it is more helpful to encourage the second person to concentrate on the situation from his or her point of view. For example:

"I can see you object to what Moira has said, Thomas, and you will get a chance to answer any points she has raised; but for the moment it will help me to understand your feelings much more if you tell me about the situation from your point of view. What do you believe the problem is?"

This example demonstrates the delicate balance between control and empowerment that a mediator has to strike. Experience and an ability to control your own feelings will assist you in judging how much to contain and process behavior and emotion, and how much to let it run on.

Balance control and empowerment

Get Feelings Heard by Both Sides

There are two major benefits in hearing positive and negative feelings.

> *Negative feelings.* When negative feelings are heard they become less pressing or dominant for the speaker and there is then room for other, more positive feelings about other people to take their place.

> *Positive feelings.* When positive feelings are heard they deepen and become integrated (Lawyer and Katz 1985).

I'm okay, you're okay

On the one hand the mediator acts like a focusing mirror, letting individuals hear and see one another clearly, and on the other hand like a pair of warming rose-tinted spectacles, helping one person to see the humanity of the opponent through the fog of his or her own hostility. This is the world of "I'm okay, you're okay" enacted by the mediation process.

Although the parties may not actually come around entirely to the belief that their counterpart is okay by the end of the session, mediations are extremely effective ways of uncovering and developing some measure of positive belief (or okayness) in and about the other party. This is often conspicuously absent at the beginning and the mediator will have to work hard concentrating on the positive. Here are two ways this can be achieved early on.

- Reflecting feelings and meanings
- Reframing

Reflecting Feelings and Meanings

Thomas and Moira reflect their feelings and thoughts in part of their opening statements.

Thomas

"I just want to do the job well. Moira is difficult to talk to sometimes, and as she is not around all the time she can be quite hard to pin down. It's almost as though she is deliberately making life difficult for me because she did not get the job. I would just about be able to make the deadlines for your financial reports Patricia, if there were not so many mistakes."

Moira

"Well, I'm absolutely furious. He's only a kid! I didn't expect to be taking orders from a kid. I really wanted and needed that job! And he couldn't really care less. Then he expects me to help him out. Why should I?"

To assist Moira and Thomas get their feelings heard by the other, and also to let them know that she is hearing, Patricia uses reflecting skills. When reflecting feelings, keep your statements open and tentative, so that the speaker can correct you if he or she wishes. For example:

Reflect feelings

> "You sound angry."
> "You look disappointed."
> "It seems as though you were hurt by that."

Build up a selection of feeling words that cover as many shades of emotion as possible.

Reflecting meanings is a way of responding to feeling and content in a single response. You connect the two with a linking word like *because, about,* or *when.* For example, Patricia could say to Thomas

> "You feel angry when you can't get your work done on time."
> "You sound confused because you can't understand why Moira is difficult to locate."

To Moira, Patricia could respond

> "You were angry at Thomas because he got the job and you did not."
> "You felt embarrassed and frustrated that a person a lot younger than you got the job."

To help Thomas and Moira hear what may be difficult sentiments for them to acknowledge, Patricia also uses reframing.

Reframing Statements

Reframing is the process of stating what has been already said in a way more likely to be heard. Blaming, accusing, or abusive statements are likely to raise the emotional tone, and little is heard when the tone is high.

When reframing do not overelaborate or psychologize behavior. For example, do not say

"So you are projecting your anger at not getting the job on to Thomas?"

Do not interpret

Also do not offer interpretations like the following two statements.

"It would seem that you are jealous of Thomas, Moira."

"Thomas, do you think Moira is being racist?"

Do not blame

Reframing consists of fitting a clear, concise statement in simple language that corresponds to the behavior or feelings the person has described; it is not blaming and encourages them to take responsibility for their own feelings. For example:

Thomas

"Moira is difficult to talk to at times."

Reframed Sentiment

"So, there are difficult feelings associated with talking to Moira as far as you are concerned?"

Moira (to Thomas)

"You're only a kid. I've got much more experience than you, I didn't expect to be taking orders from a kid!"

Reframed Sentiment

"If I understand you right, Moira, you thought your age and experience would win out over Thomas' youth, and you are now surprised and frustrated that someone younger than yourself seems to have authority over you."

Reframing is also educational for the parties as it models a form of expression that is assertive in that it

Reframing is assertive

- Expresses feelings.
- Takes responsibility for those feelings.
- Does not attribute blame or responsibility to someone else.

Notetaking

Notetaking can be useful, but bear four points in mind.

Collect Information and Background, and Get an Initial Idea About Issues

- Gain permission from the people involved first.
- Make it clear that the notes will not be kept or used afterwards since the session is confidential.
- Record only key words; your memory is much better than you think.

Record key words

- Keep eye contact with the parties, looking up from your notes frequently as you write, especially if you are mediating alone. If co-mediating, you may agree beforehand that one of you will take notes when the other is taking the more active role.

At this early stage the parties will not necessarily give you the whole picture either of their feelings or their view of the facts. The mediator is there to

- Help them decide what the key facts are.
- Assist them in describing the background and in organizing those facts.
- Facilitate initial thoughts about what the parties want.
- Ensure that each person feels he or she has had the opportunity to say enough.

Key Facts

Many facts will probably be mentioned, some of which the mediators think are relevant and others which do not seem to be. This is where the self-discipline of impartiality comes into play. The mediator's job is to help the parties identify what are important facts for themselves. This is achieved through progressive questioning techniques mentioned several times in this book already. To review, the questions move from open to focused then specifying and, if necessary, challenging. For example:

"Could you describe for us the situation between yourself and Moira?"	(Open)
"What do you mean by...?"	(Focused)
"You said several times...could you be specific about one or two examples? Where and when? How often?"	(Specifying)
"I am not sure if I understand how that is relevant. Could you explain to me how it is?"	(Challenging)

At this stage it is useful to

- Get the time frame clear.
- Clarify inconsistencies or contradictions.

Time Frame

The angry customer in Chapter 8 was exhibiting typical conflict behavior by moving from past to present and back again without much willingness to look at the future. Although disputants want to dwell on the past, for the purposes of resolution it is much better to move their thoughts from the past to the present, and then on to the future. The past is relevant in these situations only in as much as it contributes to the present and the future. The mediator can start this process during opening statements by frequently checking in which time frame the parties are operating.

"When did that happen?"
"Is there a recent example, within the last month, that you can think of?"
"So that was seven months ago; has anything similar happened since?"
"When you say 'all the time' what do you mean? Three times a day? And when was the last time this happened?"

When people are angry they remember a past event vividly and describe it as though it were yesterday. Give them the space to get the feelings off their chest first, then clarify when the event happened.

Clarification

Some people remain clear about facts and do not need to repeat themselves, nor do they say one thing first and something contradictory later. For most people, however, anger muddies expression and clouds the quality of recollection. A mediator helps the speakers to put their story in order during the process of getting an uncluttered, correctly sequenced account for themselves.

> "Sorry. I thought you said...Does that mean that...?"
> "Right, so the first time was...then...."
> "I am not sure I am clear what point you made when you said...."
> "Thanks. Now I understand that. What about...did you say...?"

Clarify story

Initial Thoughts About Issues

"What do you want?" is often a difficult question to answer, and it is dangerous to ask it too early. Mixed up in the present state of mind are often emotions from the past, memories of similar situations, frustrated desires, and habitual wants and needs. How much anger people have left, how reasonable they are prepared to be, and how much calmer they are than when they started, can all be sampled by their response to a question like

> "So, what is the key issue for you?"
> "Thanks for describing the situation as you see it. What would you say were the main issues you wanted to be addressed?"

This provides an opportunity to think in more general terms; this is the first step in moving disputants on.

Do not encourage disputants to get too much into positions at this stage. Once they take up positions, they tend to argue from them and are less open to exploration and exchange. Keep focused on facts and a very brief summary of issues. This ensures that people feel they have had the opportunity to say enough.

You may now think the disputants have talked too long, and want to call a halt.

If the parties have used up their time, or are constantly repeating themselves, then refer back to the ground rules about equal time.

"You did give me authority to say 'stop' if I thought it was appropriate. I can see you feel strongly about this, but I think you have described that part of the situation very clearly. In the three minutes remaining, is there anything else you would like to add?"

If you are firm but respectful and also remind them that they will get a chance to say more as the mediation progresses, people will respond and either move on to another subject or be quiet and give the other a chance to speak. At the end of this chapter, there are some hints for what you can do if difficult behavior continues.

If one person comes to a natural halt of his or her own accord, then thank him or her and move on. If you sense that you need to draw someone to a conclusion, then use phrases like

"Thanks for telling us that. There's only a little time, Jeff. Is there anything about your situation that you would like the other person to understand that we haven't heard yet?"

"In the next section I will be summarizing what you said. Is there anything you would like to add to help me get your situation clear?"

"When we have heard from you both, there will be another opportunity to add anything important that you may have forgotten. Have you said as much as you would like so far? Is there anything you would like to add briefly?"

Once each person has finished speaking, you can move on to the next stage, but there is always the chance that one or both of the disputants will exhibit difficult behavior, like shouting, distracting the other party and the mediators, or disrupting proceedings. If they have not done this so far, the chances are that one or the other of the parties will do so before the mediation is finished. So how do you handle difficult behavior?

HANDLING DIFFICULT BEHAVIOR

There are different views about what is difficult behavior. Mediations will, by their nature and design, contain some shouting, resisting, avoiding, and power plays. Try to think of examples of behavior that would either threaten the welfare of the other party or your own ability to manage the situation and, finally, would make it impossible to continue the mediation if it persisted. Frequent shouting at the other party; interrupting; putting the other person down; getting out of the chair and physically moving toward the other party; deliberately distracting the other party and the mediators; and provoking by taunting, using abusive language or gestures may come to mind.

For these kinds of behavior, try an incremental approach, as follows.

1. *Do not get hooked.* Control your own feelings so that you can deal with the behavior assertively.

2. *If it is nonverbal behavior, find out what is going on.*

   "I notice you keep turning away when Thomas speaks. Does that mean you find what he has to say difficult?"

   "When you keep getting up like that and leaving the room, I find it difficult to concentrate. What is going on? Are you okay?"

   A mediator reported an incident where he witnessed a demonstration mediation when this happened, and the mediators assumed this person was being disruptive. In fact the person had a bladder problem, which neither they nor the other party knew about, and had to leave the room frequently. This proved to be a very valuable piece of information for resolving that particular conflict, which was about her attending meetings.

3. *For verbal and nonverbal behavior, acknowledge the feelings behind it.*

"This must be disturbing for you."

"I didn't realize that you felt so intimidated by this."

4. *Describe the effect of the behavior.*

"When you keep getting up I find it difficult to have a dialogue with you."

This describes the effect on you as mediator. Also describe the effect on the other party.

"When you keep tapping your foot I cannot hear Moira speak, and she has to shout to get her point across."

5. *Suggest alternatives.*

"Perhaps we could make sure that we break this down into fifteen-minute sections. Could you last out that long?"

"I can understand your frustration, but you will get a chance to tell us about that in a little while. Could you keep your foot still until then?"

6. *Refer back to the ground rules.*

"You both agreed to refrain from name calling, so...."

"At the beginning you gave me authority to stop you if I thought you were getting out of hand. Well, I would ask you to stop shouting now."

If the behavior persists, move on to stages 7, 8, and 9.

7. *State the conditions under which you are prepared to continue.*

"If you continue shouting at one another we will not be able to hear anything. I will take one point at a time once you are quiet."

"I am not prepared to continue if you keep...."

8. *Take a break.* Stay in the room, and have a break. Suggest this is a "cooling-off period." Only allow

a break with people going outside if you are confident you will be able to get them to return.

9. *Issue a warning.* You must be prepared to follow
through with any warnings issued.

   "I invited you here to work toward an agreement, but you seem concerned only with fighting. If you cannot abide by the ground rules in
   the next fifteen minutes we will have to suspend
   the session."

10. *Suspend or end the session.* Some agencies have a
policy that once parties fail to heed a warning,
they end the session, rather than suspending it
temporarily. People do have to be willing and
competent to mediate. If you believe the disputants are neither, then end the session.

In business mediations much heat is often exchanged in
tough bargaining at the beginning of sessions. The ACAS
model of conflict resolution combines open sessions
with separate ones. Mediators often suspend an open
session if things are going badly and retire with each
party into separate sessions to try and break the deadlock. You may choose to use this method if you wish,
that is, suspend the open session and work with each
party separately before getting them back together again.

CONCLUSION

You may find that the participants are more than capable
of saying what they need and that the mediator does not
have to work too hard. Up until now they will either
have been speaking to mediators in private session or
through a mediator in open session. In the next three
stages, the mediator needs all the tools in the toolbox.
What happens next will determine whether there is
more conflict or change.

The Mediation Session: Stage 4— Interchange

17

The interchange stage involves

- Summarizing by the mediator of what was said in each opening statement.
- Talking between the parties.
- Dialogue, including exploration and investigation, confrontation, and challenging.
- Finding common ground.
- Identifying which issues can be managed in the next stage.

There are two different approaches to the interchange stage.

1. Mediator-led mutual problem definition
2. Party-led dialogue and structured discussion

MEDIATOR-LED PROBLEM DEFINITION

John Haynes is an experienced mediator, trainer, and writer in the field of divorce mediation. He is a charismatic, fluent, and powerful speaker and a persuasive man and his mediation style depends on his dynamism, perception, and creative thinking.

John Haynes' style of mediation is based on his concept of the conflict resolution process. Conceiving of a conflict as a problem to be solved for the two parties, Haynes (1989) argues that, at the outset, the parties do not even agree on what the problem is, let alone what the solutions are. The mediator guides them by first, getting the problem described and defined in a mutually acceptable way, and second, finding solutions to the problem.

Problem Agreement

Find Solution

What's the Problem?

Having made their opening statements, Thomas and Moira clearly see the situation very differently.

Moira

"I have worked here for two years and thought that you all believed I did well. It's not easy leaving your two children at home, but I have to be active. I take pride in my work and don't want someone accusing me of making too many mistakes. I have to work with David and Ron, so of course I am not in my office. I only work for twenty hours a week—five hours Monday, Tuesday, Thursday, and Friday."

Thomas

"I don't understand what is unreasonable about wanting the information a week earlier. Also you would think she could make time to sit down and check it through with me. Pat, you know that I work hard, and that I have a lot to do for you, and Phillip also gives me typing. I already stay late one night. There are only so many hours in a day!"

Using Haynes' model each party defines the problem as follows:

Thomas	Moira
Problem: Moira won't talk to him, is hard to find, gives him information late and with mistakes, and he gets a bad reputation.	Problem: She is upset that Thomas got the job and finds him difficult to work with. She has little time and too much work.

As yet they cannot, or will not, see one another's point of view. They also believe that this is a uniquely difficult problem which is impossible to resolve. So the mediator has three tasks, to

- Convince them that their problem is not uniquely difficult, but can be resolved.
- Locate areas of agreement.
- Concentrate on the areas of common ground and get the parties to agree what the problem is.

There are three main skills that Haynes uses to achieve these tasks.

- Mutualizing
- Normalizing
- Selective summary

Mutualizing

As the parties make their opening statements the mediator will begin to use the two unobtrusive but effective techniques of mutualizing and normalizing, and will continue to use them throughout the mediation.

Mutualizing is the process of feeding back to the parties issues, ideas, and concerns that are true for both of them. This reduces the levels of animosity and resistance to the possibility of a joint problem definition. Patricia could say

"So you both have a lot of pressure on your time?"
"I can see that you Thomas and you Moira both want to do the best job you can."
"You both seem quite frustrated by this situation."

Common ground

Mutualizing focuses on the common ground, not on differences. It does not require a response from the parties.

Patricia will begin to influence Moira's and Thomas' definition of the problem if she makes some mutualizing statements, such as those above, as she notices common ground and makes a mental or written note of them, returning to them when she makes her summary.

Normalizing

Normalizing statements are generalizations about human experience that are relevant and similar to the parties' situation. They allow the mediator to acknowledge feelings, but also inform the parties that their problem is not uniquely difficult, and consequently is resolvable.

"I know what you both mean. Making time for one another can be difficult when you're really busy."

"I can see you have had to make adjustments, which is never easy. I think it is always difficult to adjust when there has been a change in a work team, particularly an internal appointment."

"There is often a problem coordinating work for people who work together, but who are part-time and full-time. I can really understand that."

Normalizing statements are instant, gentle reminders that this is a real problem, but not necessarily a uniquely difficult one. They are a useful tool for refocusing the parties.

Patricia will make normalizing statements at times when she notices increasing hostility or despair, as a method of encouragement or if she wants to switch from the general to the specific. For example:

Refocus

"Working with someone new is very challenging. I can understand how this can be difficult to start with. Is there one particular thing you would like to change?"

Normalizing statements should be made in a tactful, sensitive way. Always frame statements in a way that acknowledges the importance of the parties' individual feelings, while also relating them to a broader picture.

Mutualization and normalization prepare the parties for mutual problem definition and solution.

Selective Summary

Haynes often questions the parties extensively before encouraging dialogue, making normalizing and mutualizing statements and building up his idea of what the common ground is. When he has formed a preliminary assessment of the problem he will reflect it back to the disputants using a selective summary. Selective summary is a method of feeding back only the information, ideas, and issues from a dispute that you believe will move the dispute forward. For example, a part of Patricia's summary is as follows:

> "Thanks very much for being so frank with me and one another. It will help me to understand and help us move on if I summarize what I have heard you say. So, Moira, you are quite pressured for time, need to be very clear about what Thomas and I expect from you, and want a clear, formal channel for communications. You need to be able to plan for any changes in your workload.
>
> Thomas, you too are very busy and would like some time to sit down with Moira each month to make sure you understand her information. You would like to know how you can take up any ongoing or immediate queries or issues with Moira.
>
> You would both like to do your jobs well and to have an effective working relationship."

Provide useful feedback

Using a flip chart to make a visual written record of the summary can be helpful at this stage.

Make a visual summary

Patricia left out information about Moira's home life (useful as background information, but not in their remit), any personal slights, information regarding the recruitment process and appointment (this cannot be changed), and any other broad references to the workplace that do not seem central to the issue.

She has provided a very different definition of the problem from that expressed by them individually at the beginning of the meeting. To recap, what was the problem initially and after the selective summary?

Thomas	Moira
Problem: Moira won't talk to him, is hard to find, gives him information late and with mistakes, and he gets a bad reputation.	Problem: She is upset that Thomas got the job and finds him difficult to work with. She has little time and too much work.

Patricia's Summary of the Problem
Not good communication between Moira and Thomas. Difficulty fitting in effective contact in a regular, structured way.
Pressure of time.
A sense of dysfunction—not able to work easily together.

Selective summary, therefore, involves

- Identifying mutual issues, ideas, and approaches.
- Excluding issues, facts, and references that are outside the remit of your aims and role.
- Understanding and identifying wants.
- Concentrating on the possible.
- Clarifying which issues you and the parties can and cannot manage.

Gain Agreement on the Problem Definition

Having presented these core issues back to the parties, the first stage is to give each party a chance to say if they think anything has been left out. Haynes says that even the most reluctant and difficult clients will challenge him if they feel his summary is unfair, misleading, or otherwise inaccurate.

Common issues first

If an issue is then brought up which only one party considers important, the mediator should make a note of it, assure the party that they will return to it, but deal with the common issues first. Often, in the process of addressing the common issues the other issue is resolved. So address those issues where there is agreed common concern first.

Check again with the parties whether or not there is agreement on the problem definition, and then you are ready to help them move toward a resolution.

PARTY-LED DIALOGUE AND STRUCTURED DISCUSSION

A party-led dialogue approach, like that of Haynes', is based on the idea that there are common issues between the parties, but that they do not recognize this.

> Look at it like a sculptor looks at a block of wood. Though the wood seems ugly and without shape at first, the sculptor knows that inside of it there is a finished sculpture...if an agreement is possible, it already exists within the two parties.

> (Cohen, School Mediation Associates 1990).

Continuing the image, the mediator's role is to "help the parties get rid of the rough edges and the hard angry feelings so that a fair agreement can be made."

Both mediator-led and party-led methods acknowledge the power and influence of the mediator, but in the party-led approach he or she is more like a facilitator, leading, guiding, and sometimes suggesting, but committed to encouraging the parties to identify the main issue themselves.

Seven Elements to Party-Led Dialogue and Structured Discussion

1. Outlining a balanced summary of people's opening statements
2. Encouraging dialogue
3. Preventing withdrawal
4. Transmitting information
5. Getting the parties to notice new information and ideas
6. Structuring the discussion
7. Pulling everything together

Balanced Summary   The mediator opens this stage with a summary which covers the main points, uses neutral language, puts events in accurate chronological sequence, and restates any positions or suggestions the parties have made. This summary should always be framed with a mixture of authority and deference to the parties. If they wish to contradict or add anything, then the mediator should modify the summary until they are satisfied.

Encouraging Dialogue   It is surprising how little people actually talk to one another, and how infrequently they listen. In this dispute, as feelings are running high, the parties may still find it difficult to actually talk directly to one another without assistance. So Patricia will need a variety of encouraging responses. Once a true dialogue begins with listening and understanding on both sides, then you have every chance of reaching agreements. Here are a variety of encouraging phrases.

Moira (to Patricia)

"I suppose I could make some time available for Thomas."

"Please go on, Moira. Could you be more specific?"   (Offering individual encouragement)

Thomas (to Patricia)

"I don't think Moira is being deliberately difficult."

"Thanks for saying that, Thomas. Could you say that to Moira, please?"   (Acknowledgement and encouraging direct communication, not through third party)

Moira

"I am prepared to work with Thomas, but I just want him to be sensitive, and understand that it's not that easy."

"Thanks, Moira. Now, Thomas, do you understand what Moira is saying?"

Thomas

"Not exactly."

"Would you ask Moira what you need in order to be clearer about what she means?"	(Checking listening, and encouraging the parties to ask one another specifying questions)
"Is there anything you would like to check with Thomas about what he has said?"	(Facilitating active listening for the parties)
"It would help us all to be clear at this stage that we are understanding one another. Moira (Thomas), could you feed back to Thomas (Moira) the key points of what he (she) is saying?"	(Facilitating active listening and summary)

Preventing Withdrawal

Difficult behavior, like persistent name-calling, interrupting, shouting, or dominating, should be dealt with early (see Chapter 16).

A manual for managerial mediation by Dan Dana (1989) has a useful checklist for preventing withdrawal. This list, along with a few added points, is included in the following checklist.

CHECKLIST	
Preventing Withdrawal	
Behavior Signals	**Examples of What to Do**
■ Not talking directly to each other	"Can you say that to…?"
■ Changing topic to something irrelevant	"How is this related to the conflict?"
■ Denying that conflict is present	"Would you like things to be different between you?"
■ Being abstract, speaking hypothetically	"Let's talk about what is really going on here."
■ Constantly going back to the past	"How does that relate to now? What would you like to change?"
■ Focusing on the meanings of words	"I think that it is more important to talk about issues than…."
■ Focusing on process	"It seems easier for you to talk about how to do this than the conflict."
■ Challenging the mediator	Listen and acknowledge and move back to the conflict.
■ Expressing hopelessness	"I can understand how you feel, but…I think we have a real chance to settle this here. If we stop now you may lose your best chance of settling." (Only if you think there is a real chance.)
■ Threatening to walk out	"Could you stay for the time we agreed?"

Transmitting Information

Whether the parties have made their opening statements in private sessions or with everyone in the room in open session, a large part of the mediator's work is expressing one party's issues to the other.

Cohen, School Mediation Associates (1990) defines the mediator's job here as "making sure that all the important issues and statements are said in the most positive way possible." It defines the following three categories of statements

1. Positive Statements Said About the Other Party

Transmitting these builds good feeling between the parties. You may think it best to use the exact words used by the other party. Timing is important, so wait and assess how the other party reacts to the statement before repeating it. Transmitting positive statements can be very timely when there is an impasse or one party begins to withdraw.

Thomas

"I know that Moira is very enthusiastic and conscientious."

Transmit positive statements

Patricia Transmits This Statement

"Thomas did say that he knew you are very enthusiastic and conscientious."

Moira

"I would like to try and arrange a good working relationship."
"Moira did say earlier that she does want to develop a good working relationship with you."

Thomas

"I liked Moira before, but now things have become difficult."
"Thomas said that he liked you before, Moira."

2. Negative Statements That Are Important to the Issue

Repeat these statements, but use neutral phrasing. For example:

Thomas

"But I think the issue of punctuality is important, and Moira doesn't care."

Rephrase negative statements

Patricia Restates This Statement

"Moira, Thomas said a while ago that he is very concerned about having things done on time."

Moira

"He always laughs and makes fun of me when I try to explain my problems with time."

"Moira said she would like you to listen to her, so that you can understand why she is under time pressure."

3. Negative Statements That Are Not Important to the Issues

There is no need to repeat these. Examples may include

"He always did think he was so clever."

"She has got enough trouble looking after her kids, let alone work."

"You've got to be stupid to think I would do that."

Getting the Parties to Notice New Information and Ideas

Although the parties may begin to address one another, they will still need some assistance with listening. In addition to using encouraging responses the mediator can be very helpful by highlighting new ideas and information as it is given.

Highlight Information

"Do you realize, Thomas, that Moira said she actually enjoys working with other people, but does not find it easy to start with."

"I just want to check, Moira, did you notice that? I think Thomas admitted that he can be a little abrupt at times."

"That's a new idea, Thomas. What about that, Moira?"

"I can now understand why.... Did you notice what Moira added there, Thomas?"

Structuring the Discussion

People will find it easier to discuss issues if the ones that seem to be the easiest are discussed first and the discussion is concentrated on issues that are important to both sides. It is also easier if each party has a chance to say what they want, rather than one or the other dominating.

Use occasional summaries to check what has been covered so far and move the discussion on. Help the parties to establish what is mediative and what is not. For example, because

- One party is unwilling to consider the issue.
- The issue concerns something that cannot be changed.
- It concerns someone who is not in the room.
- The people in the room do not have the authority to deal with the issue.

The first interchange stage of mediation is difficult since both parties struggle for position, resort to old habits, and often resist any attempt at finding common ground. Piece by piece, however, little oases of agreement may emerge in the desert of disagreement. The methods mentioned here will help ensure that the parties notice this and that these pieces of common ground on which the future agreement will be constructed do not become as illusory and transient as a mirage.

Pulling Everything Together

Before moving on to the next stage, when the parties will be looking at how to deal with these issues, the mediator should round off the interchange stage by constructing a summary in conjunction with the parties. A flip chart is useful here, because the parties can then easily read and verify the summary. At this stage the summary should include

Highlight common ground

- Issues that both parties think are important.
- Any suggested agreements that have emerged so far.
- Issues that are important and cannot be dealt with in mediation, but can be dealt with elsewhere.

Summarize

The Mediation Session: Stage 5— Movement *18*

HOW CAN THE PROBLEM BE SOLVED?

By the time the parties have identified the issues on which they can work with the assistance of the mediator, there may have been some heat, some tears, and attempts to escalate the situation back into the danger zone of conflict where nothing can be agreed. During the struggle to agree on issues, however, the skillful influence of the mediator (emphasizing the positive, ensuring listening, and providing impartial feedback) and the subtle changes in the parties (reduced levels of anger, direct conversation with one another, and seeking to understand the persons behind their positions) will be facilitating a shift in atmosphere away from conflict and toward cooperation. Robert Coulson (1991), the president of the American Arbitration Association, describes this as the creation of a "bargaining relationship." This is, however, bargaining in which everyone gains.

Win–win bargaining

Traditionally bargaining involves some give and take but is often fraught with false bids, manipulative tactics, and posturing. The kind of bargaining that goes on in a mediation begins before the mediation session even starts, at the preliminary meetings. It is characterized by exploration and facilitation, openness and honesty wherever possible, and fairness. The mediator is constantly working to check the parties' instincts to fight, distract, and dig their heels in. The kind of bargaining that goes on in a mediation is definitely win–win (Fisher and Ury 1992) rather than win–lose. It is based on the belief that people do have the capacity to understand their own needs, be open to those of others, and overcome their differences, and do not always have to defeat an opponent to get what they want.

Issues to Agreements

Fighting is a difficult habit to kick, though, especially in the business world. So how does the mediator move the parties from issues to agreements?

BUILDING AGREEMENTS

Whether or not you have adopted a mediator-led approach based on the Haynes model or used party-led dialogue and structured discussion, there will come a time when the mediator has to shift the disputants from exploration of issues to building agreements. The role of the mediator here is to facilitate the parties skillfully so that they are able to forge an agreement of their own making. The primary focus of mediation is to concentrate the positive capacities of the parties so that they can not only find resolutions to immediate and past problems, but also can learn how they might manage future disagreements. Therefore, the parties must be imbued with a sense of their own power.

Empower parties

There are several ways in which the mediator may give the parties a chance to build their own agreements.

- Generating options
- Giving the parties space to talk
- Collecting agreements
- Supporting conciliatory gestures

- No-risk narrowing of positions
- Bargaining
- Deflating extreme positions
- Dealing with resistance to settlement
- Breaking an impasse

Ask the Parties What They Could Do to Resolve the Situation

Generating Options

Asking the parties to generate resolutions to the situation prevents them from blaming one another. Patricia could do this in various ways.

- Ask open questions and suggest that they each think about two or three things they could do, for example, "to improve the situation" or "to make things easier for both of you." Then get them to feed their ideas back.

- Ask the same kind of open, general question, but take one suggestion at a time from each. Patricia could write the ideas on a flip chart or large sheet of paper if she wished.

- Ask another general question since they both may have been provoked into new thought by the other's response. For example:

  "Is there anything else you would be prepared to do?"

  or

  "Is there anything you would like to add?"

- Focus on something very specific, for example, one of the major issues.

  "Moira, l am going to ask you first, then Thomas, what you think you could each do to improve communication between the two of you."

  or

  "Thomas, first, then Moira, perhaps you could suggest ways in which you could effectively check through and clarify the figures with Moira present."

- Refer to another time when they have successfully managed a conflict. For example:

  "Do you have you ideas about what might move us forward? Maybe think of a time when you have dealt successfully with a similar situation in the past."

These questions all put the responsibility on the parties, and it is important that they specify what the person can do, not what they want the other to do, and that they are directed at both parties to demonstrate the mediator's impartiality.

Brainstorm

Brainstorming is a quick idea-generating process, useful for groups of any size. As the name suggests, it is a method of allowing ideas to storm through the mind spontaneously, without too much thought about their practicality or appropriateness. Some people find it easier than others to generate new, useful ideas in this way. Also brainstorming can produce more ideas and suggestions than you need. However, it is quick and informal, and can often unlock difficult problems if people feel safe enough to be really imaginative and creative.

Patricia Asks Moira and Thomas

"Relax and think off the top of your heads, with no commitment, what should be helpful in dealing with any of the issues?"

or

"Imagine that it were someone else in this dispute, not you. How do you think they might proceed?"

The opening question should be clear and wide enough to permit creativity, but still focused on what would be helpful. Here are a few tips for facilitating brainstorms, whether with two people or a group.

- Write down accurately what speakers say, checking the wording with them if you need to.

- Do not ask the speaker to explain.

- Do not permit questioning.

- Repeat and add creatively to suggestions as they come up to stimulate new ideas.

- Thank those who contribute.

- Ask those who did not speak if they have anything to add.

- Set a limit as responses begin to slow down (for example, "Okay, let's take two or three more."). This is better than waiting for the suggestions to grind to a halt, which will cause a sense of frustration or stagnation.

- Acknowledge contributions before you begin to look closely at the responses (for instance, "Thanks for thinking so fast....").

If this is all a struggle, and you have a blank sheet of paper, be positive and have alternative approaches for generating ideas. If Patricia decides to get Moira and Thomas to brainstorm as a first step and they cannot get any ideas, then she could use any of the other methods in this section.

Brainstorms are useful to

- Get ideas on a new subject fast.

- Give people a chance to be spontaneous.

- Reduce performance anxiety.

- Redirect people from expressing feelings into thinking about ideas.

- Lighten the atmosphere in tense situations.

- Break the ice at the beginning of difficult negotiations.

Stand in Another's Shoes

Getting people to see and understand one another's points of view is one of the key aims of positive conflict management. The image of "standing in another's shoes" says it all—imagine what it would be like, donning shoes of a different size and color, perhaps making you feel smaller or taller than you normally feel. Your feet are the only two parts of you that touch the ground, connecting you with the real world. Your contact with that world, with reality, can be quite different if you swap your black leather work shoes for someone else's blue suede shoes, red high heels, or scuffed basketball sneakers.

Another's viewpoint

At various stages in the agreement building process it can be useful to ask the parties how they imagine the others view the situation. As a way of generating options it can be a useful shift of focus for the parties to be asked what they think the other would like.

"Moira, if you were Thomas, what do you think you would find helpful for any of the issues in this dispute?"

or

"Thomas, if you could just imagine you are Moira for a minute, what do you think she would realistically like to happen to make it easier to discuss the figures with you?"

This kind of question is risky, because parties often find it difficult to truly identify with the other disputants. Answers to such questions may also give people a chance to express their worst fears. Thomas may, for example, say

"Well, I think she would like my job."

Moira may say

"Thomas would like it if I just do everything he says."

This sort of response poses the mediator with a problem that recurs time and time again in mediation sessions—do I acknowledge such a response and explore it or acknowledge it and move on?

The mediator's role is like a traveler's guide on a journey toward understanding oneself and others. Along the way there are many gates to new lands, the ideas, insights, and opinions, and if the mediator opens a gate, then the traveler will almost certainly need more help negotiating the terrain or finding a path back to the start if it is not a safe or useful place to be. Sometimes it is best to pass by a gate, or just ease it open and let the traveler sense what is there, and then close it firmly and move on. A mediator is someone who understands and is sensitive to people, and facilitates rather than controls. If, however, it is his or her considered opinion that a gate is best left closed, whether due to lack of time, danger to already agreed-on points, or because it leads to feelings that cannot really be dealt with in mediation, then a mediator should acknowledge the feelings behind the behavior, but move on.

Despite the risk, these questions can also get parties in touch with a different perspective from their own and open up more options to them.

Offering Solutions

If people are really stuck and cannot come up with any options then it is perfectly legitimate to offer solutions. Offer several solutions so that the parties feel they still have a voice in choosing the solution. You can remain neutral and make proposals, as long as you do not attempt to coerce acceptance.

Patricia obviously needs some solutions and may ultimately have to make decisions for Moira and Thomas, but at this stage she could simply make suggestions.

Make suggestions

"Moira, what if Thomas agreed to meet you the third week of the month for about half an hour so that you could discuss the figures, particularly any problems coming up?"

"Thomas, how about discussing how to prioritize your other work with me in a week's time?"

"Moira and Thomas, have you ever thought about planning three months at a time, getting together with your calendars and scheduling in meetings to discuss the figures?"

Offering solutions can lead to dialogue when the parties are stuck for answers themselves.

Ask Tough Questions

"Mediators are neutral, not neutered" (Acland 1990, p. 171) and tough, open, fair questions will often help the parties understand the situation and come up with realistic settlements.

"I don't understand that. What do you mean?"
"How exactly will you do that?'
"When is that going to be done?''
"Do you think that is an answer to Thomas' question?"
"What if you agreed to meet him next week...?"
"What is it particularly that you don't like?"

Giving the Parties Space to Talk It Through

Once dialogue is happening the facilitator should be able to assess how much the parties can be left to make their own agreements. There are several ways to give the parties more space, for example:

- Remain silent yourself and allow the parties to be silent. We all have our own boundaries of tolerance to silence, and some people cannot bear more than ten seconds of silence. However, silence can be very useful for people to think in, and also they do not need to hear your voice if they are working well alone.

- Take a break. Breaks can often be useful in this respect. Call a break in sessions when the levels of animosity cause an impasse, or when all the mediators wish to discuss their tactics and have a break themselves. Consider the security aspects carefully and do not put your clients at risk by leaving them in a room alone together.

Collecting Agreements Versus "Boulder in the Road"

Build confidence

There are two views about whether to build agreements on difficult issues first, or go for the easy ones first to prepare the climate for more difficult areas. By collecting agreements on some of the less controversial issues first, a mediator builds the confidence of the parties and minimizes the differences between them. Some mediators argue that this then makes the major issue—the boulder in the road that blocks progress—more difficult to manage. They believe that you should attack the boulder first, then the path is clear for a really meaningful way forward.

These methods are mutually exclusive. Flexibility is a key asset in mediation. If you choose the most difficult issue first, be prepared either to break it down into more manageable segments, or switch to easier issues with the promise of returning later to the major one when some progress has been made.

Be flexible

Conciliatory gestures at times of conflict should not go unacknowledged. When parties believe their concessions are recognized, they will feel empowered. If the other party can also be encouraged to notice, they will both begin to learn that making concessions can often be a more effective way of gaining power than defending untenable positions.

Patricia, by supporting conciliatory gestures, will continue to build a positive atmosphere and encourage cooperative problem solving. Below is a list based on Dan Dana (1989) to show how this can be done.

Supporting Conciliatory Gestures

Conciliatory Behavior	Examples of What to Do
• Apologies	• Ask the one who made the gesture, "Can you say more about that?"
• Expressing regret	• Emphasize and focus on the gesture: "I believe that is very positive."
• Conceding on contested issues	• Acknowledge the gesture: "Thank you for…."
• Offering to compromise	• Check that the other has heard: "What did you hear Moira (Thomas) say then?"

Conciliatory Behavior	Examples of What to Do
• Recognizing other's point of view	• Emphasize positive statements by one about the other: "Thomas said clearly that he believes you are conscientious, Moira."
• Expressing positive views about the other	• (Self-explanatory)
• Emphasizing commonalities	• (Self-explanatory)
• Accepting responsibility for self	• (Self-explanatory)
• Narrowing of positions	• (Self-explanatory)

No-Risk Narrowing of Positions

If you feel the difference between the parties is narrowing, and a hint of a concession is being made, do not just tell one party that the other is prepared to give in, but mention what you have noticed tentatively.

"What if Thomas said that he would meet in your office, rather than expecting you to come to his?"

This way, if the suggestion is rejected, it does not reflect on either party as it was framed as the suggestion of the mediator.

Bargaining

As different options emerge it can be useful to encourage bargaining, whereby the parties aim to trade off gains with one another so that they each get something they want, if not everything. Again, "what if" questions are useful.

"What if you agreed to phone Moira first to check that she has time to speak with you, Thomas, rather than just arriving in her office? And you Moira, agree to meet with him next week to take him through how the figures actually work?"

The facilitator plays an important role here as umpire, and should ensure that bargaining is done on a fair and equal basis as some people are more forceful and experienced bargainers than others.

One of the mediator's key roles, especially with conflicts in organizations where there are external considerations, such as disposition of resources, guidelines, and procedures, is to act as an agent of reality (Moore 1986).

If the positions are so extreme that they cannot be achieved, then the mediator must generate movement by ultimately making this clear. This announcement should promote movement either by ending the negotiation or facilitating compromise on that particular point, thus permitting the parties to move to the next point or by allowing the parties to disagree on that particular issue.

Deflating Extreme Positions

Agent of reality

Marian Roberts, a specialist in a British family mediation, describes the central tensions in the mediator's role (Roberts 1991). One of these tensions is the "need to settle and the lack of power to do so." There are three strategies, below, that effectively balance the mediator's power and the need for settlement.

Dealing With Resistance to Settlement

1. *Remind the parties of the consequences of nonagreement.* The consequences may include a comparative loss of their bargaining power if they hand over the decision making to someone else, prolonged stress, demotivation, and the use of extra resources if the dispute is to be settled elsewhere.

Consequences

2. *Realistically approach external pressures.* External pressures may include the need to settle within a specific time limit, deadlines for work affected by the dispute, other time factors, financial considerations, or procedural constraints.

External pressures

3. *Refer to mediation boundaries.* Refer back to the ground rules and stages of the process. For example, Patricia may say

Boundaries

"Thanks for bringing up that information Thomas, but I would rather you did not interrupt Moira, as we agreed at the start. Also, we were getting very close to establishing agreement on issue one. Why not continue with that, then we can deal with the issue you raised?"

Breaking an Impasse

Sometimes parties get in a deadlock; even mediators sometimes feel they are stuck. Here are some hints from the Erichson Mediation Institute about how to break an impasse.

Restarting

Go back through the problem in abbreviated fashion, summarizing the steps you have taken. Often, the second time through you will locate and resolve the problem that is causing the impasse.

Recheck and Obtain Extra Facts If Necessary

Ask whether or not more facts are needed. Rechecking gives the mediator a chance to obtain clues about why they may be having settlement difficulties.

Use an Expert

An expert in the issues concerned may be able to provide information or options that the parties and the mediator have not thought of. It can often be a great advantage in disputes where technical or complex procedural issues are concerned for the mediator to have an expert in the field to rely on. For example, legal and financial knowledge helps when mediating financial settlement details for divorcees.

Discuss Fairness

People who are not in agreement on a common definition of fairness will find it difficult to agree on specific issues. Thomas may think that his case should carry more weight as he is full time, but Patricia believes it is only fair that part-time and full-time workers be treated equally. To break the impasse over this, explore their individual concepts of what is fair, obtaining examples, and then establish a concept of fairness that is mutually acceptable. This is particularly important with parties from different cultural backgrounds where value systems and codes of behavior may be different.

Comment on the Give-and-Take Score

Reminding the parties of the other's concessions is a form of intervention that prevents impasse by reminding parties that they have made considerable progress. Parties in difficult negotiations will often be so consumed by their own effort that they forget to observe the concessions by the other side. Keep track of progress and draw the parties' attention to it. This strategy can also be effective in moving the more rigid party off a strongly held position.

Use Other Means of Expression and Depiction

When people are lost for words, or angry or hurt, or the stakes are so high that they cannot describe what they want, using visual depiction may enable them to express or understand what is blocking progress.

- Ask the parties to visualize how they feel—what picture or image comes to mind?

- Ask the parties to imagine what would change in this picture if the situation improved.

- Write down a summary of what has been achieved and then what is blocking progress, or get the parties to do this separately, using words and symbols (see the section on "mapping" in Chapter 11).

- Ask the parties to explain their depictions or images and translate them back into suggestions or options.

Sometimes, despite the best efforts of parties and mediator, no agreement is possible on one or more issues. Under these circumstances, rather than struggling on, the most constructive option is to allow nonagreement, particularly when

Dealing With Resistance to Settlement

- More time is available to work out agreements.
- Issues will clearly not be resolved by the end of a session.
- Process of exploration and discovery has revealed that there were more important issues than originally realized.
- Differences are deep-seated and parties should not feel that they have been coerced into shallow, unworkable agreements.

Communicate the next step

If you allow for nonagreement, though, you have to be very clear about what the next step is and gain agreement at least on that.

For example, Thomas and Moira, at the early stages of the session, are not in agreement about in whose office to work together on the financial reports. Patricia allows them to disagree, suggesting that they could come back to this issue later. As the session progresses Moira explains that she considers her work space unsatisfactory, which is why she is uncomfortable about working with Thomas there. After this, having agreed how she might secure better accommodation, Moira is prepared to accede to a provisional arrangement.

Even if there is no agreement on any issues, the mediator should inform the parties what will happen next, that is, what the next stage in the conflict resolution will be.

The Mediation Session: Stage 6— Preparing for Resolution 19

M^{*ost*} of the time in a mediation is spent working through the confrontation. As agreements on various issues begin to emerge, the mediator's role is to encourage negotiation and resolution on each issue, anticipating and mentioning problems ahead.

Agreements should be

- Responsive to the identified needs and interests of the parties.

- Realistic.

- Specific and clear.

- Framed in neutral language.

- Open to improvements in the relationships of the parties.

For example, Thomas agrees to take his claim for regrading to Surinder, head of personnel, and Moira will approach Howard about new office space. Patricia, in her role as head of customer services, will support both in their claims. This is a balanced agreement. Thomas and Moira will meet for one hour on the second Tuesday of each month for three months at 1:00 p.m. so that Moira can explain how she does the figures and Thomas can raise any questions he has. The venue will alternate between their offices. This is realistic, specific, and clear.

By the third Tuesday of each month Moira will have completed the figures, and a further one hour should be put aside, on that day, for them to go through the figures together before Thomas takes them away to type up. Thomas will type up the figures by the following Friday.

For other work that emerges requiring joint efforts, Thomas and Moira will contact one another to check availability first, then agree on a time to meet. This agreement is open to improvements in relationships.

Thomas agrees to say "Hello" to Moira when he sees her, and she agrees to reply to his memos or phone messages within a day of receiving them. This agreement looks at relationships and uses neutral language.

During this stage the mediator is particularly keen to discourage any return to negative behavior and has to keep a tight rein on behavior. Challenging and specifying questions are very useful at this stage if people slip back into confrontation. For example:

Challenging

"That's not what we agreed."
"Surely we're not going to go over all that again."
"I think it's important. Don't you?"
"Tell me exactly what you think we agreed."

Specifying

"No, that is not on this issue; we have not come to that yet. What do you think about this particular suggestion (states agreement again)?"

"I can see that this is an important issue. Could you both tell me briefly how you would change the wording of this agreement? Moira, you first."

Do not move to the resolution stage before everyone is ready, as this will often result in negative behavior, and can lead to ineffectual agreements that nobody really wanted. Keep checking on their willingness to move to agreement, and explore resistance when it does occur.

The Mediation Session: Stage 7— Closing 20

The final stage of the session is often conducted in an atmosphere of growing euphoria. People who may have been fighting all their lives shake hands, embrace, share a taxi home. This is not to say that they are permanently transformed, but the power of coming together is infectious. Throughout this stage it is the mediator's job to ensure that this euphoria is based on solid ground. There are four main tasks.

WRITING THE AGREEMENT

The language and content of the written agreement should make it easy for all concerned to know what is expected of them. This is particularly important when there are considerations of language and culture on each side, or when dealing with complex technical issues. Acland reminds us that the "single text" method, which

Mediator writes the agreement

was used at Camp David between Egypt's Anwar Sadat and Prime Minister Begin of Israel in 1975, involves the preparation, by the impartial mediator, of a text that includes all the major issues and agreements, and is presented to the parties for consideration, criticism, and modification. It is based on the notion that parties find it easier to criticize the mediator's version than to prepare separate texts of their own, and then negotiate the wording of each item. Even though the mediator writes the text, it should always include in it as much of the disputants' own ideas and language as possible.

Parties may need separate time and space to consider the written agreement, or, when representing a wider constituency or having assistance from experts, to seek the advice of others.

CONGRATULATING

Summarize everyone's achievements and offer congratulations, because people almost always work extremely hard in mediation, even when it ends in nonagreement.

ENCOURAGING SYMBOLIC GESTURES

Encouraging symbolic gestures sounds grand, but normally requires only a handshake or similar gesture, which will build on the sense of growing togetherness. Sometimes parties will request a more public display of closure, particularly in connection with heated public issues that have been mediated privately to resolution but require public affirmation and acknowledgment.

ARRANGING FOR FOLLOW-UP

The closing session should also make clear what is being done about monitoring, evaluation, progress, and future incidents.

The Mediation Session: Stage 8— Follow-up **21**

There are two kinds of follow-up to a mediation session.

- Looking after the mediator
- Looking after the parties and the agreement

THE MEDIATOR

Mediation is stressful, though rewarding. Because of the infinite nature of human experience, mediators will encounter many similar but different kinds of behavior, and also learn much about themselves and the parties. A good mediator has a powerful set of resources and skills, but is constantly in need of feedback to make the stress more manageable, and to assess how well he or she is functioning.

A solo mediator should arrange for regular meetings with someone who understands human behavior and

Gain feedback

who will listen and support. This need not be someone who is a superior in the organization, but may be a peer who you believe can offer this service. If you are able to secure the services of an experienced supervisor or trainer, then this is the most effective method of support.

Self-evaluation

Self-evaluation can also be facilitated in the same way. Use the checklist or the mediator evaluation form at the back of the book in Appendix. You may find it useful to elicit party evaluation of the process, which can be achieved by giving an exit questionnaire at the end of the mediation with another at a fixed period later to see if their reactions have changed. These evaluations may cover a variety of elements from process to outcome, including

Party evaluation

- Mediator's control of the proceedings, fairness, managing of the facts, and understanding of the issues.
- Parties' view of the process. Was there anything they liked or would like to have changed?
- Opinions of the outcome. Were people happy with what they had achieved?

Debrief

If you co-mediate, I would recommend that you allow for at least fifteen minutes debriefing after mediation to discuss the session, unload any frustrations, and give one another constructive feedback. Focus on the positive first, then move to any areas of disagreement or concern between you. If you have agreed on areas in which you would like feedback, now is the time to obtain it.

THE PARTIES AND THE AGREEMENT

When you use mediation in the workplace you will most likely have some contact with the parties after the mediation session, unless you are mediating for another department, another branch, or another part of the organization. This may happen if you become particularly skilled, as good mediators are an invaluable commodity. Although a successful mediation assembles powerful evidence of positive interaction such as a willingness to compromise, communicate, and solve problems together, the mediator should also consider arrangements for follow-up with the parties that will

- Assist the parties in the future if necessary.
- Enable adjustments to be made in agreements.
- Take new information or circumstances into consideration.
- Check how agreements are holding up and check relationships.

This can be done by

- Arranging for a follow-up open session, or private sessions at a fixed period after the mediation.
- Providing a fail-safe or emergency procedure should hostilities break out again.
- Providing other structures of ongoing support, supervision, and communication.
- Addressing any issues which came up during mediation but could not be handled there.
- Moving on to the next stage of conflict management if agreements break down.

CONCLUSION

Owing to her impartial, facilitative approach, Patricia will by now either have managed an agreement or at least have gained so much information about the problem that she will be in a far better position to make a fair decision. If she decides to make a judgment for the parties (as in arbitration, which is covered in Chapter 22) her decision will carry more weight because it has been arrived at by a fair process, and Moira and Thomas will be much more likely to abide by it.

When conflicts are resolved people's satisfaction is dependent on outcome and process. If Thomas and Moira are happy with the outcome, then they are likely to be favorable about the process. Even if they do not like the outcome, issues of procedure matter, and many surveys have pointed to client satisfaction at mediation

Outcome and process

procedures even when they have not gotten settlements they liked. The mediation process embodies the princi-, ples and combines most of the skills of positive conflict management. It is empowering for the manager who mediates and sends out a powerful affirming and motivating message to disputants—"that the authorities are not biased, that they are honest, and that they make decisions based on factual information about the case" (Tyler). These factors contribute significantly to the prospects of future peace in the workplace.

SUMMARY

Stage One: Preparation

- Attend preliminary meetings
- Get parties to mediation
- Select mediator
- Meet co-mediator
- Prepare room

Stage Two: Opening

- Present mediator's opening statement
- Make personal introductions and establish ground rules
- Get the parties to trust you
- Agree on confidentiality

Stage Three: Parties' Statements

- Decide on separate meetings or statements made in open session
- Get parties started
- Get feelings heard by both sides
- Reflect feelings and meanings
- Reframe statements

- Collect information and background and get an initial idea about what they want by notetaking, key facts, time frame, and clarification
- Handle difficult behavior

Stage Four: Interchange

- Mediator-led mutual problem definition
- Mutualizing
- Normalizing
- Selective summary
- Gain agreement on problem definition
- Party-led dialogue and structured discussion
- Encourage dialogue
- Prevent withdrawal
- Transmit information
- Get parties to notice new information and ideas
- Structure the discussion
- Pull everything together

Stage Five: Movement

- Build agreements to solve problems
- Generate options
- Give parties space to talk it through
- Support conciliatory gestures
- Encourage bargaining
- Deflate extreme positions
- Deal strategically with resistance to settlement
- Break an impasse
- Allow nonagreement

Stage Six: Preparing for Resolution

- Work through, negotiate, and close on each issue
- Make workable agreements

Stage Seven: Closing

- Write the agreement
- Congratulate parties
- Arrange for follow-up

Stage Eight: Follow-up

- Debrief mediators, evaluate, and wind down
- Consider future arrangements
- Arrange to monitor agreement
- Evaluate process and outcome

Arbitration **22**

The Advisory Conciliation and Arbitration Service (ACAS) in London describes arbitration as the "last peaceful resort" for resolving disputes. It resembles litigation, but is less formal. An arbitrator does not decide, strictly speaking, upon a winner or loser, but makes an award which is considered to be the fairest in the light of all the evidence. Unlike mediation, which helps the parties reach a settlement, arbitration is the "determination or settlement of an issue, on which the parties have failed to agree, by an independent third party" (Mackie 1991). In mediation the parties have responsibility for the resolution. The mediator helps them explore their perceptions of facts and evidence, find common ground, and determine what is best for them all around. The arbitrator hears evidence, then makes a judgment that he or she considers is the best interest in full consideration of the evidence.

USES OF ARBITRATION

ACAS suggests that "arbitration is suitable for disputes where the issues are clear cut or concerns an interpretation of an agreement. Good examples of arbitrable issues are disputes over pay or job gradings, dismissal and disciplinary matters, and demarcation of work. Issues of principle or complicated many-sided disputes are regarded as less suitable."

Contact an arbitration service

If you have such an issue in the workplace contact an arbitration service like the ACAS for advice. It may be able to help with advice or conciliation, or by providing an arbitrator. ACAS appoints arbitrators from outside the organization where the dispute is occurring. As most arbitrators' work is in the labor relations field with disputes between work force and management, employer and employee, they emphasize the need for a third party who has no connections with either side.

Impartial third party

When you have developed sufficient constructive conflict management skills, you can act as an arbitrator if you are not connected with any previous agreement on the issue and are able to remain impartial. It certainly would not be appropriate for any dispute that you were or had been involved in or had an interest in yourself.

CHARACTERISTICS REQUIRED OF AN ARBITRATOR

CHECKLIST
Characteristics of an Arbitrator
■ Has high standing in the discipline relevant to the issues.
■ Is completely impartial and independent.
■ Has sufficient presence, self-assurance, and other social skills to be able to conduct a hearing with authority, gain the confidence of the parties, and leave each side feeling that it has had the opportunity to present its case.
■ Is able to grasp the essential points of often complex and difficult problems quickly, balance conflicting submissions, and weigh more salient considerations carefully in making a decision (Mackie 1991).

If you fulfill the criteria in the above checklist, then you may consider using the process of arbitration. It has the benefit, like mediation, of being thorough and fair, and communicates to all sides that you are doing your best to bring about a resolution for the general good, rather than for one side or the other.

THE ARBITRATION PROCESS

Four Stages to Arbitration

1. Consenting to and being clear about the process and terms of reference
2. Preparation, submission, and exchange of statements
3. The hearing
4. The decision or award

Situation

Carol, David's secretary, is on a different, lower pay scale than Thomas, who works for Patricia. These pay differences are an anomaly that Surinder, the head of personnel, inherited. As he had nothing to do with the original grading procedures and was concerned to give people who felt they were on the wrong grades a chance to achieve some measure of parity, he instituted a two-tier grading procedure. Heads of department should be the first line of appeal for people who felt their grades were inadequate. If this was declined and the person wished to take it further, as in this case, then Surinder would act as the arbitrator between the department and the staff member. Heads of department and staff were consulted about this process and agreed to abide by his awards. Surinder secured funds to make possible any awards of higher grades.

CONSENTING TO BEING CLEAR ABOUT THE PROCESS AND TERMS OF REFERENCE

If you take on the role of arbitrator, you must ensure that you and the disputants are very clear about the following points.

Issues Being Decided

This dispute is simply about grading, specifically if Carol should or should not be on a higher grade. The hearing will not consider conditions of work, salary payment procedures, any past grievances connected with salary, or other issues.

Limitations of Arbitration

Arbitration facilitates decision making solely on the basis of the evidence provided. Although feelings will be acknowledged and dealt with tactfully, the arbitrator will not consider emotional factors when making an award. An arbitrator's role is to make the fairest possible decision in light of all the evidence, using experience and knowledge of the field.

Process of Arbitration

There must be an understanding of the role of the arbitrator, the expectations on and tasks of the parties, the time scale, and the status of the decision, such as whether or not it is binding.

Who the Parties Can Seek for Help

Advisors and experts can help parties strengthen their case, and are permitted.

Form of the Agreement

All parties should understand if the agreement will be given with reasons, and how soon after the hearing they will be given.

Once these conditions have been made clear to the people involved, you must gain their consent and then the process can begin.

Surinder prepared a concise written description of the process when he instituted it, and now speaks to Carol and David briefly to check whether they need clarification, and to gain their consent.

PREPARATION, SUBMISSION, AND EXCHANGE OF WRITTEN STATEMENTS

Written statements enable the parties to organize their thoughts and prepare not only their own case, but also their responses to the points their counterpart is raising. The arbitrator, on seeing these statements, can begin to prepare for the hearing.

Written reports should be concise and include

- Background information.
- Details of the claim or offer.
- Summary of facts and evidence in support.

Allow enough time

The reports are presented to the arbitrator who then ensures that each one sees them with sufficient time to prepare for the hearing. In very complex cases, in which grievances or claims have been going on for some time, at least a week should be allowed from the receipt of statements. Surinder sets the hearing date for three days after receipt of statements as the documentation is minimal.

In cases where one person is likely to have significantly lower written language skills than the other, some measures can be taken to balance their relative capacity to prepare an adequate written statement.

- Give a checklist of what to include.
- Compile a list of people within your organization who are prepared to assist with written reports.
- Encourage them to find someone for themselves who can assist them.

Reassurance should also be given to both disputants that they will have a chance to explain and document their case more fully in the oral hearing.

THE HEARING

Preparation

Robert Coulson (1991), president of the American Arbitration Association, which has a panel of arbitrators who handled 60,000 arbitrations in 1990 in fields as varied as star baseball players' salary claims to insurance claims, summarizes how parties should prepare for a hearing. His summary is presented on the checklist below.

CHECKLIST
Preparing for a Hearing
■ Study the original statement of the grievance and review its history through every step of grievance machinery.
■ Assemble all the documents and papers needed for the hearing. Make copies for the arbitrator and the other party. If some documents you need are in the possession of the other party, ask that they be brought to the arbitration.
■ Study the case from the other side's point of view. Be prepared for opposing evidence and arguments.
■ If there are witnesses, interview them beforehand. Make sure they understand your case and how the testimony relates to it.
■ Make a written summary of witnesses' testimony, which can be used at the hearing to check nothing has been overlooked.
■ Discuss your case with others if you can in order to expose weak points.
■ Check to see if there are any similar cases and what the awards or settlements have been.

Process

Listen and question

As you can see from the preparation, this is much more like a trial. The arbitrator's approach, however, is facilitative and reassuring, and uses substantial interpersonal skills to communicate a sense of fairness, openness, and respect. Key skills throughout are active listening and questioning to encourage clear and purposeful expression of the issues and the claim. People will respect and trust an arbitrator if he or she

- Ensures the parties keep within the issues and uses his or her discretion and experience to exclude information that is not relevant.

- Is balanced in the approach to each side.
- Keeps control of the process.

The three stages of the arbitration process are clear cut, unlike the stages of mediation, and are controlled by the arbitrator.

Three Stages in the Arbitration Process

1. Opening statement through the arbitrator
2. Questioning of the parties and witnesses by the arbitrator
3. Checking that everyone has said what they want

Opening Statements

The arbitrator asks each side in turn to state their case, developing their own points, and also raising points about the other's case. This is all done through the chair. In our example, David and Carol do not address one another.

Speak through the chair

While this happens Surinder takes notes of the key points and uses these, in addition to the parties' written statements, to assist in his questioning.

Questioning the Parties and Witnesses (if Required)

The questioning stage occurs when the arbitrator can elicit all the information required to make a decision. Parties should be kept to the facts, and witnesses should be constrained from performing any role, such as a character testimonial, other than providing factual testimony.

Elicit facts

For example, Surinder questions Carol and David to clarify and check their case, concentrating on the facts. If something is not relevant he uses a challenging question to make sure they are not getting confused and redirects them.

Carol

"I have waited for eighteen months to get this sorted out, and Thomas, who has only been a secretary for a short while, is already on a higher scale than me."

Surinder

"I am not sure that the time factor is important, but are you saying that you deserve to be paid on the same scale as Thomas? Why is that?"

David

"We cannot give Carol a pay rise without changing her job description and, anyway, she does not have any responsibility for cash or receipts, which I think keeps her on the lower grading."

Surinder

"In the long term, David, you may be right, but let's concentrate on the job Carol does, for the moment. What else do you believe indicates that Carol should be on a lower grade?"

The arbitrator's job is to uncover evidence and proof so that a sound, fair decision can be made. There is an assumption that an arbitrator is sophisticated enough to disregard evidence that is not helpful, relevant, or reliable. Exercising the understanding and responding skills demonstrated in this book is important in this respect.

Surinder does not prevent the venting of feelings since there is therapeutic value in that, but ultimately he should steer David and Carol back to the salient, relevant details.

In weighing the evidence an arbitrator should be aware of the following (Coulson 1991):

1. *Direct evidence* directly proves a fact, without an inference or presumption. Carol performs some duties independently, and she cites her transcription as an example.

2. *Circumstantial evidence* tends to establish the principal fact by proving other facts from which the principal can be inferred. Carol has spoken to David about handling cash receipts, but did not

undergo the training offered by the company. When David is away, Carol refuses to accept cash, as she does not want to take responsibility for it. So she does not have responsibility for cash.

3. *Hearsay evidence* is second-hand evidence or a statement made by someone else that has bearing on the case, repeated at the hearing. The reliability of a statement rests upon the credibility of the person who made it. Surinder notices that Howard's notes from the staff meeting of last month show that Carol was thanked by Patricia for doing duties beyond her immediate responsibilities, such as taking calls from customers. This seems reliable, so he could check it with Carol.

4. *Opinion evidence* is what a witness thinks about the facts in dispute. This is usually only admissible if from an expert.

5. *Inference* means a deduction of fact that may logically and reasonably be drawn from another fact or group of facts found or otherwise established. It is reasoning based on evidence. Carol says that she spends an extra half an hour in the evening on filing, and is happy to do so; that she answers the phone and takes messages for the whole finance department in their absence; and that she answers some basic inquiries about finance from other people in the organization, so it is reasonable to infer that she should not be on the same scale as a typist.

6. *Cumulative evidence* involves a repetition of evidence that has been testified to previously, and establishes the same ultimate fact. The arbitrator can limit the amount of cumulative evidence and encourage the party to move forward.

7. *Objections* oppose questioning techniques or issues raised. Parties may make objections to exclude particular questions, modify the form or manner of questioning, change momentum, or calm a witness who is being cross examined. Often these objections will point to a weakness in the material

offered, and the arbitrator should stay cool and not be shaken.

The obligation is on the disputants to have all the relevant details at their disposal, and then the arbitrator can ensure, through thorough questioning, that each side does itself justice.

Checking That the Parties Have Said What They Want

As each person will have been questioned in turn, the arbitrator should now check whether they have said enough, and give a final, time-limited opportunity for additional information. Then, thanking everyone, the arbitrator closes the hearing.

THE DECISION OR AWARD

There are two poles of opinion about whether or not to include the reasons for decisions in arbitration awards. ACAS does not give detailed reasons but frequently refers to the considerations that were taken into account, and will give a summary of the main submissions by both sides. ACAS believes that giving reasons may "possibly exacerbate the differences by transferring the area of controversy from the main issue to the reasons given for the award" (Mackie 1991).

Other arbitrators give reasons so that clients can understand their reasoning, put the award in context, and make any changes in their organization highlighted by the decision.

Having submitted to arbitration willingly, Carol and David will abide by its decision and make every effort to continue a successful working relationship afterwards.

The award should not be made at the hearing, but communicated to the parties when the arbitrator has had sufficient time to process and consider the evidence and prepare his or her report. In this instance, Surinder will be able to consider and make the award within a day or two.

SUMMARY

Useful Circumstances

- Consenting to and being clear about process and terms of reference—the arbitrator and parties should know what issues are to be decided, limitations of arbitration, how process occurs, who the parties can get to help, and what form the agreement will take.

- Preparation, submission, and exchange of written statements—parties should have checklists of what to include, and names of helpful people.

- The hearing—parties should prepare by studying the background, details of each point of view, and available documents; summarize submissions and prior interviews; and be prepared to answer the other side's points.

  — arbitrators should question fairly and thoroughly, consider the validity of the evidence, ensure full participation, and allow limited venting of feelings.

- The award—arbitrators should decide how much detail to give and ensure a quick, clear decision.

Limitations

- A decision has to be made whether or not arbitration awards are binding, that is, is it backed up by the authority of legislation or rules that will ensure the agreement is kept even if the disputants wish to reject it? This should be negotiated at the outset. A mechanism should be provided for further action in case of

  — rejection of a decision or award.

  — reneging on an agreement.

  — unwillingness to comply with the award although it has been specified as binding.

You Versus Them—Two Step-by-Step Processes for Conflict Between Yourself and Others 23

INTRODUCTION

Adopting a neutral third party approach to conflicts is effective, but it is certainly not easy. Just about every mediator admits to working with people whose general behavior, opinions, mannerisms, and arguments set them on edge.

If a conflict is between you and others, how can you resist the temptation to act out the strong emotions that other people provoke? Examples of skills which will improve your ability to remain positive even under the most challenging circumstances have already been presented. In this chapter, two step-by-step processes have been adapted from conflict management specialists John Lawyer and Neil Katz (1985), which will help you to be assertive, register fully what your counterpart is doing and what he or she wants, and work toward agreements.

FIVE STEPS TO TAKE WHEN YOU NEED TO DEFEND YOURSELF

This method is useful when you feel that others' behavior is constantly infringing on your rights, abusing your authority, or affecting you generally in a negative way when agreements are broken, tasks are not done or contracts are ignored. If the dispute is with a superior, using this method will improve your chance of getting what you want.

Situation

Previously, Helen had persuaded the heads of department meeting that she had not been treated fairly, and Howard gave an assurance that he would look into the situation. Helen checked what he meant; he suggested he would look at ways of devising structures to ensure that Helen got the information she needed and had regular contact with the other individual department heads to discuss issues of quality, and also that he would reconsider the budget allocations.

One month later nothing has happened as far as Helen can see. She is beginning to feel that Howard is the problem, and is determined to pursue the matter as these are issues that are crucial to her personally and to her department.

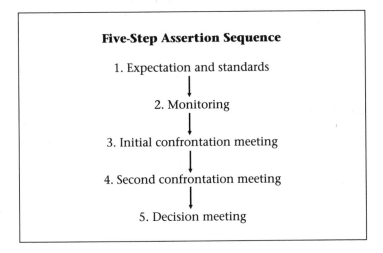

Clearly communicate your expectations, including agreements, contracts, standards, policies, procedures and rules, or understandings.

Helen has already made her case very clearly, stating her understanding of the situation and its effect on her, in the heads of department meeting.

Expectation and Standards

"I believe information is being withheld from me. I have to spend about three or four hours extra each week seeking out information. I do not consider my budget allocation to be sufficient. For example,... (gives reasons)."

Communicate expectations

Use the skills index in Appendix II to locate more assistance on how to communicate expectations clearly, including asserting with skill, reframing, I–You statements, and stating the tangible effect on you.

At this meeting Helen gained an agreement for action from Howard. As far as she is concerned this has not happened, and the problems persist.

There are two stages to monitoring.

Monitoring

Say What You Want Again, at a Later Stage

Contact the person with whom you made the agreement and repeat what you understood that to be. This will be a lot more effective if the initial agreement was clear, specific, and workable. If not, then this is an opportunity to repair any loopholes in the original agreement. Do not contact the person too late as the other person will not have time to comply if he or she has not already done so; on the other hand, contact the person too early and you may seem unreasonably hasty. For example, Howard said he would get back to Helen within a month. Three weeks later she could say

"Howard, I'm looking forward to talking to you within a week about...."

Use the Reminder Conversation

Assertively point out the continuing infringement and clarify the prior agreement. Use this conversation to check that you both have the same understanding of the agreement, and offer to help. For example:

"Hi, Howard, I thought that we agreed to meet some time this week and discuss...? What can I do to help make this happen?"

or

"Can I perhaps show you a copy of my alternative budget suggestions?"

or

"I've been talking to the other heads of department and they think that we could have regular team meetings about quality issues, say, every other month."

The aim, at this stage, is to assist the other person in complying with the original agreement, and it will be helpful if you

- Do your preparation and have some options available that will help.

- Get information together that will help your case.

- Continue using assertive, respectful language and positive body language and voice tone.

A confrontation meeting conditioned by respect for the other party, and the belief that a mutually acceptable solution can be found, requires that you do the following three steps.

Review the History of the Problem

Review the recent events that have led you to confront the other person. In this case, the broken agreement from the meeting and lack of response despite a restatement and reminder will lead to a confrontation meeting.

Believe in mutually acceptable solutions

Use a Three-Part Assertion Message

Use a three-part assertion message to work out an agreement that suits your needs. Do not forget to describe the problem; communicate what you feel about it; and describe the tangible effect on you.

Use Conflict Management Skills

Incorporate skills such as questioning, generating options, active listening, and mutual problem definition.

This should result in a renewal of the agreement, the working out of a new one or an action plan to ensure resolution of the problem. Lawyer and Katz (1985) suggest that

> Most infringements or problems can typically be corrected by assertive behavior using this sequence. In relationships based on mutuality and trust, the person is likely to modify his or her behavior before the third step.

If the problem continues, for instance, Howard still does not answer Helen's question about budget allocations and has not raised the issue of communication and information procedures with her colleagues, what should she do next?

The purpose of this meeting is to state the consequences if the problem does not get resolved or if the behavior does not change, and to give the other person time to decide whether or not he or she can accept the situation.

State consequences

This is tricky for Helen, as Howard has ultimate authority over her. In any situation that has progressed to this stage, you have to decide

- What other options are there? Check with colleagues, advisors, and people who have been in similar situations. Think through all possible ways to achieve the outcome you desire.

- What alternative action can you take to achieve your aim? Take your problem to a higher authority, or file a grievance to set disciplinary procedures in motion.

- Who can help? Enlist the support of a professional support group, union, neutral third party, or other colleagues.

- What do you do if you still do not get what you want? This might mean terminating a working relationship, job change, or, alternatively, modifying your demands or accepting a compromise.

The Decision Meeting

Don't bluff

If the problem behavior still persists and the agreement has not been kept, then you need to communicate to the other party what you intend to do next. Your credibility will evaporate if you use idle threats at this stage. From the beginning it is useful to be very clear about what will happen if you do not achieve your aim of solving the problem. Although this process is very effective, it does not guarantee success.

Be persistent, persuasive, and prepared

Helen ultimately gets her message across to Howard. By being persistent, persuasive, and prepared, she has not insulted or over-pressured Howard, who often seems harassed. Hopefully this, plus the assertive behavior of Rachel, his head of computing, will enable Howard to learn how to respond effectively to assertive women. This is the joy of constructive conflict management— not only does it solve problems, but it gives people a chance to learn from and educate one another.

SEVEN-STEP PROBLEM SOLVING

If you are feeling fed up or frustrated by a colleague or one of your team who lets you down, distracts others from their work, will not listen to advice, lowers work standards, or is constantly getting into conflicts with others, or even if there is someone who is just getting on your nerves and you cannot work out why, then the seven-step problem solving method will give you another conflict management alternative. This process will, in one meeting, help you get to the bottom of the problem, establish whether or not it can be solved, decide what to do next, and understand why you have such a problem with this person.

Situation

Phillip, customer relations officer, does not get along well with Sean, the mailroom worker. They almost came to blows two months ago, and Patricia had to separate them and calm them down. Phillip has learned to control his animosity toward Sean, but Sean keeps delivering Phillip's mail to Helen and Patricia. This has caused Phillip's important correspondence to be delayed one or two days, and recently, when Helen was away for a week,

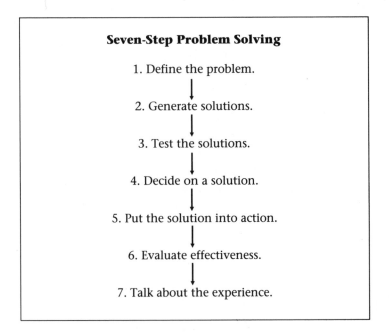

Seven-Step Problem Solving

1. Define the problem.

2. Generate solutions.

3. Test the solutions.

4. Decide on a solution.

5. Put the solution into action.

6. Evaluate effectiveness.

7. Talk about the experience.

his mail stayed in an unopened pile of Helen's letters until she returned.

Phillip thinks Sean might be deliberately making life difficult for him. If he lets this thought and the feelings of frustration that accompany it influence his attitude to Sean, then the problem will be much more difficult to solve. In situations like this, begin with the practical problem, in this case, the missing letters.

Define the Problem   Do not use blaming language, but test out your problem statement and gain agreement on the problem.

"Sean, are you aware that you have been delivering some of my letters to the wrong place for over three weeks now?"

Give examples.

"Sometimes it has taken correspondence a week to get from the mailroom to my desk, as one letter was delivered to Helen at the beginning of her five days vacation, and it was a week before I got the letter."

Describe the effect on you.

"I do not have time to chase my mail, and I never know whether or not I have received everything that is there for me."

Listen actively.

"So you thought that all mail marked for customer relations went to Patricia and that I only got the mail that was personally addressed to me? What about those that went by error to Helen?"

"You find it difficult to work out who gets what."

Ask the other to suggest solutions and add your own.

Generate Solutions

Sean

"Well, at the moment I only have names on the mailboxes, and sometimes I get confused about who is who. What if we put the person's position on the box as well?"

Phillip

"And if you're not sure, why not check with Carol, who knows everyone here."

Be honest and realistic, listen carefully to any objections, and test options so that they will work for both parties.

In this case, test that Sean understands and is able to do it. Phillip should not have any reason to be concerned about mail getting to him on time.

Test the Solutions

Restate what has been decided upon, for clarification and agreement.

Decide on a Solution

Decide specifically who does what and when.

"So Sean, I will give you a list of all the names and titles, so that you can relabel the mailboxes tomorrow, and today I will check with Carol that it's okay for you to consult her if you're not sure about who mail is for."

Put the Solution Into Action

Incorporate an evaluation stage into your action plan.

"If any letters are still slow getting to me, I will take it up with you with in a day and we can find out what happened. Let me know within a day if you have any more problems, or want anything clarified."

Evaluate Effectiveness

Talk About the Experience

Invite the other person to share what this process was like and describe your own feelings and thoughts.

"So, Sean, how are you feeling now? What did you find useful about this, and was there anything that was difficult?"

Sean

"I thought I was going to get told off, so I came prepared for a fight, but this is okay. I think I can do it now."

"Yes, I think it was useful too. I was getting frustrated about this, but I think we've sorted it out well now."

If the problem persists, then Phillip could try the five-step process outlined earlier in the chapter. Many conflicts can be resolved by using a combination of these two approaches, providing you remember to

- Describe the process clearly to your counterpart in one or two sentences.
- Invite your counterpart to solve problems in the same way.
- Maintain a positive attitude and rapport throughout.
- Be assertive with your position and interests.
- Keep listening actively.
- Be open to unusual solutions.
- Don't settle for a solution that is unsatisfactory for one party or the other.
- Be aware of your own emotional reactions during the process, and be sensitive to those of the other party.
- Be genuine and express respect and empathy.

CONCLUSION

People have problems

There is no such thing as problem people, only people whose behavior gives us problems. To think of them as the problem is to make them a lesser person. People who exhibit disruptive or difficult behavior in the workplace need to be managed, but remember that they have a whole life outside the walls of the office, factory, shop, or other premises in which they work. The part of them you never see, the thoughts and feelings they have, their family background, and their personal histories may contain intense pain and brilliant pleasure. A manager can only deal with what he or she sees, thinks, and feels about others, so it is important that this is carefully considered, balanced, and realistic. By constructive positive conflict management techniques you can at least ensure that, at work, employees can enter into an environment where they are valued, fairly treated, and where they can learn how to work with others who have their own separate, distinct cultures and private lives. In the long term you will be enabling them to perform to their capacity, be committed to your organization, and be open to your management.

Be clear if they are a problem for you

Look for the best in people

Part Four

Where and How Is Conflict Likely to Happen in Your Organization?

INTRODUCTION

If you believe in the potential of constructive conflict and develop your positive conflict management skills, you will not need to avoid or suppress the people you associate with conflict in your organization. Each successfully managed interpersonal conflict will provide additions to your notebook of behavior and your understanding of workplace interaction, and prepare you, your staff, and your superiors for a better working future.

This is quite a switch from the widely held view that conflict is a predominantly negative experience. Pascale spent thousands of hours interviewing and observing twelve top U.S. companies and found it extremely difficult to get them talking about areas of contention within the organizations. "Organizations often avoid or conceal conflict," he observed, because they do not see its positive value. In his study, those who escaped this narrow view of conflict, within Honda, General Electric, and Ford, were able to manage revitalizing organizational change utilizing the energy of conflict (Pascale 1990). These changes were driven by the same willingness to explore and learn that runs through the exercises in this book: "Problems are not just hassles to be dealt with and set aside. Lurking inside each problem is a workshop on the nature of organizations and a vehicle for personal growth." So where are your organizational conflict points and what can you learn from them?

A series of themes and questions in Part Four will help you identify the likely problem areas and understand and attend to the points where conflict most frequently occurs in your organization. You could also use the questions to evaluate your own place in the conflict culture, that is the overall pattern and character of conflicts of your workplace.

Where Conflicts Occur 24

DECISION MAKING

Decisions can be seen as instruments of closure—when debates are measured by votes for and against, wars ended by treaties, pay awards given or denied, work relationships changed or terminated. Effective decision making must take into account the practical implications of closure (for example, a change in job description, a new deadline, confirmation of an appointment, reshaping of a department, and refusal to accept a proposal), and the feelings associated with it. Decisions are also instruments of change, and affect personal and organizational boundaries. Can I do this? Can the organization take it? Where is this going to lead? A great deal of conflict is generated around decisions because of this tension between the need for closure and change.

Reviewing the decision making processes in your organization will tell you a great deal about how your organization manages this daily process of closure and change around which so much conflict occurs.

Decisions for closure

Decisions for change

Leadership Styles

Are the decisions in your organization made autocratically, through consultation, or through a group decision-making process? Do you associate any one of those styles with conflict? Are there mixed styles of decision making and does this cause problems? Do certain kinds of decision require more consultation than others?

Acceptability

Is there a need for a decision that is considered correct on principle, regardless of whether or not people like it? Is there general agreement on the quality of decisions? Do people think the right decisions are made, given the options? Is it more important for decisions to be accepted? Is there a high likelihood of conflict over some types of decision? What makes it likely for decisions to be accepted?

Methods

How do decisions happen? How are they researched, discussed, and communicated? Is this process open for all to see or behind closed doors? Are reasons for decisions given? What is the time scale of decision making? Are there delays, or conversely, hasty decisions? What are the consequences of this?

Think of specific examples of decision making methods. Do you associate any methods in particular with conflict or harmony? For example:

- Splitting the difference—deciding between two conflicting demands.
- Random procedures—tossing a coin, drawing lots.
- Majority voting.
- Using the power of individual vote.
- "The moot"—discuss an issue until consensus is achieved or pay the penalty of no decision.
- "Avoidance of undesired precedents" (Fisher 1992)—specifying that the decision is one-off and may not affect future decisions.

What concept of fairness exists in your organization? Is it based on shared values, tradition, precedent, moral considerations, established guidelines and procedures, or levels of status and authority?

    Is the concept of fairness different for different people, departments, or teams? How is feedback gained on the fairness of decisions? How are they evaluated?

Fairness

Are decisions workable? (see Chapter 4) Do they contain sufficient detail? Are they framed so that those affected can understand them? Are they understood? How do you know?

Details

Are decisions consistent with organizational aims and policies? Are they made and subsequently overturned? What is the overall attitude to changing decisions? Does the decision making process communicate a sense of the organization's overall reliability and dependability?

Consistency and Reliability

How much information is needed to make decisions? Are the circumstances adequately researched and explored before deciding? Who holds the key information and how is it made accessible? How much information is needed to make decisions work?

Informed or Uninformed

Do decisions work? How are they communicated? What resources are put behind decisions? Does this affect how well they work? Do decisions pass the test of time? On what criteria are they evaluated?

Outcomes

COOPERATIVE GOALS

Cooperation theory, initiated by Deutsch, suggests that groups and individuals exhibit different conflict behaviors dependent on whether they perceive their goals to be competitive or cooperative. Tjosvold cites later research that indicates

Conflict participants who believe their goals are cooperative rather than competitive have been found to express their opinions openly, exchange information and ideas, explore and understand each other's perspective, work for mutually acceptable solutions, influence and be open to influence, integrate their positions to create solutions, and develop commitment to their agreement. Persons who believe their goals are competitive try to win the conflict; they are suspicious, make unreasonable demands, pursue their own interests at the expense of others, and often fail to reach an agreement.

Competition is valuable

This emphasis on goals is constructive, because it does not deny the value of competition itself. Competition can be constructive, enhancing individual identity, strengthening units within an organization and providing standards, but it should exist within the context of shared goals, otherwise it can tear an organization apart.

Individual Goals

Do people believe that most problems can be solved to the satisfaction of all the people involved? Is there a sense that interests are not opposed so conflict could be beneficial? How are individual goals identified and shared? Do clashes occur over interpretations of goals? How do individual goals relate to organizational goals?

Organizational Goals

How are organizational goals communicated? How were they formed? Is there a feeling that everyone is working to the same broad purpose? Are individuals clear how these goals affect them, and how they can contribute toward them? How are these goals presented to clients, customers, and new staff? Are they reviewed regularly or used to evaluate performance? How do the broader organizational goals connect with departmental or unit goals?

CONTRASTS AND INTERSECTIONS

Within any organization there are moments when differences intersect and become obvious. Pascale (1990) talks about a "fit/split paradox": "Fit refers to the consistencies and coherence of an organization. When *fit* is absent, organizational life can be confusing." For example, if you aim to provide a quality service but evaluate it only in terms of cost, relegating quality control or monitoring to a minor consideration, you have poor fit. Split, in contrast to fit, "pertains to a variety of techniques used to sustain autonomy and diversity." These can be structural, such as splitting parts of the organization off for specialized work, or based on human networks such as project teams, expert or specialist groups, or groups differentiated by roles such as sales, marketing, and personnel. "Split helps instill vitality and focus—but too much of it diffuses energy. Fit contributes to coherence—but too much of it risks overadaptation." This is the paradox: These exist side by side in healthy organizations.

Fit?

Split?

Pascale calls the process of managing the tensions which arise "contend." It involves strategy, structure, and systems, but these take you only so far. "Inevitably one must deal with the passion and perspiration of human interaction. Organizations are, in the last analysis, interactions among people."

So where in your organization are the places where these interactions contain clear differences? How are they managed? How much are differences encouraged, or is uniformity promoted? How is the tension between these handled?

Interactions Among People

Consider these questions with regard to your organization, including the places where

- Inside meets outside—contacts with clients, customers, consultants, suppliers, contractors, trainers, and observers.
- Roles clash, overlap, combine, or are duplicated.
- Tasks are allocated, monitored, and evaluated.

- New meets old—a new manager or member joins a long-established team; new induction procedures, programs, or plans replace established familiar ones; merger; take-overs; and restructuring.

Or, there are differences in

- Conditions of work—salary, hours of work (part time/full time), pension rights, and child-care benefits.
- Affiliations—membership or nonmembership of union, professional association, club, or society.
- Culture, gender, or sexuality.
- Status and authority.

ORGANIZATIONAL CULTURE

Your organization may have a recognizable set of values, a collective understanding of norms and common responses to situations that could be described as its organizational culture. Styles of interactions, sets of jargon, and commonly held and perpetuated myths and stories become part of this culture. Yet how does one become part of the culture of an organization? Is being there enough, or do we have to undergo education, initiation, and acceptance into the culture?

Collective norms

Some aspects of the culture are enshrined and proclaimed in mission statements and aims and objectives, and are accessible and comprehensible to all. Other predominantly held beliefs and norms of behavior are woven almost invisibly into the fabric of human networks and systems that make up the organization.

How can one be sure whether one is part of the organizational culture or not? If such a culture exists in your organization, then who are its leaders and how do they influence the behavior of its members? How would you describe the culture of your organization? What behaviors, styles of language, uniform responses, and expectations do you notice? Have these caused conflicts?

Are some people excluded from the culture? Do others refuse to join? How does this affect their working relationships?

SUBGROUPS

Organizations are divided into functional groups which have practical responsibilities and tasks. Sometimes the clashes between these groups are the most difficult to deal with, and some of the differences have been mentioned above in the section on contrasts and intersections. There are also other groupings, which are influential as far as conflict is concerned, that are organized more around individual preference. How do these affect workplace interaction? There are several types of subgroups to look for, organized around

- Concepts of workers and management.
- Political interests.
- Styles of communication and interaction.
- Work habits.
- Beliefs and interests.

Handy (1990) also talks about four "tribes" to which people choose to belong: the club tribe, role tribe, task tribe, and person tribe.

1. *The Club Tribe.* The club tribe is an extension of the person at the head, who you can imagine sitting in the center of a web surrounded by ever-widening circles of intimates and influence. Some theatrical professions work like this, as do brokerages and agents of various kinds.

2. *The Role Tribe.* The organization is a "piece of construction engineering with role piled on role, and responsibility linked to responsibility. Individuals are role occupants with job descriptions that lay down the requirements of the role and its boundaries." Large administrative organizations, such as those that pay out welfare benefits, work like this.

3. *The Task Tribe.* Groups are formed to deal with a project, problem, or task. They can also be changed, disbanded, or increased as the task changes. Consultancy, advertising, and the media are examples of task tribes.

4. *The Person Tribe.* The individual is put first and the organization is made to be the resource for the individual's talents, such as artists in a studio or doctors in a group practice.

Handy emphasizes that few organizations are tribally pure. There may be a combination of tribes and groupings that make it very difficult for a person to enter the organization and adjust.

What kind of tribes exist in your organization? How does this affect relationships?

HUMAN RESOURCE PRACTICE

How you recruit, integrate into your organization, train, and promote staff also has a significant effect on the conflict pattern of your organization. Restrictive, unequal employment and recruitment practice is founded on a fear of diversity, and fear of the other.

Inconsistencies in training, support, and promotion lead to unrest, and store up potentially serious conflict.

Maintain equality

How equal are the opportunities in your organization? How would you describe the practices of recruitment, induction, training, support, and promotion? Are there some people who believe they are not allowed to be equal?

How much attention is paid to matching staff to clients and customers? What levels of retention of staff do you have? Do you find it easier to attract a certain kind of person? Are there myths, images, and prejudices in your organization around certain groups? How do they affect procedures and practice?

EXTERNAL PRESSURES

There are, of course, external factors which influence the capacity of an organization to deal with conflict. Sometimes, under extreme pressure, organizations pull together, finding new ways to work together under threat from an external enemy like recession or a new, powerful competitor.

Have any of the following factors affected your organization, and how?

- External economic factors linked with recession, shrinking markets, and reduced cash levels for services
- Structural reorganization, including layoffs, regrading, and reduction of working hours and conditions
- External inspection or audit requiring changes in practice and policy
- New competition
- Unfavorable comparison with another similar organization, or part of your own organization

How have you adjusted in the light of these factors? Have the chances and occurrences of conflict increased?

GROUP DYNAMICS AND DISPUTE RESOLUTION SYSTEMS

Finally, what are you already doing to devise systems for managing group dynamics and resolving disputes in your organization? There are many recent examples in international conflicts of effective group dynamics systems being used to ensure peaceful resolutions of conflict. These methods are equally applicable to the workplace.

Do you use any dispute resolution procedures? What methods does your organization have of managing the diverse groups and subgroups it contains? Examples cited by Fogg include

- Neutral chairperson assisting adversaries to work toward agreements.
- Controlling communication so that blaming is discouraged and perception clarified.

- Encounter groups that freely address issues, then seek to find an agreeable solution.

- Problem-solving approach where step-by-step approaches increase chances that resolutions will be found and adopted.

- Mutually acceptable restatement of arguments and opinions so that their terms are understood and conflicts over unnecessary disagreements are minimized.

- Feeling-out procedures that involve subtle discussion, checking up of needs, and giving full attention to both sides in a dispute.

These and other dispute resolution procedures, such as mediation and arbitration, can be very effective. How would you evaluate the systems your organization has for dealing with conflicts? Brett, Goldberg, and Ury (1990) suggest several questions to help you determine the effectiveness of whatever systems you have. Do procedures produce outcomes that meet the interests of disputants or outcomes that appear risky? Do parties believe they have some control over the outcome? Have disputants been given full opportunity to voice their concerns and demands? This includes the opportunity to express emotions, and opportunities for the blamed party to acknowledge the validity of the emotions. Are all parties on all sides of conflicts actively supportive of dispute resolution systems? Are the skills of the people responsible for the systems adequate?

CONCLUSION

Contending with disputes in organizations is a lengthy and time consuming process. The resolution of one problem often leads to the uncovering of another. The challenge is to find ways of resolving conflicts without fighting over them, and by doing so to create a workplace where diversity has a chance to express itself. This can be done so that you really can manage to make a difference in your organization.

Appendix —
Evaluation

EVALUATING YOURSELF AS A MEDIATOR

(Based on Beer 1990)

CHECKLIST
Myself As a Mediator
■ What strengths do I have?
■ If co-mediating, do I share the session easily with other mediators?
■ When do I have trouble staying impartial? How do I handle it?
■ Do I slip into other roles? Counselor? Parent? Advocate? Judge? Advisor? Sympathizer?
■ Is my language clear?
■ How do I react to differences between me and the disputants? Class? Race? Gender? Age? Sexuality?
■ What signals have I picked up about my mediating from disputants?
■ Do I always debrief and gain feedback with co-mediators after sessions?
■ Do I ask for and accept criticism from my co-mediators?

CHECKLIST
What Went Well? What Could Have Gone Better?
■ The process?
■ The agreement?
■ Special difficulties?
■ Mediator prejudices, opinions, advice, feelings?
■ Coworking?

MEDIATION OBSERVATION CHECKLIST

CHECKLIST			
Mediation Observation Form			
Task	**Competence Level**		
	Demonstrates competence	**Needs to improve**	**Shows serious weaknesses**

Establishing Trust
 	
■ Introduction
 	
  • Understands and accurately describes mediation
 	
  • Understands and accurately describes role of mediator
 	
■ Sessions
 	
  • Uses clear, concise language
 	
  • Asks nonthreatening questions
 	
  • Has respectful and attentive demeanor
 	
  • Establishes and maintains neutrality
 	
  • Listens actively
 	
Understanding the Situation
 	
■ Elicits facts
 	
■ Elicits feelings
 	
■ Follows clear line of questioning
 	
■ Keeps joint session orderly
 	
■ Allows for ventilation
 	
■ Clearly organizes facts, options, and interests			

CHECKLIST		
Mediation Observation Form (continued)		
Task	**Competence Level**		

Task	Demonstrates competence	Needs to improve	Shows serious weaknesses
Teamwork			
■ Plans clear strategy			
■ Contributes to side meetings			
■ Takes and uses notes			
■ Anticipates difficulties			
Managing the Negotiation			
■ Elicits and stresses positives			
■ Helps parties prioritize concerns			
■ Clarifies facts and issues			
■ Transmits information carefully			
■ Gets specific details of proposals			
■ Elicits solutions from parties			
■ Encourages movement			
■ Positive stroking			
■ Keeps realistic focus			
■ Uses nonjudgmental language			
■ Is able to see validity of both sides			
■ Exhibits patience			
■ Brings objectivity to discussion			
■ Constructs clear, balanced, diplomatic agreements			
■ Other comments			

References

Acland, Andrew F. *A Sudden Outbreak of Common Sense.* London: Century Business, 1990.

Adorno, Theodor W. *Notes to Literature.* Vol. 1. New York: Columbia University Press, 1991.

Beer, Jennifer E., Adams, Sandi, et al, eds. *Mediator's Handbook: Peacemaking in Your Neighborhood.* 4th ed. Philadelphia, PA: Philadelphia Yearly Meeting, Religious Society of Friends, Publications, 1990.

Blake, Robert R., and I.S. Mouton. *Corporate Excellence Through Grid Organization Development.* Ann Arbor, MI: Books on Demand, 1971.

Bret, J.M., S.B. Goldberg, and W.L. Ury. "Designing Systems for Resolving Disputes in Organizations." *American Psychologist* (February 1990): 62-71.

Burley-Allen, Madelyn. *Listening: The Forgotten Skill.* New York: John Wiley & Sons, 1982.

Burrell, N.A., W.A. Donohue, and M.I. Allen. "Gender-based Perceptual Biases in Mediation." *Communication Research* 15 (No. 4): 447-449.

Cohen, R. *School Mediation Training Manual.* Boston, MA: School Mediation Associates, 1990.

Coulson, Robert. *Business Arbitration—What You Need to Know.* 4th ed. New York: American Arbitration Association, 1991.

__. *Business Mediation—What You Need to Know*. New York: American Arbitration Association, 1987.

Dana, Dan. *Managerial Meditation—Seminar Resource Manual*. Connecticut: Mediation Training Institute International, 1989.

DeBono, Edward. *Conflicts—A Better Way to Resolve Them*. Mamaroneck, NY: International Center for Creative Thinking, 1990.

Deutsch, M. "A Theory of Cooperation and Competition." *Human Relations*. Vol. 2: 129-152.

Fisher, Roger, and William Ury. *Getting to Yes*. New York: Houghton Mifflin, 1992.

Fogg, R.W. "Dealing With Conflict—A Repertoire of Creative, Peaceful Approaches." *Journal of Conflict Resolution*. Vol. 29 (No. 2.): pp. 33-58.

Gendlin, Eugene T. *Focusing*. New York: Bantam Books, 1981.

Hall, J. *Conflict Management Survey: A Survey of One's Characteristic Reaction to and Handling of Conflict Between Himself and Others*. The Woodlands, TX: Telemetrics International, 1969.

Handy, Charles B. *Inside Organizations: 21 Ideas for Managers*. New York: Parkwest Publications, 1992.

__. *Understanding Organizations*. 3rd ed. Ann Arbor, MI: Books on Demand, 1988.

Harris, Amy, and Thomas Harris. *Staying OK*. New York: Avon Books, 1986.

Haynes, John, and Gretchen Haynes. *Mediating Divorce*. San Francisco, CA: Jossey-Bass, 1989.

Honeyman, C. "On Evaluating Mediators." *Negotiating Journal* (January): 23-26.

Huston, G. *The Red Book of Groups and How to Lead Them Better*. London: Gaie Huston, 1984.

Irving, H. H., and M. Benjamin. "A Study of Conciliation Counselling in the Family Court of Toronto" in Eekelaar, J.M. and S.M. Katz, *The Resolution of Family Conflict: Comparative Legal Perspectives*. London: Butterworth, 1984.

Kanter, Rosabeth M. *The Change Masters: Innovation for Productivity in the American Corporation.* New York: Touchstone, Simon & Schuster, 1985.

Kindler, Herbert. *Managing Disagreement Constructively.* Los Altos, CA: Crisp Publications, 1988.

Lawyer, John W., and Neil H. Katz. *Communication and Conflict Negotiation Skills for Ministry.* Dubuque, IA: Kendall/Hunt, 1985.

Mackie, Karl, ed. *A Handbook of Dispute Resolution—Alternative Dispute Resolution in Action.* London: Routledge, 1991.

Mintzberg, Henry. *The Nature of Managerial Work.* New York: Prentice-Hall, 1980.

Mole, J. *Mind Your Manners.* London: Nicholas Brealey Publishing, 1992.

Moore, Christopher W. *The Mediation Process: Practical Strategies for Resolving Conflict.* San Francisco, CA: Jossey-Bass, 1986.

O'Brien, Paddy. *Positive Management.* San Diego, CA: Pfeiffer & Company, 1994.

Pascale, Richard. *Managing on the Edge—How Successful Companies Use Conflict to Stay Ahead.* New York: Touchstone, Simon & Schuster, 1991.

Peters, Tom. *Thriving on Chaos.* New York: Random House, 1988.

Peters, Tom, and Nancy K. Austin. *A Passion for Excellence.* New York: Warner Books, 1989.

Roberts, Marian. *Mediation in Family Disputes: A Guide to Practice.* Wildwood House San Francisco Fire Department 1991 Peer Mediation Program Training Workbook, 1991.

Scott, Gini G. *Resolving Conflict With Others and Within Yourself.* Oakland, CA: New Harbinger, 1990.

Slembek, E. "The Vision of Hearing in a Visual Age." *American Behavioral Scientist.* Vol. 32 (No. 2):147-155.

Thomas, K. W., and R. H. Kilmann. *Conflict Mode Instrument.* New York: XICOM, Inc., 1974.

Tjosvold, Dean. "Cooperation Theory and Organizations." *Human Relations.* Vol. 37. (No. 9): 743-767.

Tjosvold, Dean, and L.C. Chia. "Conflict Between Managers and Workers: The Role of Cooperation and Competition." *Journal of Social Psychology*. Vol. 129 (2): 235-247.

Tyler, T. "Procedure or Result: What Do Disputants Want From Legal Authorities?" in Mackie, K., ed.

Vroom, Victor H., and P.W. Yetton. *Leadership and Decision-Making*. Pittsburgh, PA: University of Pittsburgh Press, 1976.

Walton, R.E. "Social Choice in the Development of Advanced Information Technology." *Human Relations*. Vol 35. (No. 12.): 1073-1084.

Whitmore, John. *Coaching for Performance*. San Diego, CA: Pfeiffer & Company, 1994.

Index